Chung Anh Tran

Role and dynamics of ‚Late-comers' in the global technology competition

Role and dynamics of ‚Late-comers' in the global technology competition

by
Chung Anh Tran

KIT Scientific Publishing

Dissertation, Karlsruher Institut für Technologie
Fakultät für Wirtschaftswissenschaften
Tag der mündlichen Prüfung: 08.02.2011
Referenten: Prof. Dr. Jan Kowalski, Prof. Dr. Ingrid Ott

Impressum

Karlsruher Institut für Technologie (KIT)
KIT Scientific Publishing
Straße am Forum 2
D-76131 Karlsruhe
www.ksp.kit.edu

KIT – Universität des Landes Baden-Württemberg und nationales Forschungszentrum in der Helmholtz-Gemeinschaft

KIT Scientific Publishing 2011
Print on Demand

ISBN 978-3-86644-648-9

Role and dynamics of ‚Late-comers' in the global technology competition

Zur Erlangung des akademischen Grades eines Doktors der Wirtschaftswissenschaften

(Dr. rer.pol.)

von der Fakultät für Wirtschaftswissenschaften des Karlsruher Instituts für Technologie (KIT)

genehmigte Dissertation

von

Dipl. Wi.-Ing. Chung Anh Tran

Referent: Prof. Dr. Jan Kowalski
Korreferent: Prof. Dr. Ingrid Ott

Eingereicht: 28.10.2010
Mündliche Prüfung: 08.02.2011

Danksagung

Mein Dank für diese Arbeit gilt meiner wissenschaftlichen Heimat dem Institut für Wirtschaftspolitik und Wirtschaftsforschung (IWW) des Karlsruher Instituts für Technologie (KIT), wo diese Dissertation während meiner wissenschaftlichen Tätigkeit entstanden ist. Dabei danke ich in erster Linie meinen beiden Doktorvätern Prof. Dr. Hariolf Grupp, der mir den Einstieg in die Wissenschaft ermöglicht hat, und Prof. Dr. Jan Kowalski, der mich nach dem plötzlichen Tod von Prof. Dr. Hariolf Grupp übernommen hat und ans Ziel führte. Weiterhin möchte ich mich bei meinen Kollegen, sowie ehemaligen Kollegen bedanken, die mir nicht nur mit wissenschaftlichen Diskussionen inhaltlich weitergeholfen haben, sondern auch durch ihre freundschaftliche Art der Zusammenarbeit immer zu einer schönen Atmosphäre für meinen Arbeitsalltag beigetragen haben. Insbesondere seien hier Inna Haller und Björn Bertram genannt, die mit mir über die Jahre am IWW das Büro geteilt haben. Ebenso Mirja Meyborg, die meiner englischen Arbeit den Feinschliff verliehen hat, und Dirk Fornahl, der mir mit seinen wertvollen Kommentaren immer zur Seite stand.

Weiterhin danke ich meiner Familie, die mir bei allen Höhen und Tiefen der wissenschaftlichen Arbeit immer stets den Rücken stärkte und mich unterstütze.

Karlsruhe, Februar 2011 Chung Anh Tran

Table of contents

List of figures

List of tables

Abbreviations

BMBF	German Federal Ministry of Education and Research (Bundesministerium für Bildung und Forschung)
BRIC	Brazil, Russia, India, and China
DEUS	Germany (DE) and the USA (US)
DIV	Diversification Index (term: 1-HHI)
DPMA	German Patent and Trademark Office
EC	European Commission
EPO	European Patent Office
EU	European Union
FDI	Foreign Direct Investment
GDP	Gross Domestic Product
HHI	Herfindahl-Hirschman-Index
INPI	Institute de la Propriété Industrielle
IPC	International Patent Classification
IPR	Intellectual Property Rights
IS	Innovation Systems
ISI	Fraunhofer Institut für System- und Innovationsforschung
IWW	Institute for Economic Policy Research
JPO	Japanese Patent Office
KSI	Krugman-Specialisation-Index
MNE	Multinational Enterprise
MOST	Ministry of Science and Technology of the People's Republic of China
NACE	Nomenclature générale des activités économiques
NIS	National Innovation System
NSF	US National Science Foundation
OECD	Organisation for Economic Co-operation and Development
OST	Observatoire des Science et Techniques

PCT	Patent Cooperation Treaty
R&D	Research and Development
RCA	Revealed Comparative Advantage
RIS	Regional Innovation System
RSCA	Revealed Standardised Comparative Advantage
RSTA	Revealed Standardised Technological Advantage
RTA	Revealed Technological Advantage
S&T	Science and Technology
SIS	Sectoral Innovation System
SNA	Social Network Analysis
TFP	Total Factor Productivity
USPTO	US Patent and Trademark Office
WIPO	World Intellectual Property Organization

1. Introduction

Research in the field of innovation economics refers to the role and impact of knowledge, science and technology on economies. Such considerations have a long tradition not only in the field of economics, but also in social studies. Marx (1862) already wrote that technological innovation is a key driver of economic and social development. In his understanding, the changes in society are also driven by the changes of the technological capabilities at his time. Later on, also Schumpeter (1911) described the important role of innovations on economies. He even states that innovation is essential to break obsolete economic structures. Innovation enables economies to transform and rise onto another level. This effect is called the 'creative destruction' (Schumpeter, 1911). These ideas are confirmed by Solow (1956). He showed that the contribution of technological progress on economic growth even exceeds the role of capital accumulation and the increase of labour. For sustainable economic growth, the construction and constant preservation of a profound knowledge base and technological pool is crucial for an economy.

1.1. The role of technological late-comers

Global economic balance is ever-changing. Developed countries are challenged by emerging ones each day. Leading economies have to face this competition to constitute their place. Faster developing cycles and economic developments created many emerging economies in the 20th century. The rise of Germany after the Second World War, the emergence of Japan in the 1960s and 1970s, and the upcoming of the so-called *Four Asian Tigers*[1] are just some successful examples for the second half of the last century. All these countries succeed to establish a competitive economy. Their economies all base on a solid knowledge and technology driven industry and most of them are among the technological leaders, at least in certain sectors.

In recent years the balance of the global economy has been challenged by new emerging economies which are different from former competitors. Since the beginning and mid-1990s the so-called *BRIC* countries, namely Brazil, China, India and Russia, experienced constant high economic growth rates and begun to evolve to solid economies which are challenging the established players. Compared to other emerging economies, these four countries do not just differ in geographical size and number of inhabitants. Moreover, they differ in other aspects, such as political power and historical background, as well as knowledge and technological background. There is no question that not all economic conditions of these countries already reached the same level as the one in the established global economies. For instance, regarding

[1] The term '*Four Asian Tigers*' stands for the countries Hong Kong, Singapore, South Korea and Taiwan.

income per capita and huge spatial differences between the rural and the urban inhabitants, these countries still have many difficulties to face in their own countries. Nevertheless, regarding the development of their *Gross Domestic Product* (GDP), they already play an important role in the global economy. Hence, it is important to answer the question, whether these countries are crucial competitors of the leading economies and challenge their leading role. Therefore, an important issue is the analysis of the technological capabilities of these countries, as knowledge and technology are the key drivers for sustainable economic growth.

This dissertation thesis consists of a profound empirical analysis of these emerging economies. As technology is the one of the last fields in which developed countries have an advantage, this dissertation focus on an analysis of this topic. It sheds light on the technological development of these countries in recent years and delivers an in-depth empirical analysis of the role of these countries in the international technological competition. The analysis focuses on the technological capabilities and gives an impression of the role in the international technology competition. Moreover, it draws implications for policy makers and shows the way they possibly will take regarding their technological capabilities. For an analysis, this dissertation refers to a general national view, and presents an analysis of one specific technological sector. The biotechnology sectors is chosen to be analysed as activities in the biotechnology sector need a broad base of intellectual capital, such as qualified workers, access to scientific research etc. This means that a detailed examination tackles typical functions of an innovation process. The dissertation thesis, thereby, examines these functions.

1.2. Research question and structure

The last section already sketches the research question. To be precise; this thesis deals with the analysis of four technological late-comers and their role in the global competition. For this reason, an analytical framework is built with well-known innovation indicators and scientific methods to define precisely the current situation of these countries and the stage of their technological capabilities. Each stage is described by a separate analytical step and answers a separate hypothesis. Therefore, this thesis employs indicators and methods, such as *Patent Analysis*, *Social Network Analysis* and *Regression Models* to answer the underlying sub-questions respectively hypothesis. The whole analysis and, thus, the structure of this thesis are arranged as follows:

Chapter 2 and Chapter 3 introduce the theoretical background. Thereby, Chapter 2 delivers definitions and descriptions regarding the state-of-the-art of studies in innovation research. In this regard, essential terms, such as ‘innovation’, ‘knowledge’, and ‘technological catch-up’ are clarified and discussed. Moreover, this chapter discusses the relevance and importance of the subject innovation and its role for economic development in detail. This chapter is rounded down by the introduction of certain innovation theories relevant for this thesis. Chapter 3 is dedicated to a description of innovation indicators which are employed in this study. In this respect, it also discusses the theoretical background of these indicators. A special part of this chapter is dedicated to patents and patent indicators, as these are one cornerstone of this analysis.

Chapter 4 presents an introduction of the countries which are analysed in this dissertation and gives detailed reasons for the selection of these countries. It also summarises economic facts and figures of these four countries derived from other studies. Furthermore, a short overview of the historical background of these countries regarding innovation policy is given. Basically, this chapter clarifies the topic of technological late-comers and early-movers and introduces the line of argumentation and, therefore, the construction of the dissertation. Finally, the hypotheses are introduced and arranged into the whole analysis. The whole analysis consists of three analytical steps which are carried out in six chapters (Chapter 5 to Chapter 10).

Chapter 5 and Chapter 6 examine the stage of entry into the technological competition. They are dedicated to the examination of the relevance of external knowledge and niches strategies for late-comers. By employing *Patent Citation Analysis* and specialisation indicators, such as the *Balassa-Index*, the entry strategies of the technological late-comers are analysed. Additionally, these analyses consider time aspects to show the development of these technological late-comers. These considerations illustrate the detection of changes within these late-comers and show whether their development shows patterns of convergences towards the technological early-movers.

The second stage of the analysis deals with the process of establishment of technological capabilities. In this respect, this dissertation thesis analyses specific aspects of the national innovation system. Therefore, Chapter 7 deals with technological diversification aspects and employs indicators, such as the *Herfindahl-Hirschman-Index* (HHI), also known as the *Herfindahl-Index*, and the *Krugman-Specialisation-Index* (KSI). In this case the development of the diversification is observed with time aspects to detect approaches towards leading countries. Chapter 8 also examines patterns of the establishment of a competitive innovation system by looking at the level of innovation players within these countries. It employs *Social Network Analysis* to illustrate the structure of the networks of innovators, as well as inventors.

The last stage of the analytical framework looks at the success of the catch-up processes of these four countries. Chapter 9 analyses the relevance of innovations originating in these countries and their impact on the global technology competition. In this regard, it is illustrated how often late-comer technologies are used for new international technologies. In addition, a *Regression Model* is constructed for the analysis of influences affecting the use of late-comer knowledge. Chapter 10 gathers all former analysis within one frame and evaluates the different technological catch-up stories of each late-comer country. It classifies the status of each country, discusses short-comings and delivers policy implications for each country.

Finally, Chapter 11 delivers the concluding remarks and closes the dissertation with an overall discussion of the results and findings. Moreover, it delivers an outlook for further research studies in this field.

2. Innovation and technological change

In today's literature on economics, the contribution of innovation and technological knowledge to economic performance and development is a well-discussed and accepted topic. The scientific work in economics to capture innovation as a factor in economic development has already started at the beginning of the 20th century. One cornerstone of modern innovation research is laid by Schumpeter (1911), who is one of the first economists who named and described innovation in a scientific work on economics. Later on, Solow (1956) argues that a neoclassical production function, which is based on the two input factors labour and capital, cannot explain sustainable economic growth. He shows this effect by analysing the economic development of developed countries. In his understanding, there is an additional factor which is responsible for the sustained economic development of most nations. He called this additional factor 'Total Factor Productivity' (TFP) which enables economies to produce on different output levels, although they might have the same amount of labour and capital input. However, it took some more years until economic literature directly referred to knowledge and innovation as factors affecting economic growth, for instance, by considering labour with different levels of experience, education and training. The works of authors like Arrow (1962a), Lucas (1988) and Romer (1986) show that the differences in the levels of human capital, which are due to their level of knowledge, can lead to disproportionally high levels of output. Hence, they deal with the influence of knowledge on economic growth, and they show that it is necessary for a national economy to create sources of new technological knowledge to protect sustainable economic growth.

In recent times, the discussion on the role played by innovation, technology and knowledge reaches an almost omnipresent status. The present era is even called 'information age' or 'knowledge society' (Alberts and Papp, 1997, p. iii). Referring to Papp et al. (1997, p.14), the third modern information revolution has been in progress since the 1980s and it '[...] significantly alters the politics, economics, sociology, and culture of knowledge creation and distribution [...]'. Knowledge and information seem to be the answer to a major part of the problems occurring in society and economy. Policy and decision makers tend to refer to it as a universal remedy. The European Union (EU), for instance, undertakes great efforts to push Europe towards a knowledge-based economy, to increase its living standards and strengthen its competitiveness within the global economy. For this reason, in March 2000, European leaders decided to begin the so-called Lisbon Agenda by which the plans and the means towards a knowledge-driven economy were fixed. It specifies precisely that the declared goal is to transform Europe into '[...] the most dynamic and competitive knowledge-based economy in the world which is capable to retain sustainable economic growth with better jobs and greater social cohesion […]' (European Council, 2004, p. 6). This kind of efforts can be observed throughout many countries and regions affected by the global competition. Rising countries, such as China and India, also fix ambitious strategies to become a knowledge-driven economies in their recent Five-Year-Plans and long-term projects, such as the Torch Project[2] in China (Ministry of Science & Technology India, 2007 and MOST, 2008). It is obvious that developed countries try to maintain their advantages within the global competition, and emerging economies make efforts to close the gap between them and the countries which are at the technological frontier.

The role of innovation and technology is conceived to be not only theoretical, but also from the practical point of view. The importance of innovations and technological change is recognised both by researchers in their theoretical and empirical work as well as by policy makers and firms trying to increase competitiveness. The aim of this chapter is to give an introduction to the theories of innovation, as well as the terms and concepts employed in innovation research. Based on these explanations, relevant theories about innovation systems are described and discussed. A deeper insight is given in specific themes concerning technological late-comers and early-movers to build a framework for the understanding of the empirical approaches of this thesis. Therefore, the next section presents the introduction of the theories concerning the topic of innovation, as well as definitions and concepts relevant for the innovation research (see Section 2.1). Second, selected theories about systems of innovation are introduced (see Section 2.2). Third, the relevance of innovation to economic development is described and discussed by giving a review of studies concerning this topic (see Section 2.3). Fourth, as all preceding sections deal with innovation Section 2.4 serves as introduction to the topic of late-comers. It implies the topic of technological catch-up. Finally, the terms and concepts of technological late-comers and early-movers used in the context of this work are explained on a national level, based on the theoretical background presented before (see Section 2.5).

2.1. Concepts of knowledge, technological change and innovation

This section begins with the description of some simple innovation models. At this stage basic terms, such as knowledge, science, technology and innovation are used without providing a profound definition. A detailed definition and discussion of these terms are delivered immediately after the introduction of the innovation models.

[2] The Torch Program is the most important high-tech project launched by the Chinese government to push China's industry towards the high-tech sector (MOST, 2008).

2.1.1. Simple innovation models

Scientific studies on innovation consider two main research focuses. First, the impact of innovation on the economy is a main issue of these studies (see Section 2.3). Second, consideration of its emergence plays an import role in innovation research. A brief overview on simple innovation models is given in this subsection to provide a better understanding of the innovation topic and to deliver a guideline throughout the introduction of the basic concepts and terms.

Linear models

In the seminal theory of Schumpeter (1911), the emergence of innovation is understood as a linear model[3]. He described the process as a sequential order of events which takes place as follows: First, at the beginning of an innovation process stand scientific results. These results can evolve to technology. Technology becomes an innovation, if it enters a market. Finally the new innovative product diffuses on the market during the diffusion process (see Figure 2-1, based on Grupp, 1998, p.14).

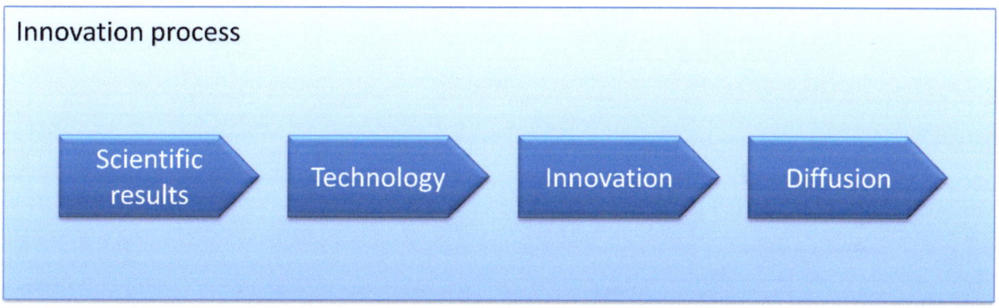

Figure 2-1: Schumpeter's innovation model

Although this concept seems to depict the innovation process just on a highly aggregated level, it delivers a basic understanding of such processes and, thus, influences technology policy discussions (Grupp, 1998, p.15). In its simplicity, it delivers the ground for later approaches, such as the 'science push' (see Bush, 1945) or the 'pipeline model' (see Schmidt-Tiedemann, 1982) which all utilise a sequential approach.

Feedback models

Improvements of the linear models are the so-called feedback models. An example is the chain-linked model of Kline (1985) (see also Kline and Rosenberg, 1986, pp.289-

[3] In his first approach innovation is understood as new products, so-called product innovations.

290). It describes the innovation process not only as a sequential progression of events, but these events stand in a relationship to each other (see Figure 2-2). Kline separates the process of innovation in two different paths which are chained to each other by feedback links and interactions. The central path (path C) is the basic path of innovation process running through the stages of the identification of a potential market, the invention and production of an analytic design, a detailed design and tests, the redesign and production, and, last but not least, the distribution and market introduction. The feedback path delivers feedbacks to preceding stages (f and F). Research and knowledge are placed parallel to these paths as a ubiquitous element (R and K). They stand in a direct link to the innovation processes (D), as they can deliver direct solutions of problems. Moreover they are also influenced by the innovation process indirectly as the stages of the innovation process can provide research instruments, tools, machinery and human resources (I and S).

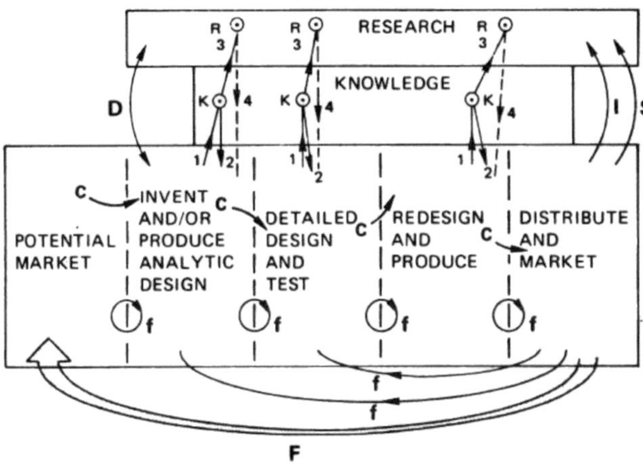

Figure 2-2: Chain-linked model (Kline and Rosenberg, 1986, p. 290)

Feedback links of the chained-linked model is also a central point of the innovation functional reference scheme introduced by Grupp (1998). Science and technology, in his sense, were separated into knowledge stock, fundamental research, applied research and experimental research, as well as the important role of standardisation. Compared to the chain-linked model, Grupp added further differentiations to the dimension of research and knowledge. He speaks of science and technology rather than research and technology which affect certain innovation stages.

All these different aspects of science and technology have a functional interplay with the innovation stages (see Figure 2-3).

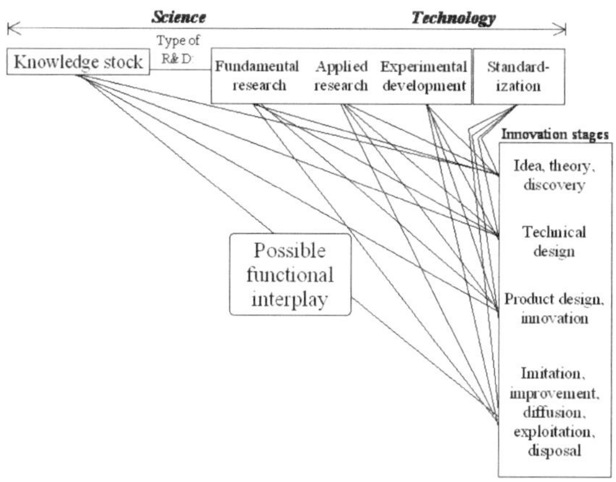

Figure 2-3: Innovation functional reference scheme (Grupp, 1998, p.18)

Hence, theories and concepts about the emergence of innovation develop through the years. Starting with the assumption that the innovation process is a linear model, later works add further interactions into the process so that it turns more and more into a system of innovations. As simple models in most cases did not satisfy complex considerations on the emergence of the innovation, many researchers discussed the shortcomings of these models. These discussions led to the introduction of the concepts of the systems of innovation which are described in Section 2.2. Since the terms 'knowledge', 'science', 'technology', and 'innovation' are used until this stage without a precise definition the following subsection deals with these terms.

2.1.2. Classification of knowledge

The understanding of the term 'knowledge' passes through many discussions and has a long history. It is a topic which was already discussed in ancient times by philosophers, such as Aristotle and Plato. However, the meaning of knowledge mainly goes along with the context it used. So, it is hard to give a general definition of the term 'knowledge', as there are many different ones depending on the context it is used for. Machlup (1980, p. xiii), for instance, states that for a general sketch-up of 'knowledge' that it is '[…] anything that people think they know […]'. Furthermore, he argues that there are no confinements regarding scientific, technological, verified, practical or intellectual knowledge. Related to economics, knowledge is often described as an entity with certain characteristics which are important for economic action. It is classified as follows:

In economic literature, knowledge is mainly examined in terms of its usability. Therefore, it is often characterised by two properties which are explained by different authors with different names. However, all these concepts are close to each other. Cowan et al. (2000), for instance, state that it is a continuum with two dimensions where the outer extremities are defined as ‘codified knowledge’, on the one side, and ‘tacit knowledge’, on the other side. ‘Codified knowledge’, on the one side, stands for knowledge which is presentable explicitly, for instance, knowledge which is written in a book. On the other side, knowledge has tacit dimension which describes all kind of knowledge which is not presentable explicitly. An example is basically given by the work of craftsmen who often do not know the reason for specific steps in their work. Cowan et al. refer in their work to Polanyi (1958) who argues that in modern understanding, knowledge generation and application is not just an explicit and conscious cognitive process; the tacit aspect of knowledge. In fact, Polanyi (1958) writes that knowledge has also attributes which are not in the permanent focus of its bearer. This means that a person may have abilities of which he is not conscious aware of and consequently can not explicitly formulate these abilities. Hence, the general use of knowledge is constraint by the ability to display it. Further, the competence to use tacit knowledge is restricted to the medium of this knowledge. A similar approach is represented by Grupp (1998), who argues that knowledge is a commodity with two characteristics. He separates knowledge into ‘embodied knowledge’ and ‘disembodied knowledge’ (Grupp, 1998, p. 335-336). This means that knowledge can be bound to certain entities, persons and machineries e.g., and is just applicable by these entities, which is a further similar understanding of ‘tacit knowledge’. On the contrary, ‘disembodied knowledge’ stands for knowledge which is, by and large, freely usable. Hence, ‘disembodied knowledge’ is in a broader sense knowledge which is possible to codify. Examples for ‘disembodied knowledge’ can be found as books, blueprints and so forth.

This subsection shows that there is no common definition of the term ‘knowledge’. In economic literature, however, it is classified by its usability. On the one hand, it is codified what means that it is understandable and freely usable. On the other hand, it can be tacit and, therefore, it is not explicitly able to display and also not freely usable. These two aspects are important for the role of knowledge concerning innovation and innovation activities. The specific effect of knowledge on economy, e.g. regarding labour force, is discussed later on in relation to innovation and economic development.

2.1.3. Science and technology

Based on the discussion of knowledge, the next step concerns the creation and application of it. One basic source of innovation is science and technology (S&T) (see Subsection 2.1.1). S&T, therefore, stands for a basic term where other terms, such as research and development (R&D), are also included. For the creation of innovation a broad S&T base is necessary. In this context, Kline and Rosenberg (1986, p.287) argue that innovation draws on science and is often introduced as 'applied science'. Thus, to give a clear definition of innovation, it is, at first, important to clarify the meanings of 'science' and 'technology'.

Dasgupta and David (1994, pp.495) distinguish clearly between science and technology. For them, science is defined as the process of knowledge creation, and technology as the output of knowledge[4]. To be more precise, science covers the '[...] creation, discovery, examination, classification, reorganisation, and dissemination of knowledge about physical, biological or social subjects' (Kline and Rosenberg, p.287). Two factors of science affect innovation mainly. The first factor is the current amount of knowledge which helps understanding and solving problems. The second one is the process of collecting, verifying, and correcting this stock of. So, it can be stated that there is hardly innovative activity without science; hence, science pushes innovation. In contrast, it should not be neglected that the demand for innovation also pushes science (Kline and Rosenberg, p.287). Thus, science does not just help to create knowledge and it influences the constant work, development and upgrade of knowledge.

Following Grupp (1998, p.9), technology is '[...] science application know-how'. He also refers to other authors, when he points to the fact that technology summarises the creation of artefacts, crafts and items of knowledge as well as various forms of social organisations[5]. Moreover, technology describes '[...] any purposive treatment, method, working method and skill in the exploitation of scientific knowledge together with the products [...]' which fulfil these characteristics. In other languages, such as German, the distinction between these products as well as artefacts (e.g. machinery) and knowledge itself is more clearly distinguished (Bullinger, 1994 and Hullmann, 2001). This separation is not given in English. So, technology is not merely applied-science. It also represents all different kinds of knowledge applications (Kline and Rosenberg, 1986, p.287).

[4] see also Hullmann (2001)
[5] See also Stankiewicz (1992), Roberts (1987) and Berry and Taggart (1994)

2.1.4. Technological change

The change in the realm of technology and its progress is called 'technological change'. The concept of 'technological change' is addressed by many important research studies on innovation. Romer (1990), for instance, implements a neoclassical model to analyse the role of endogenous technological change on economic growth. He defines technological change as '[...] improvements in the instructions for mixing together raw materials [...]' (ibid., p.S72). Grupp (1998) states that technological change does not have a priori a positive score, as the meaning of change can also be a '[...] retrograde step [...]' and, hence, do not necessarily imply an improvement. Grupp, in this case, represents a more neutral view on the meaning of change, although he emphasised that it is of greater interest to look at improvements (ibid., p.14). Technological change describes the change, respectively, the improvements in the realm of technology without the aspect of commercialisation. Hence, it can be distinguished from innovation. It focuses on the mere development of technology.

2.1.5. Innovation

Schumpeter (1911) introduces the term 'innovation' in the realm of economic science as a change in economy which brings profit to the entrepreneur (the so-called *quasi-rents* or *innovation rents*). He describes that 'mere economic growth' happens, if the population or the capital of a national economy increase. Apart from this phenomenon, there is also a '[...] fundamental change in the sphere of production [...]' which is accountable for economic growth (Schumpeter, 1911, p.95). In his words innovation must be something new, a product or a new production process, which also has an economic effect[6]. Thereby, he mentions five different kinds of innovation (see Schumpeter, 1934):

- introduction of a new product or a qualitative change in an existing product;
- process innovation new to an industry;
- the opening of a new market;
- development of new sources of supply for raw materials or other inputs;
- changes in industrial organisation.

[6] Innovation is often classified as product and process innovation (see Schumpeter, 1934, OECD, 1996, and Grupp, 1998).

Later on other authors often define innovation in similar way. Grupp (1998) refers to this approach and defines innovation as a commercialised invention[7]. The idea of 'innovation rents' is reflected by the commercial aspect. Bullinger (1994, pp.35) defines that the term 'innovation' includes two aspects; it is not only the development of something new, but also the market launch of this new 'thing'. Furthermore, he states in a detailed classification that innovation has to be separated between product innovation and process innovation. In this respect, the OECD (Oslo Manual, 1996, p.31) also defines that technological innovation '[...] comprises implemented technologically new products and processes and significant technological improvements in products and processes [...].' Thereby, the term 'implementation' means that the innovation '[...] has been introduced on the market (product innovation) or used within a production process (process innovation) [...]'.

The term 'innovation' always comprises an economic perspective. This is emphasised by most of the authors who deal with innovation research[8]. Hence, it is important that the new product or process always has to enter a market to be called an innovation.

2.2. Innovation Systems

After the definition of the basic terms concerning innovation research this section gives an introduction to another aspect of innovation topic: the innovation systems. As it delivers the background to the empirical analysis in this thesis all elements of the preceding section are linked with each other and integrated into a framework for the empirical analysis. Furthermore it also induces the understanding of technological late-comers. Following this section, the next one gives a review of works on innovation and economic growth, as well as technological catch-up processes and problems concerning innovators and imitators. Based on these models, Section 2.5 finally configures the frame around the theme of technological late-comers.

A national, regional, sectoral, and technological perspective

The term 'system' describes the idea of the interactive innovation process in a more detailed way than simple innovation models (see Subsection 2.1.1). The development towards this understanding began in the late 1980s, and at the beginning of the 1990s with the discussion about *National Innovation Systems* (NIS). Although the idea of innovation and economic systems within national boundaries already dates back to the 19th century, when List (1841) studies the problem of economic and innovative

[7] A distinction between innovation and invention is tried to given by Rutten (1959, p. 605) who states that invention stands for the subset of technical innovations which are patentable. Grupp (1998, p. 148) uses the term 'invention' in a similar way.

[8] See also Ott (1959) and Perillieux (1987)

differences between Prussia and England, the first seminal researches addressing innovation systems are published by Freeman (1987), Lundvall (1992) and Nelson (1993) (see Edquist, 2001). Furthermore, previous approaches assumed that innovations are made by a single person or firm. Researchers argued that this assumption does not hold. In addition, innovation activities are evolutionary which means that they develop over time. Countries with a higher amount of knowledge can develop faster and generate new innovation on existing knowledge. The reconstruction of Germany after the Second World War can be cited as an example. Beside of the immense economic aid delivered, for instance, by the USA the quick comeback of the German economy relayed to its skilled workers and existing knowledge stock. Over the years, other concepts evolve out of the national perspective, namely the *Regional Innovation Systems* (RIS), the *Sectoral Innovation Systems* (SIS), and the *Technological Innovation System* (TIS). A description of all three perspectives will be given after the definition of the term 'innovation system' and a presentation of the elements of this system.

One definition of systems of innovation is given by Edquist (1997). We follow his definition in this thesis. He introduces an innovation system as '[…] all important economic, social, political, organisational, and other factors that influence the development, diffusion, and use of innovations.' (Edquist, 1997, p.4) The first important fact deriving from this definition is that the focus of these approaches lies on the determinants of innovation and not on its effects. Second, the identification of these factors is crucial to understand such a system.

Elements of the innovation system

For the identification of the factors Edquist (2001, p.5) suggests that there are, first, components of the systems, namely organisations and institutions, and second, relations between the components. Thereby, organisations are formal structures with an explicit purpose. They are the players of the system. Examples are companies, universities and any kind of actors within these systems. Institutions are sets of routines and interaction rules for the relationship between the organisations. Examples for institutions are laws, habits, and policies (Edquist and Johnson, 1997, pp.46-47). Second, there are relationships within a system. These relationships could be either found between different organisations, or between organisations and institutions and institutions themselves. Referring to Edquist (1997), a successful operation of an innovation system depends on all factors, components and relations. For a precise analysis of a system, it needs to be possible to identify clear boundaries around the whole system. This leads to the NIS, RIS, SIS, and TIS.

National Innovation Systems

At the beginning, the discussions about innovation systems concentrated on NIS (see Freeman (1987), Lundvall (1992) and Nelson (1993). As the name already conveys, this approach rcgards innovation systcms, as dcscribcd bcforc, from a national perspective with respective geographical and political borders. Important components of the NIS, therefore, are national institutions, such as national laws, policies, governmental funding etc., as well as all organisations within a national boarder, such as companies, research institutes, consumers and so on. The relations in the NIS can be found between these national components. Examples are co-operation between firms or between firms and research institutes.

Regional Innovation Systems

Regional innovation systems, in turn, are innovations systems where the geographic boundaries are drawn more tightly compared to the country borders (see Figure 2-4). They are introduced, for instance, by Cooke et al. (1997) and Cooke (2001). RIS are mainly discussed within the borders of a country, although they can trespass the borders of a country. Cooke et al. (1997, p.480) define regions as '[...] territories smaller than their state possessing significant supra-local governance capacity and cohesiveness differentiating them from their state and other regions [...]'. RIS should not be mixed up with clusters which describe regions where companies, specialised suppliers, service providers, firms in related industries, and associated institutions interact with each other (Porter, 1998, p. 78). Although these definitions do not exclude each other, they focus on different topics. RIS are often considered in innovation research, because relations are local and hence, locality matters in many (but not all) innovation activities. Policies and activities to influence the innovation system within the smaller regions are easier to discover, to measure, and to show.

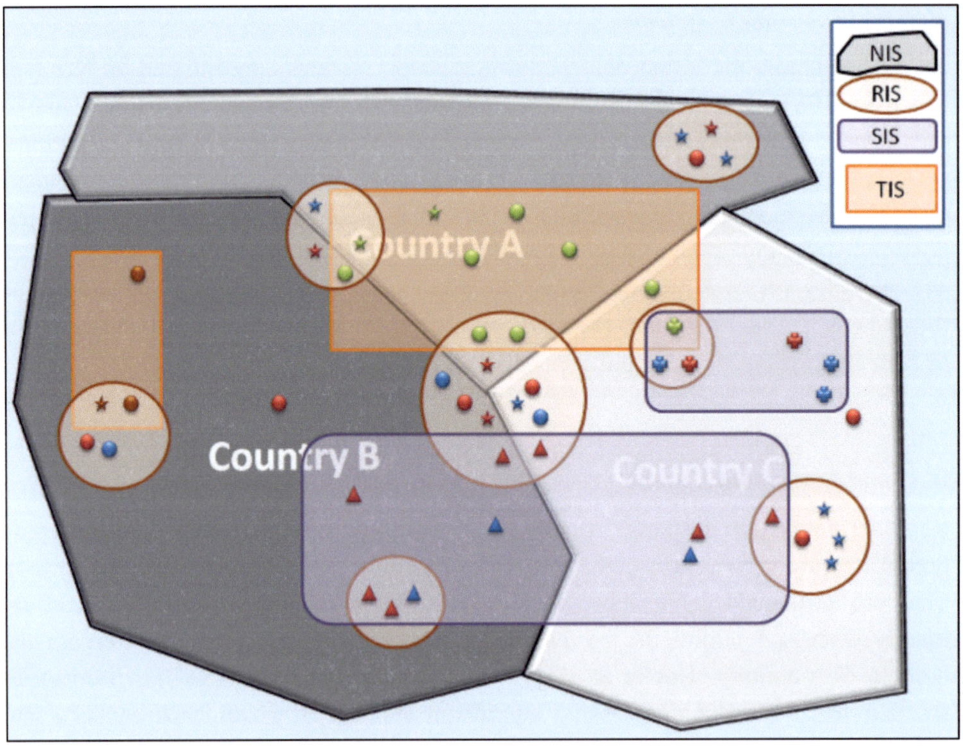

Figure 2-4: Systems of innovation

Sectoral and Technological Innovation Systems

The third and forth understanding of innovation system stresses geographical distance less and firstly looks at sectoral and technological assignments of components and relations. Thereby, the sectors are seen as industrial fields or product areas, e.g., the automotive industry and technological fields, e.g. the biotechnology area. Malerba (2002, p.247) argues that sectoral constraints always provide a key level of analysis in economics. In fact, sectoral analysis allows the examination of life-cycles of specific products and technologies. Other researchers also picked up this advantage and used it in their analysis[9].

Beside of the national, regional, sectoral, and technological approaches there are many others as well. Freeman (2002), for instance, also talks about *continental* and *sub-national* systems. These systems, however, can be derived from the former four and do not play an important role in innovation research. Furthermore, it needs to be stated that these four systems do not exclude to each other. In fact, they complement

[9] See Breschi and Malerba (1997) and Nelson and Mowery (1999).

each other and, moreover, that they co-exist with each other. Figure 2-4 shows an illustration of the coexistence of the four systems and how they can overlap with each other. The different symbols (stars, circles, and triangles) represent the components while each kind of symbol represents another sector. The colours (blue, green, red, and brown) stand for different technologies. For a simplification, it is assumed that each component just applies one kind of technology which is not necessarily true in the real world.

As aforementioned, the analysis of innovation systems focuses on the examination of the determinants of innovation and not on their effects. Niosi (2002) enriched these considerations by the analysis of the efficiency and effectiveness of different NIS. From the economic point of view, these considerations should not be neglected. The NIS, as well as SIS and TIS are needed for parts of the following analysis.

2.3. Innovation and economic development

Schumpeter's view (1911) on innovation delivers, at its early stages, the mere results of the observation that innovation has its impact on sustainable economic growth. Neither does he specify a source for innovation, nor does he formulate mathematical models to underline his observations. In one of his later works (Schumpeter, 1942), he tackles at least the aspect that innovation creates a monopoly and, hence, a certain profits (see *quasi-rents* and *innovation rents* in Subsection 2.1.5). This 'monopolistic practice' improves production and drives economic development. The statement is known as the so-called 'Schumpeter hypothesis'. Although, or just because, his works still lack the explanation of how innovation occurs, his ideas become the starting point of most innovation theories. As a complete description of all innovation theories goes beyond the scope of this dissertation, and are not used in this thesis, just the basic theories and the theories which are needed for the topic of technological late-comers are discussed.

2.3.1. Growth theory

A macroeconomic view on innovation and economic growth is provided by Solow (1956). He starts to think about the influence of innovation on production, and consequently on economic development, with a neoclassical production function[10] considering one output (Y) and two inputs, namely labour (L) and capital (C). The relation between output and input is denoted as follows (2-1):

$$Y = L^{\propto} * C^{1-\propto} * TFP \qquad (2\text{-}1)$$

[10] Solow (1956) used a Cobb-Douglas function.

With this theoretical approach he tries to describe the empirically observed phenomenon that developed countries grow constantly, although their production factors, in the same period of time, do not grow in the same proportion. Solow suspects that there must be another factor which drives this growth and considered a third input which is responsible for this growth, the so-called Total Factor Productivity (TFP). In his understanding, this third factor has to do with something that enables the same combination of labour and capital to achieve a higher level of output. He concluded that this residuum is related to different levels of technology.

A deeper insight into this approach is given in the *New Growth Theory* which analyses the factor TFP extensively. While Solow considers TFP as something exogenous, economists of the New Growth Theory emphasise an endogenous character on TFP. Lucas (1972) and Romer (1990), for instance, refer to human capital as part of TFP and state that output can be invested to build up the stock of human capital. As this factor can be increased by investments in education, schooling and so forth, TFP no longer has been black box. In addition, the *New Growth Theory* also sheds light on effects of knowledge diffusion.

Thus, from a macroeconomic approach a perceptible effect of knowledge, technology and innovation on productivity is evident, and this also influences economy. In the subsequent subsection a microeconomic view will be highlighted. Once again, the last subsection illustrates that technology and innovation is crucial for economic development. Countries which want to improve their GDP also have to invest into new technology and innovation.

2.3.2. Competition theory

Von Hayek (1978) takes over the idea of Schumpeter's 'monopolistic practice' and formulates an innovation theory by integrating concepts from competition theory. He wants to show the effect of knowledge on the economy. Thereby, he starts with an assumption that consumers always ask for new goods and services and companies try to satisfy these demands. Knowledge, however, provides companies with the ability to find new types of allocation to produce new goods or create new services and, hence, deliver new sources of income. The economy is in a permanent 'exploration process' to look for still unutilised opportunities which create new income and, therefore, economic growth. For this reason, successful companies need to foster their knowledge stock (Grupp, 1998, pp.57-58).

Another innovation theory is represented by Arrow (1962b). In the neoclassical tradition, he asks questions about welfare and perfect allocations of commodities[11].

[11] Arrow (1962b, pp.179) stated that 'information' can also be regarded as commodity.

Based on a set of assumptions, he creates a mathematical model to examine mainly the effect of market structure on innovation activities. The results show that the incentive to innovate is linked to the market structure, and he considers full competition as the most fruitful breeding ground of innovation which stands in contrast to Schumpeter's monopolistic practice.

Although there are more theories on the interaction between competition and innovation[12], already the two approaches presented above show that influences of innovation on economic growth can first be analysed with competition theories and that competition is even necessary for innovation. This underlines the importance of countries which are late-comers in technological sense, as they do not necessarily bear risks to developed countries, but also can stand for opportunities for the global economy.

2.3.3. Innovation and trade

The key concepts of competition theory can be found in the discussions about innovation and international trade. With the emergence of the questions about the economic relevance and the impact of innovations, aspects like globalisation and international trade flows are also considered. In this case competitiveness is regarded from the national perspective, rather than from the companies' point of view. The concepts of competitiveness of firms and nations differ from each other. Krugman (1991, pp.811) discussed the differences by references to Ricardian trade theory. He points to comparative advantages so that even countries with actually higher absolute productions costs can participate in international trade (see also Ricardo, 1817). In addition, international competition does not drive countries into bankruptcy. This also distinguishes competition on a national and a firm level. The strength of domestic industries results from their so-called 'external economies'. Krugman (1991, p.813) introduces these effects as *technological external economies* and *pecuniary external economies*. Thus, he states that comparative advantages are self-reinforcing and countries have to maintain productivity and technological change.

Another approach on international trade and technological change is laid by Grossman and Helpman (1990). They create a method to analyse the relationship between trade, knowledge accumulation and endogenous growth based on a regression model. In their analysis, they refer to the *New Growth Theory*, in which technological progress is generated endogenously. They show that the national knowledge stock positively affects the long-term growth performance and trading activities. Furthermore, they emphasise that international knowledge diffusion is not self-

[12] See also Grossekettler (1985)

supporting. Thus, similar to Krugman, they attest that knowledge and technological change are important for trade and competition on the national level.

Section 2.3 summarised theories and approaches regarding the relationship between innovation and economic development. It shows that innovation is important for economic development in a direct and indirect way. The *Growth Theory* and the *Competition Theory* emphasises this importance and this also justifies the relevance of this thesis. Following the line of argumentation, the next section will deal with the topic of technological catch-up processes to tackle the problem of those who are not innovators and try to follow the innovators.

2.4. Technological catch-up

Economic growth base on production cost advantages and cost advantages for raw materials. This kind of growth, however, last mostly just for a short period of time. As sustainable growth relates to innovation, the pursuit of economic growth also drives innovation activities. Thus, the creation of innovation is a must for firms and countries. The definition of innovation (see Subsection 2.1.5), however, implies that only one firm or country can be the innovator of a certain innovation. All others have to follow and catch-up with this novelty. This section deals with the topic of technological catch-up in a broader sense. Therefore, it tackles the differences between innovation and imitation, the discussion of technological gaps, absorptive capacities and learning processes.

2.4.1. Innovators and imitators

Innovators and imitators are not, per se, antipodes. They often appear in combination with each other, because innovators profit from the so-called *innovation rents* (see Subsection 2.1.5) and imitators try to catch-up with this advantage. An imitation, thereby, needs not to be an exact copy of an innovation, although this is the common understanding of imitation. In this respect, Hauschildt (1997, p.61) states that imitations have a highly negative touch. In his definition of imitation, he refers to Schwartz (1978, p.46) who writes that imitations are the manufacturing of a product or a process which has the same characteristics like a product or process which was already developed by another firm. Furthermore, imitations always follow innovations and are based on a similar technology. In fact, imitations do not always result out of intentional replicating processes and it can be seen as a rival innovation which means that it is not new to the world, but new to a firm and country (Grupp, 1998, p. 20).

Referring to these two perspectives the term ‘imitation’ is defined for the remainder of the thesis as a process and a product which has similar characteristics as an existing innovation. An imitator is the user or producer of such a process or product.

The generation of the imitation does not necessarily have to be an intentional replicating process of the imitator.

2.4.2. Technological gap

The term 'technological gap' is strongly related with the discussion about innovators and imitators. Abramowitz (1986) addresses this topic by looking at technologies embodied in a country's capital stock, meaning, for instance, the technological ability to produce certain goods. He argues that the gap represents the time span a country needs to establish the current stock and, hence, abandon the older one. Leaders who are at the technological frontier try to renew their stock whenever possible. Needless to say that a follower tries to close the gap by installing new technology too, and, thus, attempt to introduce imitation or even new innovation (Abramowitz, 1986, p. 386). Fagerberg (1987, p. 88) introduces his technology gap approach along with four hypotheses[13]:

i. There exists a close relationship between the economic performance and the technological level of a country.
ii. The economic development of a country influences its change of the technological growth level.
iii. Countries which face a technological gap, which means that they are on a lower technological level than the countries at the technological frontier[14], can increase their economic growth by imitation.
iv. The rate at which a country exploits the possibilities which are offered by the technological gap depends on its ability to use resources for the transformation of social, institutional and economic structures.

The definition of the technological gap is implicitly given in hypothesis (iii). Although Fagerberg (1987) induces an explanation on how the gap is influencing an economy and, the other way round, how the economy affects technology, his description about the gap remains vague. Abramowitz (1986) delivers a more precise description to this term. Later studies, such as Glass and Saggi (1998) and Fagerberg and Verspagen (2002), talk about technological differences when they tackle the topic of technological gaps. They, however, do not state a clear definition of this term.

2.4.3. Absorptive capacities and learning processes

As stated before, it is important for sustainable growth that a country needs to upgrade its technological capabilities permanently. For this reason it is crucial to avoid technological gaps. As Fagerberg (1987) says imitation can be one solution to exploit

[13] Fagerberg (1987) derived his four hypotheses from other authors, such as Posner (1961), and Gomulka (1971).
[14] The technological frontier is defined as technological state-of-the-art.

economic opportunities. Even if countries are technological followers, it is still necessary for these countries to understand how to imitate an innovation. This leads to the discussion on absorptive capabilities and learning processes.

The relevance of learning processes are part of the research work of Arrow (1962a), Romer (1986, 1990), and Lucas (1988). All three authors emphasise the role of technology for economic growth and the role of learning processes to generate new technologies. Learning processes can have a twofold effect: the can either generate new-to-the-world or new-to-a-firm, respectively new-a-country knowledge. Arrow, Romer and Lucas, however, state that it is possible to make efforts with respect to these processes. For the understanding of technological catch-up, however, learning processes can be seen as active processes to learn from innovation of countries at the technological frontier.

In contrast to the generation of new-to-the-world knowledge, firms and countries also often use existing knowledge from external sources which are new-to-the-firm, but are not new from an absolute perspective. In this respect, nowadays, technology is often regarded as non-trivial and imitations of innovations are not straight-ahead activities. Thus, followers often have to deal with the generation of absorptive capacity in the first stage as it is a necessary requirement for imitation processes. Cohen and Levinthal (1990, p.128) introduce the term 'absorptive capacity' to state the ability to exploit external knowledge. They argue that the ability to evaluate and utilise outside knowledge and technology depends on related knowledge located in the organisation. Further, they say that absorptive capacities are composed not only of the knowledge of most recent scientific or technological developments, but even of basic skills and shared language of a firm[15]. Hence, imitation processes also require investments in research and development, since they rely on a certain level of internal knowledge.

To summarise this section, it can be stated that technological catching-up processes can be regarded as learning and imitation processes. Technological catch-up aims at the narrowing of technological gaps and the convergence to the technological frontier. With this understanding the next section approaches the main topic of this dissertation and a definition of late-comers is derived from the previous sections.

2.5. Technological late-comers

The term 'technological late-comers' is used in economic literature in a broad sense. In many analyses of regions, countries, such as Asian emerging economies and, firms it is used vaguely and without precise definitions. For this reason, this section deals with

[15] Cohen and Levinthal (1990) just regard absorptive capacity on firm level. This approach can also used on country level.

this short-coming and delivers a more clear definition of late-comers. It also introduces into the main part of the theme of this dissertation. To do so, a brief overview of the work on late-comers will be given. Additionally, a distinction between the discussion on leaders and followers and early-movers and late-comers will be stated. At the end of this subsection, a definition of late-comers applied in this work is given.

2.5.1. Technological late-comers in economic literature

Technological late-comers have been discussed in economic literature since the second half of the 1990s. In most of these papers, Forbes and Wield (2000), Chang and Tsai (2002), Furman and Hayes (2004), Sampath (2006), and Krawczyk et al. (2007) e.g., the term 'late-comers' names countries which lag behind the technological leaders in the world. Technological leaders are countries such as the USA, Japan or Germany. These works aim at analysing technological catch-up processes of the late-comer countries. Such processes are determined by the specific environmental constraints, mainly the *National Innovation Systems*, but also managing strategies of these countries, for instance, a clear technological orientation in specific niches (see Chang and Tsai, 2002). Conspicuously, these works all examine the rise of the East Asian countries, namely South Korea and Taiwan, in the 1970s and 1980s and compare them to countries at the technological frontier.

Firm level analysis on this topic appeared at the same time[16]. It is observable that mainly East Asian firms from South Korea and Taiwan, but also from Singapore and Hong Kong are analysed regarding their innovation activities. In fact, the analysis of the catch-up process and innovation activities do not highlight *National Innovation Systems* anymore, but they also try to shed light on the catch-up process with a focus on management and R&D strategies. A case study on this topic shows that late-comer firms from the East Asian (South Korea, Taiwan, Hong Kong, and Singapore) electronics sector are already able to present innovations on the international market. These innovations, however, are rather improvements and incremental innovations than cutting-edge innovations (Hobday, 1995). The same findings apply to the result of a later analysis. Choung et al. (1999) show in this empirical approach for Korean semiconductor firms that their focus on adoption and improvement of existing innovations is quite successful. In another investigation Cho et al. (1998) also find that a clear focus is helpful to become successful late-comers. They show for Japanese semiconductor firms, especially Toshiba, that their focus on a certain segment of the semiconductor sector and an aggressive investment into the improvements of the special technologies belonging to these segments has a positive effect on Toshiba's success.

[16] See Hobday (1995), Cho et al. (1998), and Choung et al. (2000).

These analyses, however, bear some short-comings. First, some of them do not distinguish between 'followers' and 'late-comers' in a precise sense. These two terms are sometimes even used as substitutes. Second, most of them lack a clear definition of late-comers. Moreover, the examinations on country level deliver as evidence to the existence of the technological gap. This may hold for static analyses, but leads to problems in a dynamic environment, e.g. when late-comers succeed to catch-up and move towards the technological leaders. Hence, a general definition at this stage is obligatory. The firm level analysis mostly defines a firm as lagging behind based on its location or origin. Hence, firms from countries which lag behind are by definition also lagging behind without taking into account the heterogeneity of the firm population. This also does not hold for a general definition on firm level late-comers. Thus, the next subsection will deal with these two problems.

2.5.2. '*Early-movers* and *late-comers*' vs. '*leaders* and *followers*'

The approach of technological early-movers and late-comers has to be separated from the one of technological leaders and followers. In general, the follower in the understanding of innovation research is thematically linked to the understanding of imitators. In Schumpeterian tradition the followers are imitators of innovations. They try to participate in the innovation rents of the monopolistic innovator[17]. This means that followers do not innovate, but they imitate. This basic characteristic is the main difference between followers and late-comers. Late-comers also take part it the innovation activities, as they are identified by a later entry into a certain market with their own innovation, even if these innovations are no cutting-edge innovations. This distinction is also used by Forbes and Wield (2000), Chang and Tsai (2002), and Furman and Hayes (2004).

In fact, a distinction of these two approaches remains unclear, as the relation between followers and late-comers cannot be stated precisely. Late-comers naturally emerge from followers. Late-comers, however, bear the touch of successful followers as they leave the status of imitators behind and introduce their own innovation.

2.5.3. A definition of technological late-comers

Cho et al. (1998, pp. 490) state that given definitions to the term of late-comers are very vague. In their work they characterise early-mover and late-comer firms by advantages and disadvantages in regard to market, competition, learning-by-doing, and enhanced level of information that they have to face. Hobday (1995, p. 1172) used a quite similar idea. In his definition, late-comer firms are manufacturing companies

[17] The imitation activities are also the reason why these monopolistic rents are also called ‚*quasi rents*, because they are temporary and just last until imitation enters the market.

which have to face two competitive disadvantages. First, they are located in developing countries (such as East Asian countries at that time) and, thus, they have no direct access to main international sources of technology and R&D. Second, they have disadvantages concerning the international market, as they are not directly situated in a leading-edge market. Furthermore, late-comer firms are characterised by focussing on minor and incremental innovations. During the establishment of a usable level of absorptive capability, they are still in transition from technology users to technology generators (Choung et al., 2000, p.969). On the country level, Sampath (2006) simply states that late-comer countries are countries which are not at the technological frontier.

For this thesis, the term 'technological late-comer' for firms and countries is defined by the following characteristics:

i. Technological late-comers enter the technological competition with their innovations.
ii. Technological late-comers enter existing industrial and technological sectors.

Based upon this definition the unit of the empirical analysis is derived in the next chapter.

2.6. Summary

Chapter 2 aims at giving a general overview on the theoretical background by clarifying the terminology, introducing relevant innovation theories and defining the basic concept of 'technological late-comers'.

For this reason, the first section deals with the definitions of knowledge, science, technology, technological change, and innovation (see Subsection 2.1). It shows that knowledge, science and technology do have many different definitions. However, since economists more and more gain interests in these topics, the OECD decided to generate standardised definitions (see OCED, 1996). Furthermore, it shows that the emergence of innovation can be shown in an aggregated level by simple innovation models. Nowadays, it can be taken for granted that innovation does not appear from nowhere. Thus, modern research efforts try to explain the emergence of innovation with more sophisticated approaches (see *Innovation Systems*). The four perspectives on innovation systems, namely the *National Innovation System*, *Regional Innovation System*, *Sectoral Innovation System*, and *Technological Innovation System* are referred to in the following empirical analyses (see Section 2.2). In the next section the relation between innovation and economic development is discussed once more through the view of different theories, such as the *New Growth Theory* (see Section 2.3). In addition, the relevance of innovation for innovators, as well as for firms and countries which lag behind is discussed. In this respect, terms like ‘technological gap’, ‘innovators’ and ‘imitators’ are tackled. So, it is important for the discussion about innovation that not just innovators are analysed. Moreover, analyses of innovation do also have to deal with countries that face technological gaps (see Section 2.4).

Finally, the last section develops the basic concept of ‘technological late-comers’ (see Section 2.5) for this thesis. After the review of the literature dealing with this topic, it draws clear lines for the theoretical concept of ‘late-comers’ based on the terminology and theoretical background delivered in the preceding sections. This distinction separates the approach concerning ‘early-movers’ and ‘late-comers’ from the research line concerning ‘leaders’ and ‘followers’.

3. Indicators of innovation and data background

The last chapter provided the theoretical background on technological change and innovation in general, and summarises the relevant innovation theories for the approach of technological late-comers and technology competition. In this chapter the tools to measure innovation activities and their theoretical background are introduced. Furthermore, a description of the data used for the analysis is given.

After the introduction of theories which deliver insight into the emergence of innovation and show how they affect economic development, researchers also look for different ways to empirically capture innovation and technological change. As the creation process of innovation on a first stage uses immaterial and intangible factors, such as knowledge (see Subsection 2.1.2), it is not a straight-forward process to develop commonly accepted indicators to measure them. Therefore, Chapter 3 deals with this topic. Additionally, it introduces the data background for the empirical analysis. First of all, a general overview of innovation measurements and indicators is outlined (see Section 3.1). Within the next step, patent indicators, one of the most recognised innovation indicators, are described in more detail. Additionally, these indicators are reflected upon from many perspectives. Therefore, pro and cons are discussed. As patent indicators are also the most important instrument for the analysis of this work, a precise introduction to them is given (see Section 3.2).

3.1. Measurement of innovation activities

The measurement of innovation activities is a topic which is rarely addressed in detail after the discussion in the late 1990s. Today the existence of innovation indicators is regarded as given. Freeman and Soete (2009), for instance, state that the development of innovation indicators changes through the last forty years. However, the most indicators can be separated into input and output indicators. Hence, innovation and technology are measured, before they even exist and afterwards when they emerge or when their emergence has a certain impact on the economy. An overview on different kinds of innovation indicators is often not explicitly given. One overview is delivered by Grupp (1998) who also follows a separation into input and output indicators. According to him, input and output indicators are called resource indicators and R&D results respectively. Furthermore he introduces progress indicators which reflect the impact of innovation on economy (see Figure 3-1). These indicators refer to a functional scheme of the innovation process which is introduced in Subsection 2.1.1. As the overview of Grupp relates to other studies on innovation indicators[18], these indicators are explained in detail referring to his scheme. According to Grupp, the

[18] See Oslo Manual of the OECD (1996), OECD (2005) and Freeman and Soete (2009)

innovation process needs inputs (namely resources) that can generate outputs. These outputs, then, affect the economy.

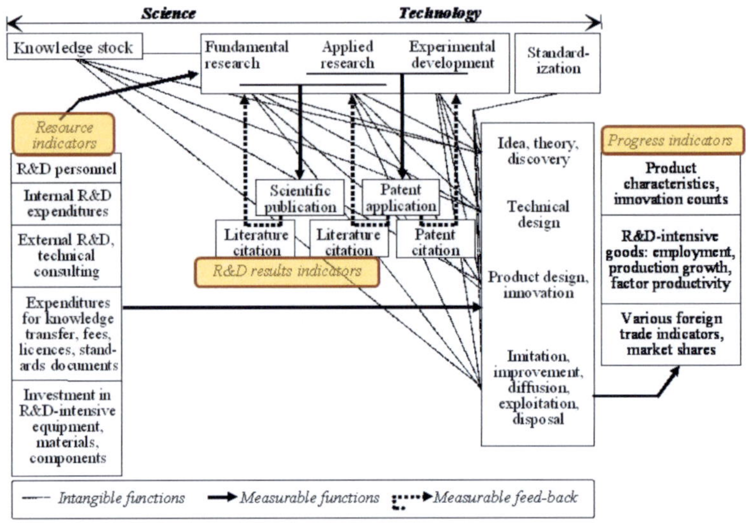

Figure 3-1: Survey of important innovation indicators and their typology (Grupp, 1998, p.143)

Resource indicators

The first category of indicators, namely resource indicators, can also be denoted as input indicators, as they depict the measurable inflows into an innovation process. In this respect, resources are, for instance, R&D personnel, internal and external R&D expenditure, technical consulting, and all kind of expenditures and investments of knowledge transfer, fees, licenses, standards, as well as R&D-intensive equipment, material and components, i.e., all factors which can be used to fuel the innovation process. In most cases, these indicators can be measured unambiguously in monetary units, even in different countries. These kind of input oriented measurement are also supported by clear definitions, e.g. of R&D personnel and, therefore, established by the OSLO Manual (OECD, 1996, Grupp, 1998 and OECD, 2005).

R&D results indicators

R&D result indicators are also known as output indicators. They complement the resource indicators as they measure the output of an innovation process. The most typical and commonly used indicators are patents, as the outcome of applied science and experimental development, and scientific publications, as the outcome of scientific work and fundamental research. Scientific works on innovation activities mostly use these indicators, as evidence of success of innovation activities and, hence, a part of these activities which could be relevant for economies. In this case, patent and scientific publications can be seen as rich sources of information as they make it possible to measure an almost incalculable commodity (see 'knowledge' in Subsection 2.1.1). In fact, this is not the whole story about output indicators, but as they, patents in particular, play an important role for this thesis, they are explained in detail in Section 3.2. (Grupp, 1998 and OECD, 2005)

Progress indicators

Last, progress indicators complete the set of innovation indicators, as they measure the effect of innovation on the economy. They are a special kind of indicators as they do not measure direct effects and influences of innovation activities. Progress indicators are furthermore classified in direct and indirect indicators.

Direct indicators are represented through measurements such as the evaluation of product characteristics and innovation counts[19]. Since they try to show the influence of innovation with comparisons of product characteristics or surveys of firms and their new products and processes these indicators are considered as direct ones. These kinds of indicators are also a rich source of information. However, their evaluation implies problems as it is arduous to carry out such surveys. Furthermore, long-run surveys are often not possible because of panel mortality and changes in the panel, such as insolvencies or mergers and acquisitions.

Indirect progress indicators imply evaluations of production growth, factor productivity, and various trade and market share indicators. These indicators are considered to be indirect ones, as they measure innovation in an indirect way, i.e.; they refer to trade with R&D-intensive commodities. Compared to the direct evaluations, these indicators are easier to carry out. Trade numbers can be, for instance, extracted from federal ministries or annual reports of large multinational enterprises. Disadvantages, in turn, are approximations to the real value of innovations which have to be made. Moreover, these approximations can comprise many different external effects and accounting biases.

Innovation indicators are already established in economics, although the debate on innovation in economics is still a vital one, and it is a 'young' field of research. This section delivered the overview of a possible classification of these indicators. As this thesis uses output indicators to conduct the empirical analysis of technological late-

[19] See also the discussion on so-called Technometrics (e.g. Grupp, 1998, p. 99).

comers, the subsequent section gives a deeper insight into the field of patent indicators. (Grupp, 1998)

3.2. Patent statistics

A patent is an industrial property right on an invention which secures the owner of the patent the exclusive right to use this invention commercially for a certain period of time and in a certain region (OECD, 2009, p. 14). In most cases this regional protection is defined by countries, but it also can have institutional boundaries, for instance, the Intellectual Property Department of Hong Kong. Thus, the owner can be considered as a monopolist regarding the commercialisation of this invention. Patents, however, do not just have the legal function of a property right; moreover, they are a rich source of information in two different aspects. First, they hold the knowledge about the invention described on the patent specification. Second, as aforementioned, they stand for a successful outcome of innovation activities and hold detailed information, such as names and addresses of applicants and inventors, as well as information of day of filing, patent classification etc.

As the empirical analysis and major parts of the econometric models of this dissertation are based on patent data, this section delivers an extended introduction into this topic. First of all, the basics, such as historical insights and basic concepts of patents are described in Subsection 3.2.1. The next Subsection 3.2.2 is dedicated to the functions of patents as innovation indicators. Therefore, an overview of the literature on patents in economics is given, as well as an introduction into the development of modern patent indicators. In the next Section 3.3 a brief summary on the crucial impact of modern information technology, such as computer-based databases, is given. For this reason, this subsection introduces the work on *PATSTAT* database[20] which is implemented in the course of this dissertation at the *Institute for Economic Policy Research* (IWW[21]).

3.2.1. Historical insights and basic concepts

Patents are the most known and most accepted Intellectual Property Right (IPR) in the world. They have a long tradition and history. The origin of the word ‘patent’ stems from the Latin term ‘litterae patentes’ and means, in general, ‘open letter’. In mediaeval times, this kind of letter was issued by the King to grant privileges, such as a monopolistic right to exploit mines or even a title of nobility. In the 15th century, the

[20] The *PATSTAT April 2007* database is known as The *EPO Worldwide Statistical Patent Database April 2007* and it is delivered by the *Patent Statistics Task Force* (Members of the Task Force: European Commission (EC), the European Patent Office (EPO), the Japanese Patent Office (JPO), the US National Science Foundation (NSF), the US Patent and Trademark Office (USPTO) and the World Intellectual Property Organisation (WIPO)).
[21] The abbreviation *IWW* stands for *‚Institut für Wirtschaftspolitik und Wirtschaftsforschung‘*.

first technical 'patent' appeared in Venice. In these patent letters, the exclusive commercial right to use a certain invention was formulated for '[...] men of great genius who invented or discovered ingenious devices [...]' (Kaufer, 1989 cited by Grupp, 1998, p.145). That was the first time that patents, as we know them, occurred. Later, other countries adopted this law to protect inventive ventures. In Europe, France introduced them in the 16th century, and England followed by 1623. The USA did not follow until the 1790s, although Massachusetts already had a similar patent law by 1641. Germany, or rather the territories which were going to be the German Reich after 1871, did not support patent laws, as patents were supposed to hinder the circulation of a new invention. So, the patent law in Germany was not established until 1877 (Grupp, 1998, p.145 and Murrmann and Homburg, 2001).

Basic concept of patents

The resistance of the German territory against a patent law can be reduced to a simple fact. At that time, it was already known that inventions need to circulate and has to enter a market in order to realise profits. People in Germany, however, hold the view that a monopoly on an invention would just help the monopolist and not the whole economy[22]. Thus, this fact would not help to increase welfare of the whole nation. Despite of other reasons, such as the fact that Germany was not unified before 1870/71, it can be stated that this misunderstanding lasted until 1877.

Basically, a patent can be seen as a kind of deal. On the one side, an inventor offers his knowledge to a legal authority. On the other side, this authority offers the protection of the exclusive commercial use of this knowledge for a certain time within its legal sovereign border. So, a patent tries to generate a win-win situation. In fact, from an economic point of view, an inventor would not see the necessity to bare his knowledge. Without the exclusive right to use it, he would rather keep his knowledge a secret. Hence, a patent motivates to bare knowledge and rewards this with the profit one could earn with the monopoly, the so-called innovation rents. In contrast, a nation, country, kingdom, and so forth can also profit as knowledge is diffused and offered to its economy. Other inventors can, then, use this knowledge to generate new knowledge and new inventions.

Premises of patent filling

As described in the last subsection, a patent can generate monopolistic rents. Thus, many applicants try to file patents. To get the legal right on patents, the patent application needs to fulfil certain standards. Meanwhile, these premises are close to

[22] This discussion has also a tradition in Britain.

each other in all main patent authorities all over the world and can be reduced to the following three criteria (OECD, 2009, p.42)[23]:

i. *Novelty* which means that an invention has to be new-to-the-world at the moment when it is filed. If the knowledge, described in the patent application, is already known, e.g. a scientific publication, even in a totally different context, the applicant will not get this application granted.
ii. *Non-obviousness,* or also known as the inventive step which means that the invention needs to enrich existing inventions or knowledge with a certain new aspect. Furthermore, the term of non-obviousness also means that the invention is not considered to be obvious to a person with ordinary skills. This aspect also comprises that the invention is technically and not a disclosure of something naturally existing, such as an animal. However, this criterion is the most crucial one. Patent offices in different countries define this step which has to be made differently. Application numbers at the JPO, for instance, are higher than application numbers at the DPMA, because the inventive step is considered to be lower in Japan (Grupp and Schmoch, 1999).
iii. *Industrial applicability* which means that a commercial use is implied. This criterion aims to distinguish between aesthetic and scientific inventions.

These three criteria are checked during the application process at the different patent authorities by the experts in the field of certain inventions. However, it needs to be mentioned that not all patents are innovations and, vice versa, not all innovations are protected by patents. Figure 3-2 shows the relation between inventions, innovations and patents. If all inventions are considered, just a subset of these inventions is patentable due to the three criteria. However, not all patentable inventions are filed for patents, as the owner of this invention rather wants to keep his invention secret. Innovations lay within these three subsets, as it is a commercial used invention (see Chapter 2).

[23] See also Griliches (1990), (Schmoch, 1990) and Grupp and Schmoch (1999).

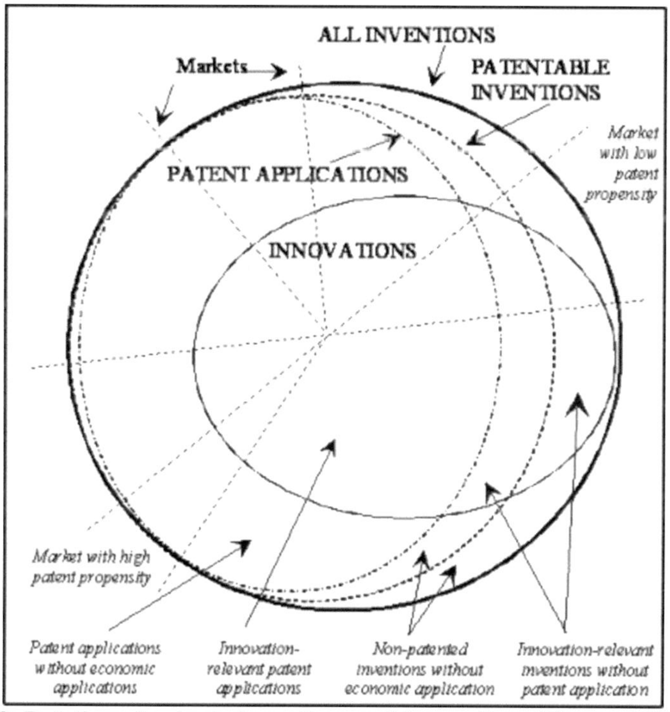

Figure 3-2: Relation of patents, inventions and innovations (Grupp, 1998, p. 148)

Functions and properties

Despite of the three premises of patents, they also have three basic technical properties. The patent law, as mentioned before, as the legal property right, is the first property. This function is the most interesting part for applicants as they seek profits; it gives the holder of the patent the temporal monopoly. Second, patents have an information function which is the most interesting function for the patent authorities and the competitors. The information function represents the disclosure of knowledge by the patent specification. It informs about the state-of-the-art. Both functions are discussed before, as they are the two sides of the basic concept of patents. This function is the desired effect of patents, as the disclosure amplifies the diffusion of knowledge and, hence, its positive effects on the economy. Finally, patents have a return index function. This function is the most interesting one for economic research, as this represents the return, respectively, the output of an innovation process (see Section 3.1), and thus, is also discussed in more detail in the next subsections.

3.2.2. Patents: indicator of innovation

Patent indicators have developed since its first appearance in the middle of the last century. As one of the first references to patents in economic literature, the dissertation of Schmookler (1951, cited by Griliches, 1990, p.1670) has to be mentioned. He tries to show growth of TFP in an economy by measuring patents. Although his first attempt to prove a correlation between TFP and patent statistics does not show the expected effect, it already can be considered as a milestone in innovation research. His work paves the way to patent based economic analysis. Over one decade later, Schmookler uses patents as an indicator also known for in recent times. He introduces patents as an output indicator of innovation processes (Schmookler, 1962, p. 2).

The main work on patent indicators, however, comes up in the 1980s and at the beginning of the 1990s with the rise of computer-based data processing technologies[24]. The innovation research community realises that they have many advantages. Schmoch (1990, p.13) summarised these advantages of patent information as follows:

- Patents provide a broad documentation of nearly all fields of technology.
- They have a complete geographic coverage.
- The collection of exclusive technological information is possible.
- It is possible to collect the important global innovation in [German and[25]] English.
- They have a simple retrieval due to the fine classification.
- Patent data have a good availability due to existing databases.
- Patents are rich in technological details.
- They have a strong relatedness to certain applications.
- They make it possible to collect bibliographic information, such as applicant, inventor, application years, etc.
- They deliver up-to-date information.
- Statistical analyses based on patent data are less cost-intensive.

With the help of electronic databases, it is possible to make use of these advantages so that they influence the development of patents towards a well-accepted innovation indicator. In general, patents make it possible to illustrate innovation activities by time and through a geographical, technological, sectoral, and legal perspective.

[24] See among others Carpenter and Narin (1983), Griliches (1984), Pavitt (1985), Jaffe (1986), Pavitt (1988), Schmoch et al. (1988), Griliches (1990), Schmoch (1990), and Grupp (1998).
[25] Schmoch (1990) was referring to the German Patent and Trademark Office (DPMA).

Anyhow, apart from the advantages, it should be kept in mind that all these information are delivered 'automatically'. Patents are not designed to show innovation processes, but they are an intellectual property. Thus, the information delivered by patents has to be used carefully and with certain consideration. An explanation to these considerations is given according to the information which can be drawn from a patent letter.

Time perspective

Analysing the innovation process from the perspective of time, it is necessary to distinguish between certain dates which can be found on a patent letter[26]:

- **Application filing date:** The filing data, also known as the application date, is the date when the patent application is filed at the patent office.
- **Priority date:** If the applicant wants to have patent protections in different entities the patent has to be filed at different offices. This often takes different amount of time for preliminary work, such as translations etc. To avoid problems with the constraint of novelty due to ones own patent application the priority year was introduced. This means that within a year the same patent applicant is allowed to file the same invention at different authorities without losing its claim of novelty. Hence, the priority date is the earliest date of a patent application.
- **Publication date:** Most of the patent authorities publicise the patent application 18 months after the filing date to disclose the knowledge. This date often goes in line with the grant date of the patent application. *In some cases the application is not granted and, hence, has no grant date.*

According to the listed dates a patent statistic has to use different dates depending on the evidence of the analysis. In most cases, innovation analysis refers to the application filing date, respectively the priority date as this date is the closest date to the moment an invention was made[27].

Geographical perspective

From a geographical perspective patent analysis can obviously base on the country of a patent authority. For a more detailed analysis, however, one should rather use addresses of applicants and inventors, because they show the locations relevant for

[26] This refers to European patents from the EPO.

[27] Multiple priorities are neglected in the description of priority dates as they may confuse the reader who is not in the discussion about patent statistics. Multiple priorities have the meaning that it is also possible to have different priority patents as different offices uses different standards for the inventive step. However, they are not used in the analysis of this thesis.

innovation[28]. At this stage these two kinds of persons should be explained more precisely. First, there are patent applicants who are the holder and owner of the patent. They can be any kind of legal persons regarding the law which means that they can be an individual person, as well as a firm or an institute. In most cases the applicant is represented by a firm or organisation. Second, there are inventors which are the real human creator (or the whole team) of an invention. Thus, they are real persons (and not just legal persons).

For the localisation of places where inventions where created or where the rights on these inventions are, analysis based on patent data uses, mainly, the addresses of applicants or inventors. In addition to the mere localisation of innovation creation, applicants and inventors also deliver the data source to analyse other aspects of the innovation process, such knowledge transfer, patent networking and inventor mobility[29].

Technological and sectoral perspective

For analyses of certain technological and industrial sectors with patent data it is possible to refer to the *International Patent Classification* (IPC). The IPC is a classification used by the patent offices to characterise the patents for their retrieval. So, they are not a per se classification into commonly known international classifications of industrial sectors. Due to the work of Hinze et al. (1997), Schmoch et al. (2003) and Schmoch (2008), it is possible to classify patents in certain technological fields and industrial sectors. The work of these researchers introduced certain concordances to link the IPC with industrial sector classifications, such as the NACE[30], and technological sector classifications. Meanwhile, these classifications are accepted by supranational institutions, such as the OECD (2009). For the identification of the biotechnology sector this thesis refers to the OST[31]/INPI[32]/ISI[33] Concordance (see sector 12, Appendix).

Legal perspective

Finally, patent analysis can focus on a legal perspective which means that they examine patent activities at different offices. As the protection of a patent is always limited to a certain country or even region (e.g. the Hong Kong Intellectual Property Department), applicants always have to keep in mind where they want to receive this protection. Therefore, analyses of different patent offices deliver different evidence. It

[28] See also Jaffe, Trajtenberg and Henderson (1993).
[29] See also Breschi and Lissoni (2003), Cantner and Graf (2006) and Fornahl and Tran (2009).
[30] Nomenclature générale des activités économiques
[31] Observatoire des Science et Techniques
[32] Institute de la Propriété Industrielle
[33] Fraunhofer Institut für System- und Innovationsforschung

is, for sure, much more relevant, to have a patent on the North American or European market than holding the same patent for African, Asian or South American markets. Furthermore, local competitors in the latter markets often just ignore the legal protection. For this reason, patent analyses should have a certain standard and, hence, use information of relevant offices.

Grupp and Schmoch (1999) argue that patent statistics should use applications which are filed at the USPTO, EPO and JPO, as these three offices cover the most important markets. This approach is known as the *Triadic Patent Family*. For the global market, a later approach of Frietsch et al. (2008) shows that the important inventions are filed at EPO or go through the filing process of the *Patent Cooperation Treaty* (PCT) of the *World Intellectual Property Organization* (WIPO). They called this approach the *Transnational Patent* approach which is also used in this thesis.

3.3. Patent information and patent databases

Analyses based on patent data are difficult to perform since these examinations have to deal with mass data. For instance, looking at the three most important national patent offices (USPTO, JPO and DPMA), there have been 795,526.5 patent applications[34] per year between 1986 and 2005. Figure 3-3 shows immensely increasing numbers of applications at the USPTO. They start from nearly 90,000 patents in 1986 and go up to over 430,000 in 2005. The JPO has a decreasing numbers of patent applications from 520,000 in 1987 down to 400,000 patents. Applications at the DPMA first increase from about 80,000 up to 155,000 patents in 1999, but decrease again down to 75,000 patents in 2005.

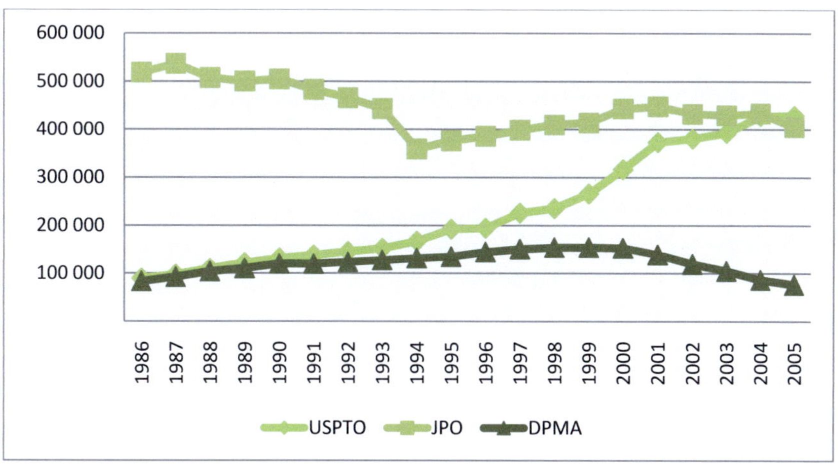

Figure 3-3: Patent applications at the USPTO, JPO and DPMA, 1986-2005

[34] 229,375.5 in the US (USPTO), 444,588.25 in Japan (JPO), and 121,561.75 in Germany (DPMA).

The high numbers of the JPO patents refer to the lesser inventive step of JPO patents (see Subsection 3.2.2). The high growth of USPTO patents refers, firstly, to a general increase in patent activities all over the world and, secondly, to globalisation effect of the world economy which pushes MNE to protect their inventions in the most important national economy (OECD, 2007). The decrease of applications at the German Patent Office refers to the rising acceptance of the supranational patent offices, such as the EPO. Foreign applicants, as well as German applicants which search for patent protection in Germany begin to file their patents at the EPO.

PATSTAT

The handling of patent data needs sophisticated data processing techniques. For this reason, statistical investigations of patent information are often based on computers and modern software, such as database systems. Even though it is possible to collect these data, as all patent information is accessible at every patent office (see e.g. esp@cnet of the European Patent Office[35]), it needs tremendous efforts to do this work. To analyse global patenting activities, however, one needs aggregated data. One of the first patent information databases for researchers is introduced by the *Patent Statistics Task Force*.

The official name of *PATSTAT April 2007 database* is *EPO Worldwide Statistical Patent Database April 2007*. It delivers patent information of almost every patent office of the world. For all these offices, it contains nearly complete information about their patents (e.g. applicants' and inventors' information, any kind of filing dates, etc.). The most important fact, however, is that this information is delivered in an easily accessible and aggregated raw format. Building on this raw format, it was possible to generate a relational database (see Appendix) for the statistical work. *PATSTAT* has 16 relational database tables with almost 530 million datasets. In the course of this work, these tables were enhanced with further information and new tables where added[36]. Therefore, all patent data and statistics in this thesis arise from the work with *PATSTAT*.

This chapter gives an insight into innovation indicators and the classification of these indicators, namely the input indicators, output indicators and the progress indicators. In addition, it gives a brief introduction into patent statistic as one of the most known output indicator of innovation activities. Furthermore, *PATSTAT*, the source of most of the data used in this thesis, is also explained.

[35] www.espacenet.com

[36] Operating *PATSTAT* is explained in detail in the manual *'PATSTAT in a nutshell'* by Tran et al. (2009).

4. Characteristics of technological late-comers and discussion of hypotheses

Referring to patents and economic key indicators, such as *Gross Domestic Product* (GDP), the characteristics of technological late-comers are described in this chapter. This empirical approach helps to strengthen the understanding of late-comers and explains the choice of countries to represent the late-comers, namely Brazil, China, India and Russia, in this thesis (see Section 4.1 and Section 4.2). In a separate section a brief overview of these countries with a focus on their innovation characteristics is given (see Section 4.3). Moreover, the hypotheses of the empirical work are introduced based on existing literature (see Section 4.4). A detailed development of each hypothesis is given in the following chapters. As different econometric methods are used to handle these hypotheses, the theoretical backgrounds of these methods, as well as the background of the interpretation of the findings are not explained in this chapter. They are illustrated in the following chapters. Finally, a summarising section closes this chapter (see Section 4.5).

4.1. Global economy

The globalisation process of the last decades has influenced the international economy in many respects. The balance of economic power changed essentially regarding the national economic performance and output. According to the World Bank (2009), the GDP of some emerging economies already exceeds the GDP of the so-called industrialised countries. Regarding the GDP in 2008, for instance, China (3rd), Brazil (8th), and Russia (9th) entered the top ten world economies. India still lags a little bit behind and occupied the 12th position (see Table 4-1). In fact, the ranking changes, if it refers to the GDP per capita and the GDP per capita according to purchase power parity (PPP). However, these countries still describe an ascending process and they are going to play a major role in the future global economy

Ranking	Economy	GDP in mio. $	GDP per capita	GDP per capita (PPP)
1	United States	14 204 322	47 580	46 970
2	Japan	4 909 272	38 210	35 220
3	**China**	**4 326 187**	**2 940**	**6 020**
4	Germany	3 652 824	42 440	35 940
5	France	2 853 062	42 250	34 400
6	United Kingdom	2 645 593	45 390	36 130
7	Italy	2 293 008	35 240	30 250
8	**Brazil**	**1 612 539**	**7 350**	**10 070**
9	**Russian Federation**	**1 607 816**	**9 620**	**15 630**
10	Spain	1 604 174	31 960	31 130
11	Canada	1 400 091	41 730	36 220
12	**India**	**1 217 490**	**1 070**	**2 960**

Table 4-1: GDP in US$ 2008 (Source: World Bank, 2009)

The industrialised countries are more than ever faced with the competition of these upcoming economies. Emerging economies, however, have been the focus of many economic analyses during the last two decades. In particular, Brazil, Russia, India and China (the *BRIC*s) can be stated as four out-standing ones. In fact, these countries have very different industrial structures backing their economic development. The major part of Russia's economy is driven by the energy and resources sector (see Guriev and Rachinsky, 2005). The gas and oil sector even holds for over 20% of the GDP between 2001 and 2004 (see Kuboniwa et al., 2005). Nevertheless, with an average economic growth of at least 5-8% per year since the beginning of the new millennium, these countries perform much better than some developed counterparts. This dynamics occurred due to the aforementioned globalisation effects, such as cost advantages in low-tech production, or rising prices of raw materials. On the other hand, these emerging economies do not just serve as the production line of low-cost production and suppliers for raw materials. They, in particular the Asian countries, also increased production of knowledge-intensive commodities (Goldstein, 2002, Schaaper, 2004, Gu and Lundvall, 2006, Altenburg et al., 2008, Kowalski et al., 2008).

Chapter 2 argued that for the establishment of constant economic development, countries need to build up a knowledge-based economy. Sustainable economic growth and development cannot be based on factors such as comparative cost advantages and exportation of raw materials. Policy makers of the *BRIC*s are also aware of these effects originating from a knowledge-based economy. The creation of technology parks and support of R&D facilities and universities were just a few efforts to strengthen their NIS and, in the case of scientific output, these efforts already seem to be fruitful. Krawczyk et al. (2007) investigated the relevance of emerging economies in the global technology competition. In internationally recognised journals, it is shown that, especially in Asian countries, the scientific publication output experienced strong growth rates. Furthermore, patent activities, in particular from China and India, are not only recorded at national patent offices, but also increasingly at patent offices abroad. Hence, the *BRIC* countries have begun to build up their own knowledge stock. In this respect, India and China, in particular, use the financial advantages of their economic growth to build up a profound knowledge-base. On the one hand, these efforts boost competitive pressure on the developed countries. On the other hand, the developed countries might, in turn, profit from knowledge flows generated by the *BRIC*s. Hence, developed countries should not only keep their interest in the economic development of the *BRIC*s, but also observe the development of their knowledge-stock.

With these upcoming technological activities, the *BRIC*s can be considered as technological late-comers (a clearer classification referring to the definition of technological late-comers follows). As aforementioned (see Section 2.5), many analyses have been conducted for technological late-comers (see e.g. Hobday, 1995, Choung et al., 2000, Wong, 1999, Forbes and Wield, 2000, Chang and Tsai, 2002, Furman and Hayes, 2004). The focus of such analyses, however, lies on smaller emerging economies, such as Korea, Taiwan, and Singapore. Although these countries also developed well, they do not have the same impact on the global economy as the *BRIC*s (see Table 4-1). Hence, a profound examination of the *BRIC*s regarding their role as technological late-comers is reasonable, as they already have stronger influence on the global economy, and might bring a new order in the global economic balance. This can be seen in the dynamic ascension into the top global economies (see Table 4-1). Hence, concerning their ascension and their still lingering status as technological late-comers, the question arises, whether they are going to play an important role in the technological competition.

The next section presents an overview on the global technology competition during the last two decades based on patent indicators. The findings provide a rationale on the importance of the *BRIC*s. Further, it strengthens the definition of the *BRIC*s as technological late-comers in respect to the definition given in this thesis. Afterwards a brief historical and technological profile of the *BRIC*s is delivered.

4.2. International patenting activities

During the time from1986 until 2005 patent applications at the EPO and WIPO increased all over the world (see Appendix). For these two patent offices, Figure 4-1 and Figure 4-2 show the weighted count[37] of patent applications classified by the origin of the applicants (Figure 4-1) and inventors (Figure 4-2) for some selected countries. They are grouped by priority date into four time periods to give a clear overview.

[37] A weighted count is necessary to avoid multiple counts of a patent, if this patent has more than one applicant. In such cases a patent is allocate to each of the countries of the applicants weighted by the numbers of applicants from this country.

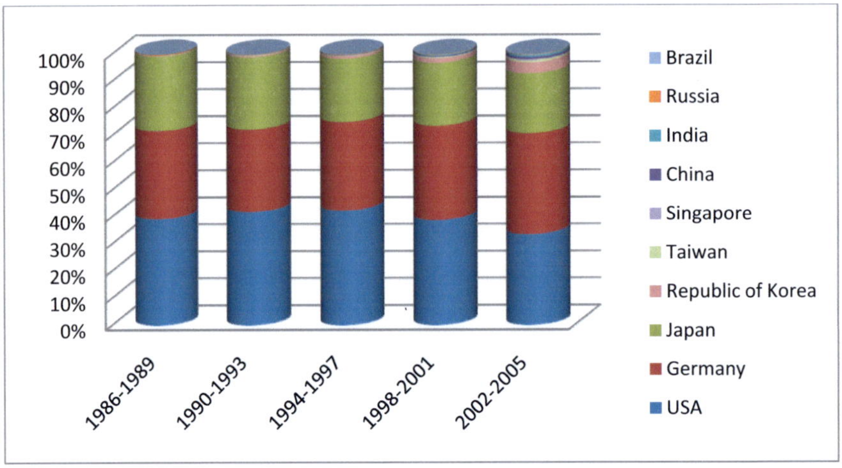

Figure 4-1: Patent application applicant weighted at EPO and WIPO

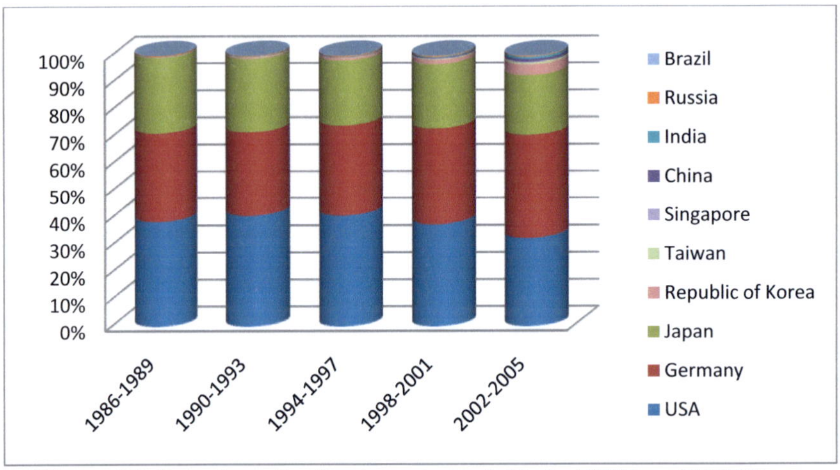

Figure 4-2: Patent application inventor weighted at EPO and WIPO

Compared to the three strongest patenting countries, namely the USA, Germany, and Japan, applications of the *BRIC* countries play a minor role. The major part of the global applications is made by these three global players. They are responsible for nearly 2/3 of all patent applications at the EPO and the WIPO (see Appendix). Interestingly, the share of patents made by Korean applicants and inventors has increased constantly since the first period and already has remarkable numbers of patents in the last period (12,951.46 according to applicant weights and 12,790.90 according to inventor weights, see Appendix). Considering the rankings from 1986 till

2005, the *BRIC*s show a more dynamic development (see Table 4-2). In this case China and India show the most dynamic development. Referring to applicant weighted counts China improves from the 28th rank in 1986 to the 17th in 2005. India starts at the 30th rank and reaches the 19th in 2005. Brazil, at least, rises to positions from 31st to 29th, while Russia falls from the 20th position to the 30th position. Similar movements can be observed for inventor weighted counts; rising development are made by China 27th to 15th, India 28th to 19th, Brazil 31st to 30th and Russia, once again, falls from 19th to 27th.

Applicants	86	87	88	89	90	91	92	93	94	95	96	97	98	99	00	01	02	03	04	05
USA	1	1	1	1	1	1	1	1	1	1	1	1	1	1	1	1	1	1	2	3
Germany	2	2	2	2	2	2	2	2	2	2	2	2	2	2	2	2	2	2	1	1
China	28	29	29	30	29	29	31	32	30	32	30	29	27	24	21	19	20	20	19	17
India	30	32	31	31	32	32	34	34	34	34	34	34	26	22	22	20	19	19	20	19
Russia	20	18	16	19	26	26	24	24	23	24	24	25	28	30	30	29	30	30	30	30
Brazil	31	30	30	33	28	30	28	28	33	30	33	30	33	31	31	32	31	29	32	29
Inventors																				
USA	1	1	1	1	1	1	1	1	1	1	1	1	1	1	1	1	1	2	2	3
Germany	2	2	2	2	2	2	2	2	2	2	2	2	2	2	2	2	2	1	1	1
China	27	26	25	31	27	28	29	29	27	26	26	25	25	24	21	19	20	19	18	15
India	28	31	29	27	29	32	31	30	34	30	30	30	24	25	25	22	19	20	20	19
Russia	19	18	16	19	21	21	20	20	20	20	20	20	21	21	22	25	26	26	26	27
Brazil	31	27	30	29	25	26	26	25	28	25	29	26	29	28	29	28	28	28	28	30

Table 4-2: Ranking of patent applications at EPO and WIPO

The dynamics of patent applications from the *BRIC*s can also be shown by their development. Figure 4-3 presents the development of patent applications of the three major players (green shades, right axis) compared to the *BRIC*s as a whole (red, left axis), and to each *BRIC* country (blue shades, left axis). Since the middle of the 90s of the last century, the two Asian emerging economies show tremendous growth rates regarding their patent applications, even if in total numbers they still lag far behind the big players.

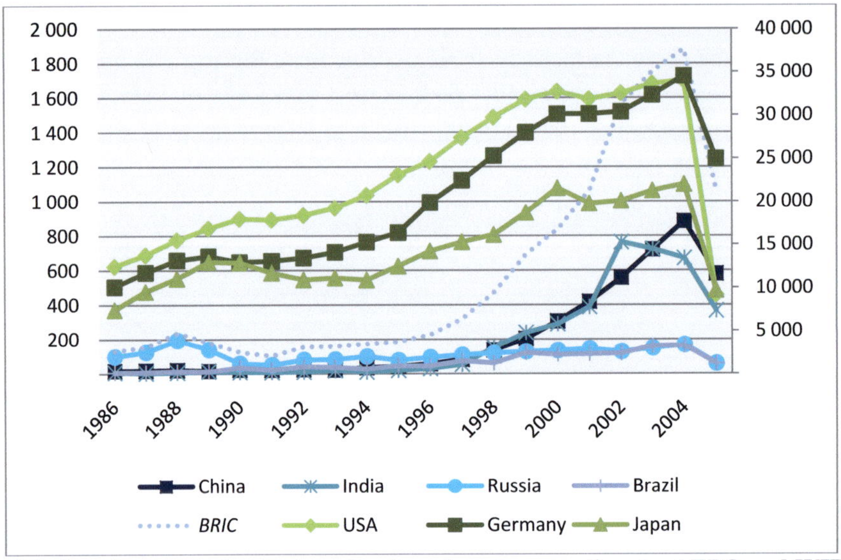

Figure 4-3: Development of patent applications based on applicants at EPO and WIPO 1986-2005

These findings are confirmed by other studies on emerging economies (see Mitusch et al., 2010). In fact, the Asian countries show the most interesting development during the last decade, as they improve their technological skills in those fields which are highly relevant for the future (see Mitusch et al., 2010). Compared to the developed countries, this result of the *National Specialisation Report* emphasises that the developed countries, and in particular Europe, needs to improve their efforts in the global technology competition to not fall behind in the future.

4.3. Profile of the BRICs

The abbreviation *BRIC* dates back to an analysis of emerging economies from Wilson and Purushothaman (2003). They implement a model for analysing the global economic development within the next decades. According to the model, the GDP of these countries is going to exceed most of the G7 countries by 2050. The six leading economies will consist of the USA, Japan, and the *BRIC*s. With respect to the economic size and growth, incomes and demographics, global demand patterns and currency movements, the global economy will change dramatically (Wilson and Purushothaman, 2003). Although their study is not a scientific paper, it shows the interest of economic studies in the *BRIC*s. Furthermore, policy-makers also realise the importance of these four countries for the global economy. In the recent past, decision making processes concerning global economic strategies also involve decision-makers from these countries (G20, 2008).

Brazil

Innovation policy has a long tradition in Brazilian history. In 1809, the country had already established its first patent law. This was almost 70 years earlier than Japan (1871) and Germany (1877). Policy-makers in Brazil early realised the need for technological progress in order to achieve sustainable economic growth rates.

Trade numbers show that exports of high-technology products have risen. Yet, the majority of Brazilian exports still consist of raw materials, resources, agricultural products and manufactured products. As an outstanding success within the Brazilian high-technology sector, the aviation sector should be mentioned. Starting as a project with defence and military background in the mid-20th century, Embraer nowadays vies with its Canadian archrival, Bombardier, for the third place of all aircraft manufacturers (Goldstein, 2002, p.98).

Although many efforts have been made to improve the conditions for innovative activities, Brazil is still far away from achieving constant economic growth rates through technological progress (Lattimore and Kowalski, 2008).

China

Starting as the 'working bench' of the world, China is associated with imitation rather than with innovation.

After the opening of the Chinese mainland in 1978, its economy grew at an average rate of 9.7% per year for more than 25 years. Additionally, China has also pursued a strategy of acquiring new technologies at the beginning of the 1980s. The defined long-term plan was to catch up with the developed countries. These plans, among them the so-called Torch Program and other innovation strategies, were created to push the "[…] strengthening [of] indigenous innovation capacities and [the] building [of] an innovative country […]" (MOST, 2008). Lattimore and Kowalski (2008) show that these efforts also seem to be successful. Export shares of the high-technology sector could constantly rise up to 30.6% of the total exports. Although the net trade of this sector is negative, it is still a notable achievement for an emerging economy.

India

The introduction of *Intellectual Property Rights* (IPR) in India started lately compared to countries such as Brazil. The first decisive efforts were not introduced until the 1970s. Great efforts such as market liberalisation, activities to strengthen IPR, and supporting efforts regarding foreign direct investment (FDI) in the early 1990s, show that the Indian government tried to foster an innovative environment during the last decades. These efforts are also reflected by current programs of the Ministry of

Science & Technology which focus on R&D-intensive sectors, such as biotechnology, space science and nuclear science (Ministry of Science & Technology India, 2007).

It can be stated that decision makers in India try to push their innovation performance in many respects (Kowalski et al., 2008).

Russia

After the collapse of the Soviet Union, the Russian government was faced with many national problems. The national economy was struggling with an imminent collapse and needed public funding to survive. The dilemma of having to choose between preventing an economy collapse and investing into innovation activities reduced state-controlled innovation efforts at the time of transition to a minimum. Government-funded innovation activities remained at a low level limited by the small public budget (Saltykov, 2007). Additionally, the transition from a state-owned and state-dominated R&D sector to market-driven innovation efforts turned out to be very difficult. Due to the uncertain situation of the Russian economy during the 1990s, R&D plans of the private sector were kept at a low level (Narula and Jormanainen, 2008).

According to the current trade statistics, Russian exports are dominated by petroleum and petroleum products, natural gas, wood and wood products, metals, chemicals, and a wide variety of civilian and military manufactures which are not, with the exception of military manufactures, part of the high-technology sector (Tarr, 2008). Nevertheless, the Russian economy can use its financial advantages of the economic growth to strengthen their innovation activities.

In summary, innovation efforts differ within the *BRIC*-countries. For all, it has been anticipated that they will have a positive future within the global economy. Despite this forecast, there are more dissimilarities than similarities within this group. Therefore, an analysis showing the differences regarding their technological performance and the relevance of technology originating from the *BRIC*-countries is necessary. The empirical analyses in this thesis deal with these differences, as they shed light on different aspects of the innovation processes. As an encompassing discussion on all innovation activities of the *BRIC*s bears many difficulties, a detailed analysis of their status as technological late-comers will focus on the biotechnology sector. The next section introduces the hypotheses of this dissertation. Further, it shows the line of argumentation throughout the analytical steps and gives a guideline throughout the next chapters which each comprise one analytical treatment of each hypothesis.

4.4. *Early-movers* vs. *late-comers*

Each analysis starts from a comparison between the country groups, *BRIC* and *DEUS* (Germany and the USA). Afterwards, the analyses also contain detailed views on a national level, on the one side, for Brazil, China India and Russia, when possible, and Germany, as well as the USA on the other side. The USA, as one of the leading biotechnology countries (see Cooke, 2001a, Phene et al., 2006), is a benchmark to the biotechnology approach. Germany, which is a global technological leader, however, serves as a benchmark in two different ways. On the one hand, it is a technological leader and can be a positive benchmark. On the other hand, Germany is also a technological late-comer in the field of biotechnology (see Cooke, 2001a).

For the sectoral approach, all patents that belong to the field of biotechnology (see Hinze et al., 1997) are extracted. Furthermore, to give the analysis a dynamic perspective, patents between 1986 and 2005 are examined. In this case, the priority dates of the patents are decisive. In order to be able to consider patents with a certain economic value, the studies concentrated on patents which are filed at EPO or go through the Patent Cooperation Treaty (PCT) filing process at WIPO. Frietsch et al. (2008) show that such an approach covers inventions with a certain economic importance. Additionally, the sectoral approaches consist of examinations of the top players in the field of biotechnology which are identified through their patenting activities.

Line of argumentation

The line of argumentation throughout the analysis follows a top-down approach. All analyses start at a national level and are broken down, where possible, to the biotechnology sector. Deriving from the theoretical background delivered by the preceding chapter, the first block of hypotheses deals with technological late-comers and their entry into the technological competition:

Hypothesis 1: Technological innovators start their innovation activities by introducing incremental innovations. For this reason, innovation activities of late-comers use external knowledge to a greater extent than early-movers.

Hypothesis 2: New entrants into the technological competition face established players which have a broad technological base. Late-comers pursue niche strategies to enter the technological competition.

Hypothesis 1 analyses the usage of external knowledge of technological late-comers. As late-comers are assumed to try to catch-up, they need to learn from existing knowledge. Meanwhile late-comers need to enter the technological competition in certain fields which are not already utilised by the established players and nations, such as Germany and the USA. This is expressed by *Hypothesis 2*.

The next block of hypotheses deals with the establishment of technological late-comers in the global competition. As the whole analysis covers a range of 20 years, a dynamic view can be applied in this approach. Therefore, late-comers and early-movers are compared in the same time period to each other what means that the early years of technological late-comers are compared to early-movers when they are already established in the global competition:

Hypothesis 3: Technological early-movers have more technological experience than late-comers. Due to their broader knowledge base, they can generate a broader scope of innovations. For a competitive innovation-based economy late-comers have to diversify their technological portfolio. Thus, after the phase of entry into the international technology competition technological late-comers develop towards early-movers in respect of technological.

Hypothesis 4a: Late-comers have fewer resources, such as human capital, for the generation of new knowledge and technologies. They need more external knowledge at the beginning of their innovation activities and, have, therefore, more linkages to external sources.

Hypothesis 4b: Innovation networks of late-comers develop towards early-movers with regard to their network characteristics and the role of major players. Major players become more central and gain importance.

These hypotheses focus on the establishment of technological late-comers which emerge after they enter the competitive markets. In fact, in these cases the question is more relevant for 'successful' late-comers. This point is also discussed in the examinations.

Finally, the last set of hypotheses consists of econometric analyses on the role and the dynamics of technological late-comers. Hence, they consist of the following hypotheses:

Hypothesis 5a: Late-comers develop to a source of international knowledge flows.
Hypothesis 5b: Influences on knowledge flows originating from these countries are based on geographical and technological closeness, as well as cultural similarities and a close language background.
Hypothesis 6: Successful technological late-comers follow certain steps in their catch-up process. They develop towards early-movers in respect of technological diversification, centrality, niche strategies and scientific linkages. Hence, successful technological late-comers follow specific patterns of success.

Figure 4-4 summarises the structure of the analysis and visualises the line of argumentation.

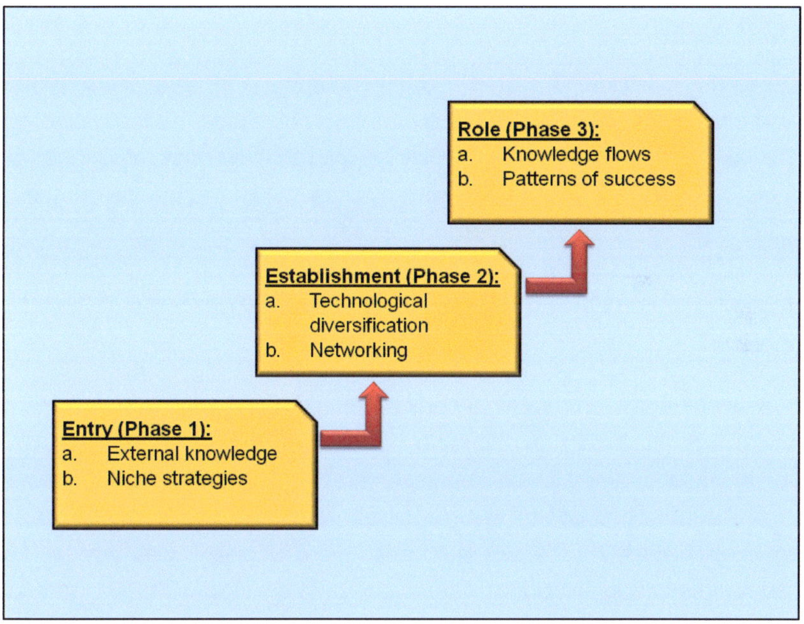

Figure 4-4: Structure of the analyses of technological late-comers

To sum up, the line of argumentation follows the three steps entry, establishment, as well as role and dynamics of technological late-comers in the global technology competition. For the different perspectives of the examinations, namely the national and the sectoral[38] one, the next subsections give a definition for the proceeding parts of this thesis.

National approach

Technological late-comers on a national level are represented in this thesis by the *BRIC* countries. They have been chosen as the most dynamic economies of the last decades regarding their GDP and their emerging innovation activities (see Section 4.1 and Section 4.2)[39]. The USA and Germany are included in the analyses as benchmarks. Thereby, Germany even plays a two-edged role, as it represents technological early-movers, on the one hand, but also a late-comer in the biotechnology sector, on the other hand. The national classification of EPO and WIPO patents is delivered by the address information of the applicants and inventors. As the national patenting activities are already presented in Section 4.2, the focus in this subsection is on the sectoral examination.

Sectoral approach

For the sectoral approach, the field of biotechnology is chosen. Biotechnology is a typical example for a knowledge-based technology. Dealing with biotechnology needs a broad base of intellectual capital, such as qualified workers, access to scientific research etc. It has been shown that in such a sector, typical functions of an innovation process, for instance, relations of institutions and firms (see Haug, 1995, and Zucker and Darby ,1996), interaction of scientists and other actors etc. (see Malmberg and Maskell, 2002, and Fornahl and Tran, 2009), can be analysed. Some of these topics are part of this work.

The biotechnology sector, as aforementioned, could be identified through the patent classification. Actors in the field of biotechnology, hence, are identified as applicants of biotechnology patent applications. Figure 4-5 presents the development of patent applications counted by applicants. For sure, patent applications by American and German applicants (right scale) outnumber the *BRIC*s (left scale) by far. However, the numbers of patent application in China and India develop with the beginning of the new millennium impressively.

[38] This is based on the approach of the systems of innovation (see Section 2.2).
[39] See also Tran (2009).

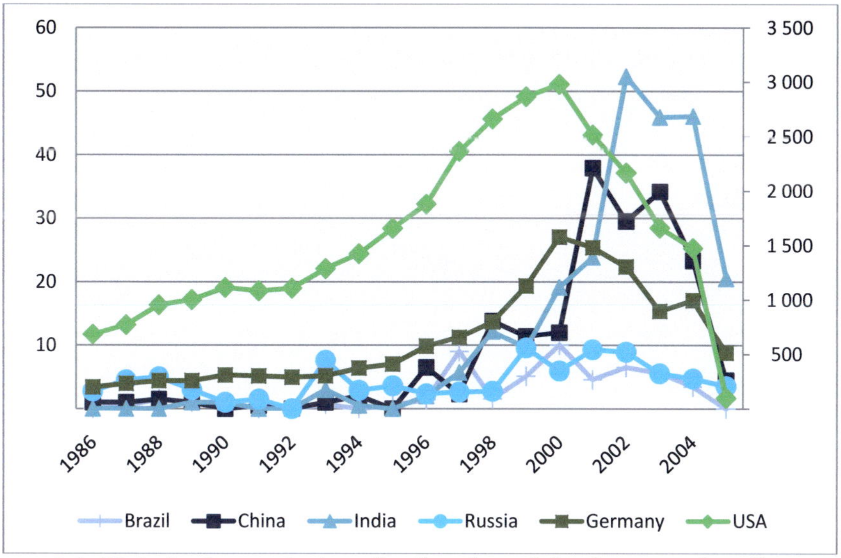

Figure 4-5: Biotechnology patent applications by weighted-counts of applicants

The same picture can be drawn from the inventor-based counting of patent applications (see Figure 4-6). American and German inventors are, by far, more active than *BRIC* inventors. However, the Asian *BRIC*s also have a positive trend. Interestingly, Russian inventors are more active than Russian applicants. This fact could have negative effects on the Russian economy, as they do not hold the legal right on their own inventions.

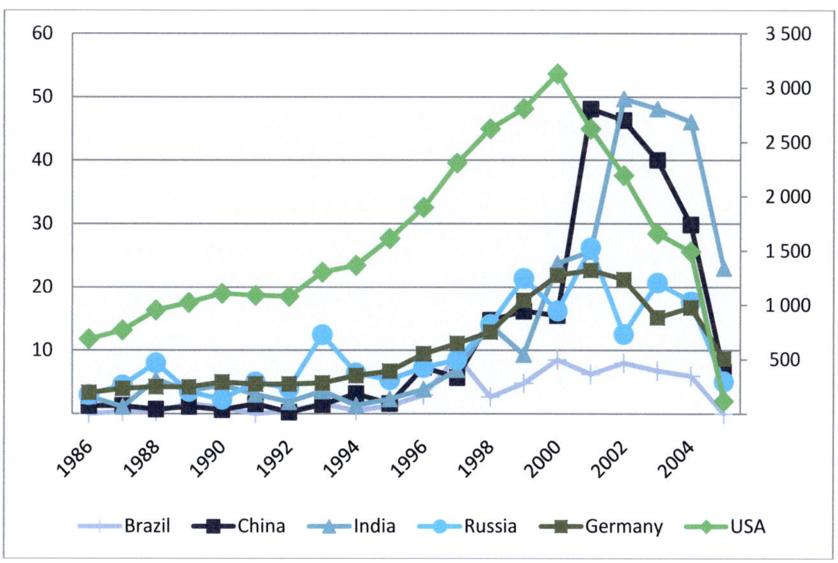

Figure 4-6: Biotechnology patent applications by weighted-counts of inventors

The sectoral approach also shows that *BRIC* patent applications in the field of biotechnology are very different for each *BRIC* country. Therefore, it is necessary to have a deeper insight into the specific analysis of the innovation process for all these countries.

4.5. Summary

To summarise this chapter, it can be separated into two parts. First, the area of analysis is sketched by conducting the first empirical examinations. Sections 4.1 and 4.2 described the countries by referring to the global economy and technology competition. Afterwards Section 4.3 gives an overview of the *BRIC*s.

Second, this chapter draws the line of argumentation by stating the hypotheses which are examined in the next chapters (see Section 4.4). Furthermore, it explained the two different approaches, namely the national and sectoral ones, which are also used in empirical analyses (see Chapter 5 - 10). To be precise, the analysis of technological late-comers is comprised of the *BRIC*-countries on the national level and their biotechnology sectors on a sectoral level.

Finally, this chapter close the introduction of theoretical background of this thesis. Some backgrounds to methods are delivered in the different steps of the empirical analysis; however, the next chapters mainly consist of the examination of the induced hypotheses.

5. The role of external knowledge for innovation activities of late-comers

This chapter consists of the examination of the first hypothesis how technological late-comers enter the global competition. The key issue of this chapter is based upon the assumption introduced in Chapter 4.4 which states that late-comers need more external knowledge to generate innovations than early-movers. In the following section the rationale of this hypothesis is developed in more detail (see Section 5.1). In doing so, it firstly refers to the theoretical background worked out in Chapters 2 and 3. The subsequent section introduces the methods which are used to analyse the hypothesis (see Section 5.2). Furthermore, this section also consists of a literature review of the specific scientific works which deal with the methods. Afterwards, Section 5.3 shows the empirical approach and the findings. Finally, these findings are discussed in Section 5.4.

5.1. Innovation activities and the necessity of external knowledge

The role of knowledge is important for innovation activities. This means that, for instance, a firm, institute or nation needs to have a knowledge stock to generate innovations (see Section 2.1 and 2.4). This stock can be delivered by internal sources, meaning that a firm, institute or nation possesses an own source of knowledge; e.g. skilled inventors, construction plans and blueprints; just to mention some. Moreover, innovation activities use external knowledge which means that the innovator bases his new product or process on already existing knowledge which is not developed and owned by him and, hence, has to be explored externally. It is also possible that innovators have internal knowledge, but still refer to external sources. The ability to understand and use external knowledge, so-called absorptive capacities (see Subsection 2.4.3) is not tackled in the analysis of this thesis.

With regard to technological late-comers, Hobday (1995) states that their innovation activities are mainly defined by incremental innovations. So, these innovations improve existing products or adapt products for local markets to satisfy local needs and requirements. Normally they are not ground-breaking innovations (see Choung et al., 2000). Thus, innovations made by late-comers build upon radical innovations which were originally introduced by others[40]. For this reason, this chapter analyses the following hypothesis:

[40] For further references see Section 2.4.

Hypothesis 1: Technological innovators start their innovation activities by introducing incremental innovations which are based on other innovations. For this reason, innovation activities of late-comers use external knowledge to a greater extent than early-movers.

To test this hypothesis, the analysis in this chapter refers to patent data and uses patent citation data. This approach and the background to this kind of examination of external knowledge are discussed in the next section.

5.2. Patent citations as indicator for external knowledge

Citation analysis can be employed to identify knowledge spillovers; they show references from one patent to another one. Although they are not identical to citations known from publications they are a well-accepted proxy for spillovers between patent applicants, inventors, and between inventors and applicants (see Carpenter and Narin, 1983, Schmoch, 1993, and Jaffe et al, 1993). However, they are still only a proxy for the following reasons. Authors of scientific publications have to add their references to other publications. The same procedure is just valid for patents which are filed at the USPTO. In the USA, the patent applicant and inventor has to make sure that their patent application refers to the state-of-the-art technology. So, citations of USPTO patents appear similar to citations of scientific publications. Patents filed at other offices, particularly the EPO, WIPO, DPMA, and JPO have, in turn, a different process. Here, citations are also listed by applicants and inventors, but they are mainly added during the filing process by patent attorneys and patent examiner. Hence, the assumption that knowledge spillovers from the applicants and inventors of the cited patent to the applicants and inventors of the one who cites does not necessarily hold. Maurseth and Verspagen (2002), however, argue that even if applicants and inventors do not know about the cited patent in advance, the knowledge spillover can be initiated by the externally added citations. Therefore, it stands for a potential spillover and, hence, represents a 'noisy' indicator for spillover effects. This finding is verified by Jaffe et al. (2000) who show on a basis of an inventor survey that the knowledge represented by the cited paper is known by the inventors of the one who cites.

5.2.1. Citation rates as a measurement of knowledge spill-over

The method to use patent citation rates as an indicator for knowledge spill-over is applied by different researchers. Carpenter and Narin (1983), for instance, proof that citation analysis based on patent data of the USPTO can be used as indicator of external knowledge. In their work, they compare findings of interviews, which they carry out with R&D managers, with a patent citation analysis. The results confirm that it is possible to trace foreign knowledge dependencies of US patents by counting citations of US patents to foreign patents. The results reflect a high agreement of the managers' opinion of dependencies on foreign technology and the findings of the citation analysis. Other scientific works strengthen these findings with their studies. These papers also state that the references which can be found on patent documents represent knowledge transfer from other patents and, hence, the use of external knowledge. Jaffe et al. (1993) underline these facts by using patent data of the USPTO. Meanwhile, Schmoch (1993) finds the same evidence for patents of the DPMA and the JPO.

In addition to the references of external knowledge, citations can disclose a second fact. As patents do not only cite other patents, but also scientific papers, the last kind of citations can also stand for scientific linkages (Carpenter and Narin, 1983, Schmoch, 1993, Jaffe et al. 1993, and Grupp, 1996). In this case, the mean values of the so-called non-patent literature, namely scientific literature, is used to show different levels of relevance of scientific work. Schmoch (1993), for instance, states that patents in specific technology fields, such as laser medicine and polyimide in electronics, have more scientific citations than the average. Hence, they are 'closer' to science than other technologies. The same holds for technologies, such as optics, information storage, organic chemistry, genetics, and pharmaceutics (Grupp, 1996). Therefore, it is possible to show a relative closeness to science within technological fields by analysing different kinds of patent citations.

5.2.2. Problems of patent citations analysis

The use of citations also encompasses several problems which have to be considered. One important short-coming is that citations can just be considered as a noisy indicator for the use of external knowledge. This mainly refers to the two ways how citations are made. First, they are not necessarily added by applicants and inventors, but by the patent searchers or patent attorney. As aforementioned, this might doubt the use of patent citations as an indicator for external knowledge. Nevertheless, it can be assumed that external knowledge is still transferred (see Maurseth and Verspagen, 2002). Second, citations are normally made by applicants and inventors themselves. However, it often turns out that many applicants and inventors cite themselves, the so-called 'self-citations'. This fact occurs, because inventors refer to their own patents as this implies a higher value of these patents[41] (Trajtenberg, 1990, Harhoff et al., 1999,

[41] A higher value in this respect refers to different aspects. Trajtenberg (1990) considers the social value and the contribution to new inventions. Harhoff et al. (1999) rather speaks of private economic value meaning the earnings which can be realized with a patent. Last but not least, Hall et al. (2005) look at the value of the patent holder meaning the value of the companies.

and Hall et al., 2005). Applicants have a commercial motivation to cite their own patents. In doing so, they make it harder for competitors to use important inventions as they need to avoid more than one patent protection (Shapiro, 2000). Hence, analysis based on patent citation has to consider this problem (Jaffe and Trajtenberg, 1999) and self-citations have to be eliminated.

5.3. Citation activities of technological late-comers

This chapter adopts patent citation data to examine the use of external knowledge. Therefore, the citation rates of the technological late-comers and the early-movers during 1986 and 2005 are compared to each other in a statistical manner, applying mean values and t-tests to test the hypothesis. In the first step, this is done on a national level. Later on, technological late-comers and early-movers in the biotechnology sector are examined in detail. Furthermore, the test also considers different time periods as late-comers enter the global technology competition with a time lag, compared to the early-movers. The first results which are presented in this section are from a national point of view. They show citation rates of the *BRIC*-countries, as well as the rates of German and US patent citations over the time period of 1986 to 2005.

5.3.1. Citation rates on a national level

Table 5-1 comprises the mean values for all citations, citations of other patents, and citations of non-patent literature of the *BRIC* countries and German pooled with US patents (*DEUS*). These citations are not separated into foreign and home country citation, because usage of external knowledge is given in both kinds of citations. At first glance, the mean values of these two groups differ by about 0.4 citations. This difference, interestingly, refers mainly to non-patent citations. As the mean values of the citations to other patents just differ by about 0.1, the non-patent citations have a difference of about 0.3 (see Table 5-1). A further consideration of citation rates of different technological sectors, which can also influence these rates, as well as the consideration of self-citations in the analysis on national level, is neglected, because of the high numbers of patents and consequently high numbers of applicants which needs to be treated manually.

	All citations	Patent citations	Non-patent citations
BRIC	4.046	2.935	1.111
DEUS	3.648	2.848	0.799

Table 5-1: Mean values of *BRIC* and *DEUS* citations per patent 1986-2006

Further examinations disclose that the citation rates develop steadily between 1986 and 2005. This can be seen in Figure 5-1. It shows that the citation rates of the *DEUS* patents are quite stable, but have a decreasing development with two exceptions, namely in 1994 and 2005. *BRIC* patents, however, start with lesser citations compared to the *DEUS* patents. With the beginning of the 1990s, the citations on *BRIC* patents overtake the citations on *DEUS* patents for the first time. Comparing the two different groups of citations, namely citations to patents and non-patent literature, the development of citations to patents is close to the latter findings. At the beginning of the examined time period, the citations to patents of the *BRIC*-countries are also below the *DEUS* citations, but the numbers exceed the *DEUS* numbers already at the beginning of the 1990s. The non-patent citations of *BRIC* patents, however, are over the whole period below the numbers of the *DEUS* non-patent citations (see Figure 5-1). The low rates of citations of *BRIC* patents at the beginning can refer to the fact that their patents at the beginning still have a local focus. Hence, their innovations just build on some other patents which are also relevant for the local markets. Moreover, the absorptive capacities and the possibilities to exploit foreign knowledge in these countries are still on a very low level. Late-comers first had to learn how to use the external knowledge. Interestingly, this is not true for non-patent citations. Hence, this leads to the implication that these countries achieve to build up the absorptive capacities to use scientific knowledge first and afterwards gain the ability to exploit technical knowledge.

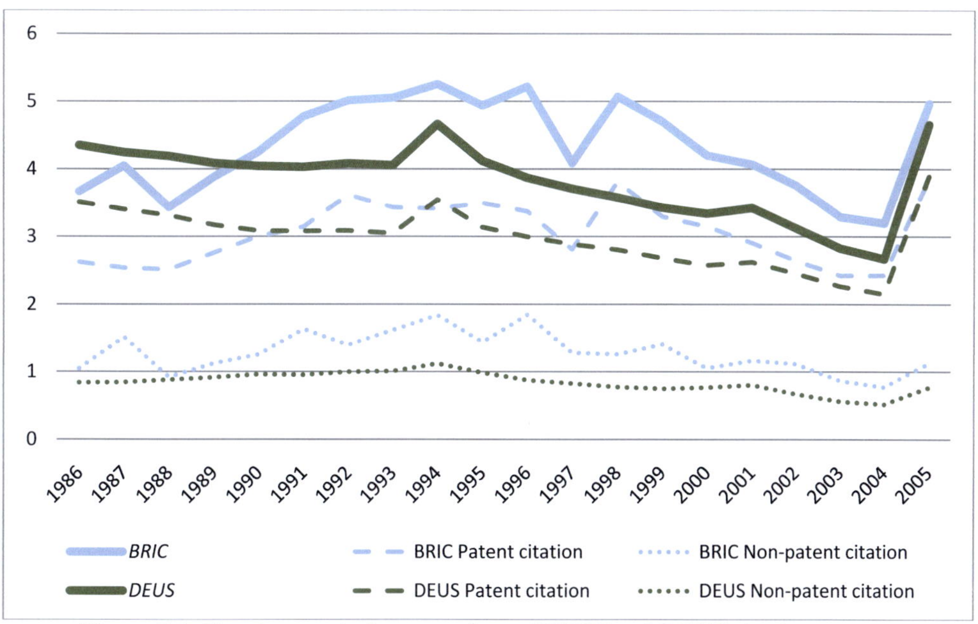

Figure 5-1: Development of mean values of *BRIC* and *DEUS* citation rates

The findings described so far in this section are also strengthened by statistical tests. Table 5-2 summarises the results of these tests which do not only compare the two groups, but also each *BRIC*-country with the USA. The t-value of the t-test comparing the mean values of the *BRIC*-countries with the ones of the *DEUS* show a value well over 2.0[42]. Hence, the mean values of the *BRIC*s are significantly higher. Within the group of *BRIC*-countries, this significance does not hold for everyone (see also Appendix). Compared to the USA, the Russian citations deliver a t-value of 1.41, what means that Russia and the USA do not differ from each other significantly, even if the degree of freedom at a level of 35.8 is considered. The other three countries, however, have significant t-values. The Asian late-comers even have t-values which are well beyond 2.0 (see Table 5-2).

	Obs.	Mean	Std.Dev.	t-value				
				DEUS	Brazil	Russia	India	China
BRIC	20	4.34	0.67	2.66*				
DEUS	20	3.82	0.55					
USA	20	3.51	0.81		2.43*	1.41	6.03*	4.55*
Brazil	20	4.29	1.18					
Russia	20	3.93	1.04					
India	20	5.23	0.98					
China	20	4.97	1.19					

Standard errors: *p<0.05

Table 5-2: t-test of citation rates

The further analysis of citation to patents shows that the difference between *BRIC*s and *DEUS*s is not significantly high (see Table 5-3).

[42] The t-value can be considered as significant, if a limit of 2.0 is exceeded in a confidence level of 95% and a degree of freedom of at least 5.0. These two terms hold for all tests conducted in this chapter. Hence, a significant difference between two mean values is given and the null hypotheses can be rejected (see Bosch, 1998, pp. 766).

Patent citation	Obs.	Mean	Std.Dev.	t-value				
				DEUS	Brazil	Russia	India	China
BRIC	20	3.06	0.46	0.52				
DEUS	20	2.98	0.44					
USA	20	2.63	0.61		3.04*	-0.22	4.43*	3.95*
Brazil	20	3.39	0.95					
Russia	20	2.58	0.70					
India	20	3.59	0.75					
China	20	3.56	0.86					
Non-patent citation								
BRIC	20	1.28	0.30	5.88*				
DEUS	20	0.84	0.15					
USA	20	0.88	0.24		0.09	4.28*	5.29*	4.31*
Brazil	20	0.89	0.49					
Russia	20	1.34	0.42					
India	20	1.64	0.60					
China	20	1.42	0.50					

Standard errors: *$p<0.05$

Table 5-3: t-test of citation rates distinguished between patent citations and non-patent citations

Once again, Russian citation of patents does not differ from the US ones significantly. Referring to non-patent citations, however, the test also strengthens the first impression of the development over the twenty years. It shows a significant difference between the *BRIC*s and *DEUS*s according to the non-patent citations of nearly each *BRIC* country and the USA (see also Table 5-3). Interestingly, Brazilian non-patent citations do not show a significant difference to the US ones.

Time lag

Late-comers enter the market, as their name already reveals, later than early-movers. For this reason, a comparison of the citation numbers also has to consider this time lag between these two groups. Table 5-4 lists the statistical test values of late-comers and early-movers with regard to a time lag of ten years. According to the consideration of the time lag, it is possible to say that differences of usage of external knowledge vanish and the late-comer countries approach the citation rates of early-movers. Except for India, all other late-comers do not show significant differences to the early-movers anymore. In the case of India this effect is due to higher rates in the non-patent citations (see Table 5-5). A reason may be the specialisation in scientific related technologies (see Chapter 6) and therefore a higher rate of scientific research results. Please note again that a separated consideration of all technological sectors is not possible and a control of this finding is made in the sector of biotechnology.

	Obs.	Mean	Std.Dev.	t-value				
				DEUS	Brazil	Russia	India	China
BRIC	10	4.25	0.23	0.29				
DEUS	10	4.19	0.06					
Germany	10	4.31	0.07		-1.47	-0.92	2.07*	-0.49
USA	10	4.10	0.06		-0.89	-0.34	2.90*	0.18
Brazil	10	3.77	0.36					
Russia	10	3.97	0.36					
India	10	4.84	0.25					
China	10	4.15	0.31					

Standard errors: *p<0.05

Table 5-4: t-test of citation rates between different time periods

The classification between citations to other patents and to non-patent literatures delivers an interesting finding, as the citation rates to other patents also do not have significant differences to the early-movers anymore. However, differences of the citation rates of non-patent literature are still highly significant high for most of the late-comers (see Table 5-5). Once again, Indian innovations have a high linkage to scientific work and the role of a scientific knowledge-base plays an important role for Indian patents.

Patent citation	Obs.	Mean	Std.Dev.	t-value				
				DEUS	Brazil	Russia	India	China
BRIC	10	3.07	0.16	-0.98				
DEUS	10	3.24	0.06					
Germany	10	3.52	0.05		-1.59	-3.59	0.03	-2.83
USA	10	3.02	0.07		-0.09	-1.57	2.72*	-0.31
Brazil	10	2.99	0.33					
Russia	10	2.63	0.24					
India	10	3.52	0.17					
China	10	2.96	0.19					
Non-patent citation								
BRIC	10	1.19	0.09	2.44				
DEUS	10	0.95	0.03					
Germany	10	0.79	0.03		-0.09	3.96*	4.13*	2.92*
USA	10	1.07	0.02		-3.28	1.95*	1.93*	0.87
Brazil	10	0.78	0.09					
Russia	10	1.35	0.14					
India	10	1.32	0.12					
China	10	1.19	0.14					

Standard errors: *p<0.05

Table 5-5: t-test of citation rates between different time periods distinguished between patent citations and non-patent citations

On the national level, the *BRIC*s mostly show that their rates of external knowledge measured by patent citations are significantly higher compared to the *DEUS* citations, although late-comers do not show a higher citation rate in the first years. The reason for this finding can refer the low numbers of patents of late-comers at the beginning of their patent activities, as well as a lack of experience in exploiting external knowledge. Moreover, this may also be caused by different levels of absorptive capacity. The results for Russia strengthen this finding. The general differences the Russian citation rates do not differ significantly to the early-movers, because Russia can look back to a longer tradition of science and research pushed by the former Soviet Union. In an examination of citation rates separated into citations to other patents and non-patent literature, it is possible to say that differences between the citation rates mainly refer to differences in the use of non-patent literature. The only exception in this case is Brazil where the scientific link seems not to play an important role.

In an additional analysis of different time periods due to the later entry of technological late-comers the findings show that with a time lag of ten years citation rates of the late-comer countries become, in general, more similar to the rates of the early-movers and no clear difference between the earlier rates of Germany and the USA is detectable anymore. In this case, India is the only exception as it is the only country which still shows differences in citation rates. In a further differentiation it can be shown that India's higher citation rates occur from the higher numbers of non-patent citations. Moreover, according to the division between the two kinds of citations, it can be stated that most of the late-comer countries still have significant high usage of external scientific knowledge. This fact seems to result from the still governmental driven national innovation systems of the Asian late-comers (e.g. see Ministry of Science & Technology India, 2007 and MOST, 2008), as well as a specialisation on science-based technologies. For this reason an in-depth analysis of one science-based technology, namely the biotechnology, is made in the next part of this chapter.

5.3.2. Patent citation in the biotechnology sector

The examination of the biotechnology sector reflects similar findings as the national analysis. Table 5-6 shows a comparison of the mean values of *BRIC* and *DEUS* biotechnology citation rates. Once again, the *BRIC*s have higher mean values in all categories. Here, the general difference is about 0.8, what is higher than in the national examination; an even higher difference is observable between the citations to other patents (about 0.2). The latter finding is different to the national examination. Regarding the non-patent citations, a second effect can be shown (see Section 5.2). As biotechnology is known as a knowledge-intensive sector (see Cooke, 2001a, and

Fornahl and Tran, 2009), a stronger link to fundamental research can be expected. This fact is also reflected by the mean values of the non-patent citations covered in Table 5-6. Contrary to the national examination, the mean values of non-patent citations are higher than the mean values of the citations to other patents. Furthermore, the difference between the two country groups is about 0.6 which is also higher than the measured value at the national level. This implicates the following interpretations: A relationship of certain technological sectors and the differences of the citation rates are given. Especially science-based technological sectors, such as the biotechnology sector, have higher citation rates of non-patent literature in late-comer countries than in early-mover countries. This may be caused by the fact of the stronger governmental controls in these countries, a still smaller base of industrial driven R&D and still lacking experience in the exploitation of external knowledge sources.

	All citation	Patent citation	Non-patent citation
BRIC	4.642	1.825	2.818
DEUS	3.872	1.643	2.229

Table 5-6: Mean values of *BRIC* and *DEUS* biotechnology citations per patent 1986-2005

Figure 5-2 shows that the development from 1986 to 2005 is more unsteady for the biotechnology sector. Especially the *BRIC*s experience an unsteady development. In the years 1988, 1990, 1992, 2002, and 2004, the citation numbers even fall below the *DEUS* citations. The non-patent citations of the late-comers, however, are above the numbers of the *DEUS* non-patent citations.

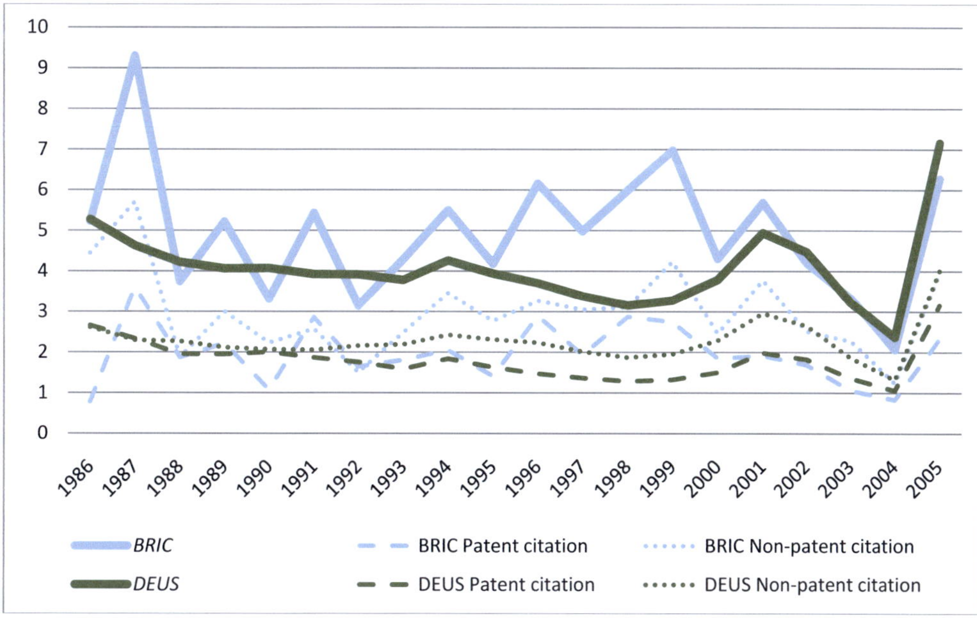

Figure 5-2: Development of mean values of *BRIC* and *DEUS* biotechnology citation rates

The statistical analysis of the biotechnology sector discloses that there is also a significant difference between the *BRIC* patents and the *DEUS* patents (see Table 5-7). However, this finding does not hold for all countries. Once again, the USA is taken as benchmark. Brazil and India do not share the findings for the whole *BRIC* group, as they have no significant t-values. The most significant difference can be seen between China and the USA (3.10). Germany, which is also considered as a biotechnological late-comer, has also significant differences of mean values compared to the USA. Adopting the same statistical tests with each *BRIC* country and Germany also shows that they do not have clear differences to each other. Hence, the general assumption that late-comers use more external knowledge is also strengthened by the analysis of the biotechnology sector in general.

	Obs.	Mean	Std.Dev.	t-value					
				DEUS	Brazil	Russia	India	China	Germany
BRIC	20	4.96	1.61	2.11*					
DEUS	20	4.08	0.98						
USA	20	3.76	1.41		0.60	2.00*	1.14	3.10*	3.54*
Brazil	20	4.89	8.36						-0.04
Russia	20	4.97	2.32						0.01
India	20	4.45	2.33						-0.96
China	20	5.75	2.52						1.36
Germany	20	4.97	0.60						

Standard errors: *p<0.05

Table 5-7: t-test of biotechnology citation rates

Patent citation	Obs.	Mean	Std.Dev.	t-value					
				DEUS	Brazil	Russia	India	China	Germany
BRIC	20	1.97	0.75	0.86					
DEUS	20	1.79	0.50						
USA	20	1.65	0.71		0.06	1.70*	0.09	2.11*	3.43*
Brazil	20	1.68	2.81						-0.88
Russia	20	2.10	0.97						-0.62
India	20	1.68	1.25						-1.96
China	20	2.36	1.32						0.37
Germany	20	2.24	0.32						
Non-pat. citation									
BRIC	20	2.99	1.06	2.68*					
DEUS	20	2.28	0.53						
USA	20	2.11	0.72		0.83	1.99*	1.80*[43]	3.24*	3.32*
Brazil	20	3.20	5.87						0.37
Russia	20	2.87	1.55						0.40
India	20	2.77	1.48						0.14
China	20	3.40	1.63						1.80*
Germany	20	2.72	0.40						

Standard errors: *p<0.05

Table 5-8: t-test of biotechnology citation rates distinguished between patent citations and non-patent citations

[43] A significant difference can be accepted in these two cases as the limit of the t-value is lower, if the degree of freedom is higher. In this case the degree of freedom is high enough (> 10) to give these values significance.

Regarding the two groups of citations, namely citations to publications and to other patents, this sector also shows that citations of patents are quite similar to the general findings for this sector (see Table 5-8). However, the mean values do not differ significantly between the two groups of countries (0.86). The difference between the two groups and the differences between each *BRIC* country, as well as Germany, and the USA are again driven by differences in the mean values of the non-patent literature citations. The statistical tests of these mean values firstly show that the group of countries differ significantly to each other (2.68). Additionally, the Chinese (3.24) and German (3.32) non-patent citations also differ significantly to the US ones.

Time lag in the biotechnology sector

Regarding different time periods in the sector of the biotechnology, the comparison of the time periods considers a division into three steps. It is assumed that Germany, as a biotechnological late-comer, follows in a time lag of five years after the USA and the four *BRIC* countries with the general time lag of ten years (see Cooke, 2001a, and Fornahl and Tran, 2009). Due the few numbers of observations a clear statement can not be made in this case. This is presented in Table 5-9 where almost all countries do not show significant t-values in comparison to the USA. Germany is the only exception.

	Obs.	Mean	Std.Dev.	t-value				
				Brazil	Russia	India	China	Germany
USA	5	3.79	0.09	-0.59	0.97	-0.07	0.74	5.28*
Brazil	5	3.05	1.23					
Russia	5	5.52	1.78					
India	5	3.75	0.53					
China	5	4.42	0.85					
Germany	5	4.68	0.14					

Standard errors: *p<0.05

Table 5-9: t-test of citation rates of the biotechnology sector between different time periods

The special status of Germany persists in the detailed investigation of the two different kinds of citations, as Germany is, once again, the only country which has significantly higher citation values in comparison to the US biotechnology sector. A reason may be the special effort which was undertaken by the German Federal Ministry of Education and Research (Bundesministerium für Bildung und Forschung (BMBF)) in the late 1990s to strengthen the German biotechnology sector. The so-called *BioRegio* contest tries to push Germany towards the world leaders of the biotechnology and may enhanced co-operations between German biotechnology players which also led to more citations as existing knowledge is shared among the collaboration partners (see Fornahl and Tran, 2009). According to the differentiation of the two kinds of citations, the *BRIC* countries also do not show a significant difference to the US biotechnology sector.

Patent citation	Obs.	Mean	Std.Dev.	t-value				
				Brazil	Russia	India	China	Germany
USA	5	1.62	0.06	-1.92	0.80	-1.29	0.05	5.28*
Brazil	5	0.95	0.34					
Russia	5	2.09	0.59					
India	5	1.35	0.20					
China	5	1.63	0.34					
Germany	5	2.02	0.05					
Non-pat. citation								
USA	5	2.10	0.06	0.00	1.08	0.86	1.29	4.49*
Brazil	5	2.10	0.92					
Russia	5	3.43	1.24					
India	5	2.40	0.34					
China	5	2.79	0.53					
Germany	5	2.67	0.11					

Standard errors: *p<0.05

Table 5-10: t-test of citation rates between different time periods distinguished between patent citations and non-patent citations

The evidence delivered by the statistical test can be summarised as follows. The t-values of the mean comparison between the two groups of countries are significantly higher for the late-comers on the national level, as well as for the biotechnology sector. The differences between the mean values are mainly driven by non-patent citations which are significantly higher for the late-comers, while the citations of patents do not show a clear difference between the late-comers and the early-movers. This points to a higher scientific linkage of the late-comer countries. In an in-depth examination of the citations of each country, the tests show that on a national level all late-comers except from Russia differ significantly from the benchmark (USA, see Chapter 4.3). This also holds if the citation rates are divided into citations to other patents. Non-patent citations, however, are more important in Russia, as the mean values of these kinds of citations are significantly above the US ones. The deeper insight into the biotechnology sector reveals that Brazilian and Indian citations do not show significant differences from the US ones while the other two *BRIC*-countries do. Interestingly, German citations also differ significantly from the US counterparts. Looking at the two groups of citations, it is once again observable that citations to other patents do not differ significantly, this holds especially for Brazil and India. Non-patent citations, however, still show significant differences. This even holds for Indian patents (see Table 5-10).

5.4. Use of external knowledge in technological late-comer countries

As main result of this chapter, it is possible to conclude that late-comers do have higher rates of patent citations in general. This is verified by means of patent citation and statistical tests. Hence, the general hypothesis of this chapter is confirmed to a certain degree. Not all variables show clear and significant results. In general, however, late-comers use more external knowledge than early-movers.

All in all, the rates of citations which refer to other patents do not differ significantly from each other; this holds not only for the country groups, but also for the *BRIC*-countries compared to the USA. The higher rates originate from citations to non-patent literature, what means that the use of external knowledge is basically deriving from the use of scientific knowledge. Late-comers use this kind of knowledge to a greater extent and, therefore, have a higher scientific linkage. Especially the Asian late-comers use science more than others. This fact may be due to their investment in science and technology. This investment includes, for instance, international exchanges which could be a driver for a higher linkage to the science network (see Chapter 8). A special consideration of a time lag for technological late-comers shows that after ten years the differences in the citation rates become more similar to the early-movers. Hence, late-comer countries show patterns of learning processes and an adaption to early-mover countries. A higher linkage to scientific knowledge, however, is also detected in the time lag approach which shows that late-comers still use more scientific work to introduce their innovations. This effect may be caused by the higher governmental driven innovation efforts, as well as a focus on more scientific based technological sectors. This result is also mirrored by the exploration of the biotechnology sector.

In general, the biotechnology sector shows higher numbers in non-patent citations for all countries. This emphasises the stronger link to science. It also underlines the fact that biotechnology is a knowledge-based technology. Concerning the differences between the late-comers and the early-movers, it is still observable that in this sector the use of external knowledge for the late-comers is also significantly higher compared to the early-movers. However, Brazil and India do not show significant differences anymore. In case of Brazil, this may be due to the low numbers of patents in this sector and hence, some patents with lower citation rates already have a higher impact on the mean. India, however, seems to profit from their concentration on life science since the beginning of their innovation activities. Interestingly, the assumption that late-comers have a higher link to external knowledge also holds for the German biotechnology sector. Hence, regarding the biotechnology sector, Germany is also at the stage of a late-comer, although the mere counting of patent activities would deliver different evidence. The special considerations of the time periods do not discover significant differences between the *BRIC* and the US biotechnology sector. This may also point to the adoption of both biotechnology sectors. Unfortunately the fewer numbers of observations makes it impossible to draw clear implications. Special attention is attracted by Germany where the citation rates are still significantly higher for both kinds of citations. As mentioned before, this finding can be caused by the efforts of the BMBF to push the German to become a world-class biotechnology country.

6. Entry into the global technological competition with niche strategies

This chapter deals with the second hypothesis of this work. It covers the entry of the late-comers into the global competition and, therefore, illustrates the first analytical block together with the examination of the usage of external knowledge (see Chapter 5). In doing so, it is assumed that activities of players in technological competition are comparable to activities of players in a certain kind of market, for instance, for a specific product or a whole industrial sector. In general, such markets consist of established players, as well as newer and smaller competitors. The first ones basically possess the major share of a market, providing basic products of the specific market or whole mainstream portfolios to satisfy a broad bandwidth of demand. In this respect, new and small entrants try to find their niches to enter a market as it is more difficult to challenge established big players in their dominion. The same process can be assumed for the technology competition. Established players, here, early-movers are major players in certain technological fields. As well-known examples, the German automotive and machine tool industry can be named, or the electronics industry in Japan, as well as biotechnology in the USA. Hence, technological late-comers have to find niches to enter the technological competition. This does not just hold for the national level, but also for specific sectors, such as the biotechnology sector.

This chapter presents an analysis of the occupation of niches by technological late-comers. It, therefore, examines national and sectoral level technological patterns of innovation activities. The analysis gives rationale for the question why late-comers need to use niches to enter the technological competition (see Section 6.1). Then, in Section 6.2, the methods by which a niche is identified are presented. The next sub-chapter (Section 6.3) tests the empirical evidence of the hypothesis. Finally, the findings are discussed in Section 6.4.

6.1. Rationale for niche strategies

New entrants basically face established competitors. Of course, new technology can originate from an existing technology within the same field. Technological late-comers still look for niches to introduce their innovations (see Forbes and Wield, 2000 and Chang and Tsai, 2002). Forbes and Wield (2000, p. 1097) argue that late-comers should not try, or even hope, to compete with early-movers, as they do not have the same options regarding their production methods and R&D capacities. Hence, it is crucial for technological late-comers to follow a different strategy. Chang and Tsai (2002) share this point of view also for specific sectors, as they investigate competition strategies of Taiwan's integrated circuit design industry. They state that the strategy of being a *superior quick follower* with a focus on a niche turns out to be successful. This strategy emerges as a result of the Taiwanese lack of a deep-rooted scientific foundation in research on semiconductor technology. It is not surprising that the USA and the European countries have long dominated specifications for integrated circuit designs, as their engagement in this field began much earlier, and, hence, control the major part of this market. However, Taiwan managed to establish itself in this market (ibid., p. 103). This was achieved by the development of specific core competences in this sector[44].

To sum up, although niche strategies are not per se crucial for the introduction of a new technology, late-comers often follow this strategy. Therefore, this chapter deals with the analysis of the following hypothesis:

Hypothesis 2: New entrants into the technological competition face established players which have a broad technological base. Late-comers pursue niche strategies to enter the technological competition.

For future economic and technological development, this assumption is very important as technology underlies an ever-changing development. The successful emergence of technological niches also offers opportunities to transform or break existing patterns of technological development, the so-called technological regimes (van de Poel, 2003, p. 49). Therefore, it is stated that niche technologies can be incubators for future transitions, undo technological lock-ins or even provide a sustainable development of technologies (Smith, 2003, Agnolucci and McDowall, 2007 and Nill and Kemp, 2009). It is possible that technological late-comers take advantage of the strategy to enter technological niches for future technology competition. Taking advantage of the impulses of these niches, as well as their transformation to established technologies, late-comers can develop to future main competitors.

6.2. Identification of technological niche

The examination of technological niches is done by a twofold analysis. First, the technological focus of late-comers is analysed by means of a distance measurement, the so-called *Cosine Index* which is also used by Jaffe (1986) for the first time employing patent data. Second, to consider the total strength of patent activities, the additional analysis uses relative measures, namely the *Balassa Index*, also known as

[44] See also Smith (2003), Agnolucci and MacDowall (2007) and Nill and Kemp (2009).

the *Revealed Comparative Advantage* (RCA). The latter analysis gives additional insight into the specialisation profiles of each country. Both indices are discussed in detail in the following subsections.

As the focus of the analysis lies on technology, this examination uses technological classifications of patents. Unfortunately, such classifications are not given by patent data directly. Although, there is a patent classification delivered by the EPO and WIPO, it is not a straight-forward process to identify technologies based upon the *International Patent Classification* (IPC). To classify patents into technological sectors, it is necessary to use concordances to link the IPC classes to the sectors and technologies. The analysis of the niche strategies on a national and biotechnological level uses the 30 technological sectors of the *OST/INPI/ISI Concordance*[45].

6.2.1. Distance between late-comers and early-movers

As early-movers are already established in the market, their technological portfolio represents a mainstream portfolio (see Section 6.1). A niche and specialisation strategy can, therefore, be observed, if a technological portfolio or profile is different from the mainstream. In contrast to geographical distance between countries, technological distance is not measured by common metres. It is rather an examination of similarities than a direct distance measure. On a technological level, such distances can be measured by the *Cosine Index* using patent data (Jaffe, 1986[46]). This index is defined as follows:

$$d_{ik} = \frac{\sum_{n=1}^{N} p_{in} * p_{kn}}{\sqrt{\sum_{n=1}^{N} p_{in}^2 * \sum_{n=1}^{N} p_{kn}^2}} \qquad (6\text{-}1)$$

The distance d_{ik} between the two countries *i* and *k* is calculated by the numbers of patents in each country and each sector *n* (p_{in} and p_{kn}). Hence, the more patents two countries possess in the same sector, the more similar they are and the *Cosine Index* delivers a value close to 1. The other way round, the fewer patents two countries possess in the same technological sector, the less similar they are and the index delivers a value around 0. Hence, late-comers which focus on a few technologies have a lower similarity to early-movers. Thereby, the *Cosine Index* does not refer to absolute amount of patents in certain technologies, but to the mixture of the portfolio. If both countries have the same inner-country shares of patents in the same

[45] A detailed discussion to this topic is given in Subsection 3.2.2. See also Hinze et al. (1997), Schmoch et al. (2003) and Schmoch (2008).

[46] See also Maurseth and Verspagen (2002) and Breschi et al. (2003).

technological fields, the *Cosine Index* also delivers a high similarity even if one country has a higher total amount of patents.

6.2.2. *Revealed Comparative Advantage*

The second method deals with the problem of relative strengths of certain sectors. Comparisons of countries, regions and industrial sectors always comprise external circumstances which influence these comparisons. Two countries with different sizes regarding their population, national economy etc. are hardly comparable to each other. A comparison of the total amounts of patents between the USA and Korea, for instance, would lead to the finding that the USA file more patents than Korea in nearly every technological sector. Consequently, the USA has a technological advantage compared to Korea. This finding, however, does not reflect Korea's strength in some specific fields, such as the semiconductor industry (Choung et al. 1999). Moreover, it is also not possible to draw implications on specific specialisations of a country. Korea, whose focus lies in specific technological sectors, would not reveal this specialisation, if the total amount of patents is compared with the USA. For such cases, comparative advantage structures need to be exploited. In the field of exports and trade, Balassa (1965) introduced such a measure the *Revealed Comparative Advantage* (RCA) or the *Balassa Index* which is defined as follows[47]:

$$RCA_{ij} = \frac{x_{ij} / \sum_j x_{ij}}{\sum_i x_{ij} / \sum_i \sum_j x_{ij}} \qquad (6\text{-}2)$$

The RCA reveals comparative advantages of a country *i* in a certain sector *j*, such as the biotechnology sector. In doing so, it uses export numbers classified by industrial sectors which is represented by *x*. Hence, exports of a specific sector, for instance the biotechnology sector, of a country (x_{ij}) are compared to the total exports of this country (see enumerator of *6-2*). This term, in turn, is compared to the share of global exports in this sector (see denominator of *6-2*). If the RCA equals 1 in a given country and a given sector, it is identical with the global average. In general, the denominator is a referent and is not necessarily the global export. It can also be a benchmark group of countries, such as the OECD, depending on the comparison which is wanted. For technological considerations this indicator is used employing data of scientific publication counts and patent numbers instead of export numbers (Grupp, 1994 and Laursen, 1998).The RCA in such cases is also denoted as *Revealed Technological*

[47] See also Guerrieri and Iammarino (2003).

Advantage (RTA) or *Revealed Patent Advantage* (RPA) (see Grupp, 1994, p. 187 and Mitusch et al., 2010).

Standardisation

Calculations of term *6-2* deliver results from 0 to ∞. As aforementioned, a RCA value of 1 represents a specialisation which is the global average. It is not easy to draw straight-forward implications because values in the co-domain [0; 1) stand for under-average advantages or disadvantages and values in the co-domain (1; ∞) stand for over-average advantages. Hence, the following standardisation of this index is proposed to make it symmetric and, therefore, easier to draw interpretations[48] (Vollrath, 1991 and Grupp, 1994).

$$RSCA_{ij} = 100 * \tanh \ln RCA_{ij} \qquad (6\text{-}3)$$

These *Revealed Standardised Comparative Advantages* (RSCA) deliver results in a co-domain (-100; 100), while the average is represented by a value of 0. Furthermore, it is argued that this standardisation is needed for econometric analyses, not just to give the indicator a more appealing range, but also to have an easier statistical handling (Laursen, 1998, p. 6). For the analysis of technological niches, the approach of RSCA is used with a technological focus. Hence, for the remainder of this work the term 'specialisation' stands for the *Revealed Standardised Technological Advantage*.

6.3. Niche strategies of technological late-comers

In this section, the findings of the *Cosine Index* and the *Revealed Standardised Technological Advantages* are presented for the national and sectoral levels.

6.3.1. Distance from early-movers

The *Cosine Index* offers a view on the development of the technological similarity over time. Hence, the technological distances between the late-comer countries and Germany, as well as the USA are calculated and compared to the technological distance between the early-movers.

[48] Another standardisation is proposed by Laursen (1998) which delivers results in the co-domain of (-1;1):

$$RSCA_{ij} = \frac{RCA_{ij} - 1}{RCA_{ij} + 1}$$

Distance to Germany

Figure 6-1 shows the distance between late-comers and Germany. To present a clear trend, a weighted[49] sliding window over three years is used to smooth the yearly distance values. The orange line represents the distance between Germany and the USA which is between 0.91 and 0.82. As a value of 1 stands for a perfect match between two technological portfolios, these values are close to a similar portfolio. This relative close similarity between these two countries refers to the fact that both countries have many patent applications in all technological sectors and, therefore, a relative balanced portfolio without extreme outliers with no prevalent specialisations in certain sectors (see Subsection 6.3.2). It can be stated that the distance values between them are reducing which means that their technological portfolios move away from each other. The distance between Brazil, as well as Russia and Germany describes an upward trend. Both countries begin with lower values (Brazil: 0.65 and Russia: 0.71) and rise to maximum values of 0.84 for Brazil in 2002 and 0.85 for Russia in 2002. From 1995 onwards, Brazil firstly shows a decreasing trend down to 0.71 in 1998. Afterwards, an increasing trend can be observed. The Russian similarity values to Germany also decreased slightly in 1996 and 1997, but overall increased nearly in all other years. Hence, despite of the slightly decreasing years in the middle of the 1990s and at the end of the analysed period, Brazil's and Russia's portfolios show high similarity values compared to the German technology portfolio. Their distances (DE-RU and DE-BR) move towards the distance between the two early-movers (DE-US) and arrive at this level in 2002 and 2003.

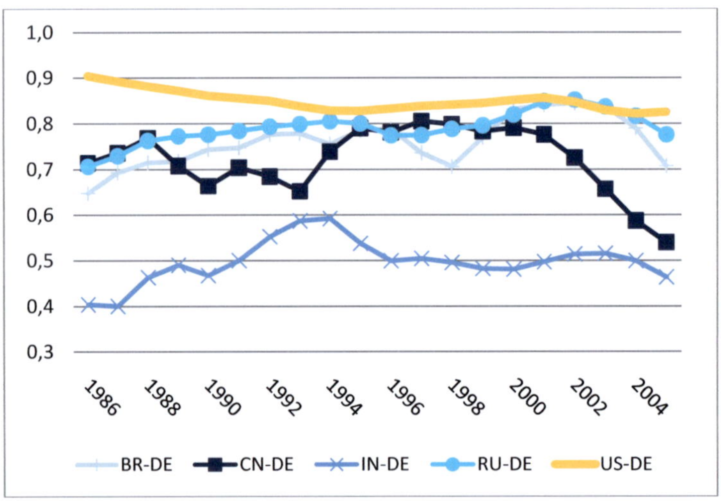

Figure 6-1: Technological distance between the four late-comers and Germany

[49] The weighted sliding window ($d^*_{ik,t}$) is calculated:

$$d^*_{ik,t} = 0.25 * d_{ik,t-1} + 0.5 * d_{ik,t} + 0.25 * d_{ik,t+1}$$

The development of the Asian late-comers is different to the Brazil and Russia ones. The Chinese technological portfolio converges towards the German one between 1986 and 1988. After 1988, it shows again a decreasing trend until 1994. Even though China could approach their portfolio towards the early-movers until 2000, its technological similarity to Germany decreases rapidly to a minimum of 0.54 in 2005. India, compared to the other late-comer countries, is an outstanding exception. It has the lowest level of similarity to Germany. At the end of the 1980s until 1994 this similarity increases, but never exceeds a value of 0.60. After 1994, it decreases again and ends at a level of 0.46. Hence, the Asian late-comers show less similarities to the German technology portfolio compared to Brazil and Russia. This finding shows interesting aspects of niche occupation of the four late-comer countries and they are interpreted at the end of this Chapter (see Section 6.4)

Distance to the USA

Looking at the US technological portfolio, the findings are similar for Russia (see Figure 6-2). The Russian technological distance values increase during the whole period, starting at a minimum of 0.64. In 2001, Russia reaches its peak with a value of 0.91. Hence, Russia and the USA are quite similar in a technological sense. The same can be stated for China and the USA; their distance levels start at 0.70 and rise up until 2001. At its maximum in 2000, the distance value between China and the USA is 0.88 which stands for a very close similarity.

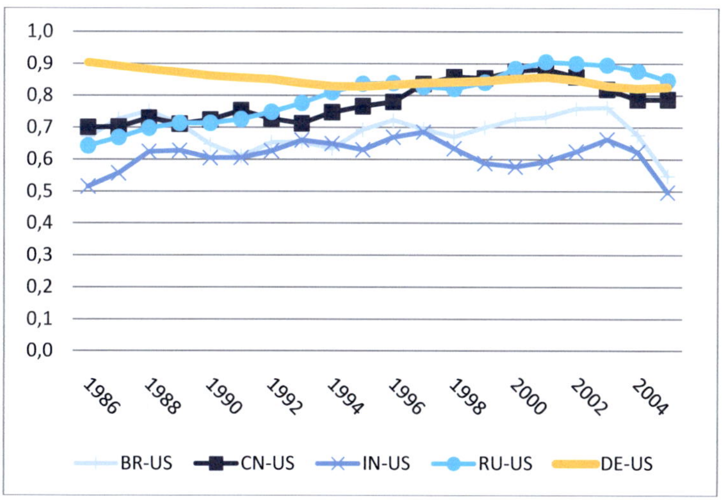

Figure 6-2: Technological distance between the four late-comers and the USA

The *Cosine Index* shows ever-changing trends for Brazil and the USA within the whole time period. However, it ranges between 0.55 in 2005 and 0.76 in 2003. India, once again, shows the lowest similarity to an early-mover as it is also technologically ‘far away’ from the USA. Like the Brazilian distance values, India also shows a variable development. It begins with 0.52 and rises up to a maximum of 0.66 in 1993. In summary, it is possible to say that Russia also develops towards the second early-mover. China, however, converges towards the technological portfolio of the USA. Brazil shows an unclear development, while India has once more the lowest similarity.

	Obs.	Mean	Std.Dev.	t-value
				DE-US
Brazil-Germany	20	0.76	0.05	6.81***
China-Germany	20	0.72	0.07	7.60***
India-Germany	20	0.50	0.05	29.61***
Russia-Germany	20	0.79	0.04	6.27***
Brazil-USA	20	0.69	0.05	12.50***
China-USA	20	0.78	0.06	4.66***
India-USA	20	0.61	0.05	19.85***
Russia-USA	20	0.80	0.08	2.72***

Standard errors: *p<0.1, **p<0.05 and ***p<0.01

Table 6-1: t-test of Cosine Index

A statistical test shows the differences of the *Cosine Index* of the two early-movers compared to the *Cosine Indices* of a late-comer and Germany or the USA respectively. It shows that these values are significantly different from each other (see Table 5-7). This means that the late-comer portfolios are still different from the mainstream and a tendency to niche strategies can be assumed.

Biotechnological similarity

The examination of the *Cosine Index*, as well as the *RSCA*, is based on the technological classification of patents delivered by the patent offices (see Subsection 3.2.2). They are given on the patent applications of each patent specification. Figure 6-3 shows an example of a European patent specification with seven different IPC classifications (red frame). In Table 6-2 the IPCs which belong to biotechnology sector are listed. This also refers to the *OST/INPI/ISI Concordance* (see Subsection 3.2.2).

C07G	C12M	C12N	C12P
C12Q	C12R	C12S	

Table 6-2: IPC classes of the biotechnology sector

The calculations of the *Cosine Index* for the biotechnology sector are based on the different sectors given by the classifications on one patent. As aforementioned, a patent belongs to the biotechnology sector, if one or more IPCs on this patent belong to the biotechnology sector.

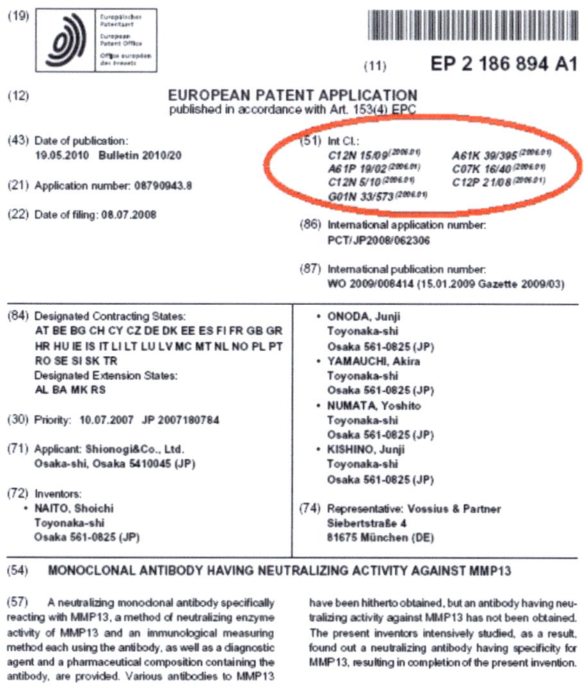

(19) Europäisches Patentamt / European Patent Office / Office européen des brevets

(11) EP 2 186 894 A1

(12) EUROPEAN PATENT APPLICATION
published in accordance with Art. 153(4) EPC

(43) Date of publication:
19.05.2010 Bulletin 2010/20

(21) Application number: 08790943.8

(22) Date of filing: 08.07.2008

(51) Int Cl.:
C12N 15/09 (2006.01) A61K 39/395 (2006.01)
A61P 19/02 (2006.01) C07K 16/40 (2006.01)
C12N 5/10 (2006.01) C12P 21/08 (2006.01)
G01N 33/573 (2006.01)

(86) International application number:
PCT/JP2008/062306

(87) International publication number:
WO 2009/008414 (15.01.2009 Gazette 2009/03)

(84) Designated Contracting States:
AT BE BG CH CY CZ DE DK EE ES FI FR GB GR HR HU IE IS IT LI LT LU LV MC MT NL NO PL PT RO SE SI SK TR
Designated Extension States:
AL BA MK RS

(30) Priority: 10.07.2007 JP 2007180784

(71) Applicant: Shionogi&Co., Ltd.
Osaka-shi, Osaka 5410045 (JP)

(72) Inventors:
- NAITO, Shoichi
Toyonaka-shi
Osaka 561-0825 (JP)
- ONODA, Junji
Toyonaka-shi
Osaka 561-0825 (JP)
- YAMAUCHI, Akira
Toyonaka-shi
Osaka 561-0825 (JP)
- NUMATA, Yoshito
Toyonaka-shi
Osaka 561-0825 (JP)
- KISHINO, Junji
Toyonaka-shi
Osaka 561-0825 (JP)

(74) Representative: Vossius & Partner
Siebertstraße 4
81675 München (DE)

(54) MONOCLONAL ANTIBODY HAVING NEUTRALIZING ACTIVITY AGAINST MMP13

(57) A neutralizing monoclonal antibody specifically reacting with MMP13, a method of neutralizing enzyme activity of MMP13 and an immunological measuring method each using the antibody, as well as a diagnostic agent and a pharmaceutical composition containing the antibody, are provided. Various antibodies to MMP13 have been hitherto obtained, but an antibody having neutralizing activity against MMP13 has not been obtained. The present inventors intensively studied, as a result, found out a neutralizing antibody having specificity for MMP13, resulting in completion of the present invention.

Figure 6-3: European patent application form

The findings of the *Cosine Index* of the biotechnology sector based on the technological sectors are difficult to interpret as there are certain technologies which are highly related to this sector (e.g. pharmaceuticals). This relation does not differ strongly in different countries and also leads to a quite close biotechnological portfolio for all countries (see Table 6-3). Although the biotechnology sector consists just of seven IPC classes (see Table 6-2), the examination of this sector bases on a set of 337 different IPC classes and all 30 technology sectors of the *OST/INPI/ISI Concordance*.

A weighted count[50] of the patents according to their technological sectors leads to the technological top five rankings which are very similar to each other (see Table 6-3)

Brazil		China	
11	Pharmaceuticals, cosmetics	11	Pharmaceuticals, cosmetics
10	Organic fine chemistry	10	Organic fine chemistry
13	Agriculture, food chemistry	7	Analysis, measurement, control technology
7	Analysis, measurement, control technology	13	Agriculture, food chemistry
17	Chemical industry and petrol industry, basic materials chemistry	18	Chemical Engineering
India		**Russia**	
10	Organic fine chemistry	11	Pharmaceuticals, cosmetics
11	Pharmaceuticals, cosmetics	10	Organic fine chemistry
7	Analysis, measurement, control technology	7	Analysis, measurement, control technology
13	Agriculture, food chemistry	18	Chemical Engineering
17	Chemical industry and petrol industry, basic materials chemistry	13	Agriculture, food chemistry
USA		**Germany**	
11	Pharmaceuticals, cosmetics	11	Pharmaceuticals, cosmetics
10	Organic fine chemistry	10	Organic fine chemistry
7	Analysis, measurement, control technology	7	Analysis, measurement, control technology
13	Chemical industry and petrol industry, basic materials chemistry	17	Agriculture, food chemistry
18	Agriculture, food chemistry	13	Chemical Engineering

Table 6-3: Technological sectors occupied by biotechnology patents 1986-2005

The findings of this investigation are shown in Figure 6-4. Again, the US biotechnology sector is taken as benchmark. It becomes clear that the biotechnological similarity between the USA and Germany, as well as between China, India and Russia is generally very high. The *Cosine Index* of the similarity between the USA and Germany has the highest values. During the twenty years it is always between 0.98 and 0.99 which stands almost for a perfect match. The same holds for the major part of the late-comers, too. However, it is considerable that the *Cosine Index* has an increasing trend. Hence, the similarity of these countries compared to the USA is also increasing. Brazil shows a different development. The biotechnology sector in Brazil starts with a very low similarity and increases for the first four years. During the twenty years, it

[50] The weight is given by the amount of classifications on one patent. The example of Figure 6-3 gives a weight for the biotechnology sector of 3/7 and 4/7 in other technology sectors.

has for some years (e.g. 1991 and 2004) very low values. These values derive from the low numbers of Brazilian biotechnology patents in these years.

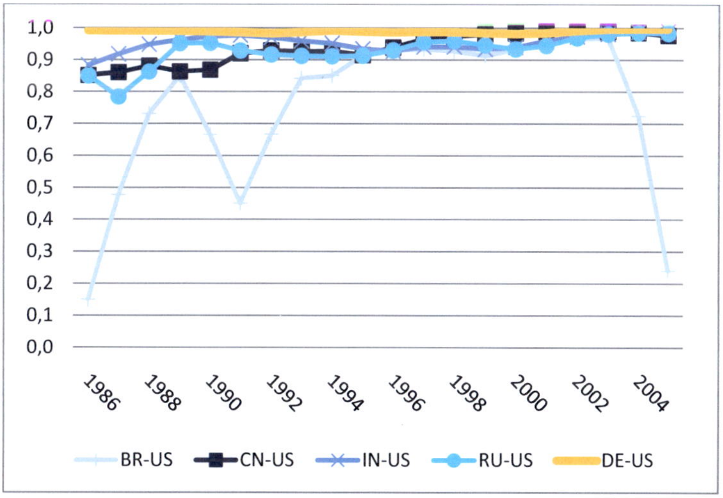

Figure 6-4: Technological distance in the sector of biotechnology between late-comers and the USA

As mentioned before, the similarity of biotechnology portfolios is, apart from Brazil, very high. A clear distinction to the early-movers and, hence, a clear niche strategy in this case cannot be discovered for late-comer countries by use of the *Cosine Index*. However, according to this index, the overall technological similarity shows significant differences which means that late-comer countries have other focuses. A detailed discussion including findings of both analyses is given after the analysis explained in Subsection 6.3.2, as the analysis of this Subsection does not deliver clear findings for the niche strategies yet.

6.3.2. Technological specialisation

To cross-check and enrich the analysis of technological niche occupation, the second analysis of this chapter employs a relative measurement of technological focus. In doing so, the RSTA for the whole technological portfolio of the late-comer countries, as well as of Germany and the USA are examined for the whole time period between 1986 and 2005. In Figure 6-5, the overall view on the technological profiles is depicted with the range between -100 and 100 (see Subsection 6.2.2).

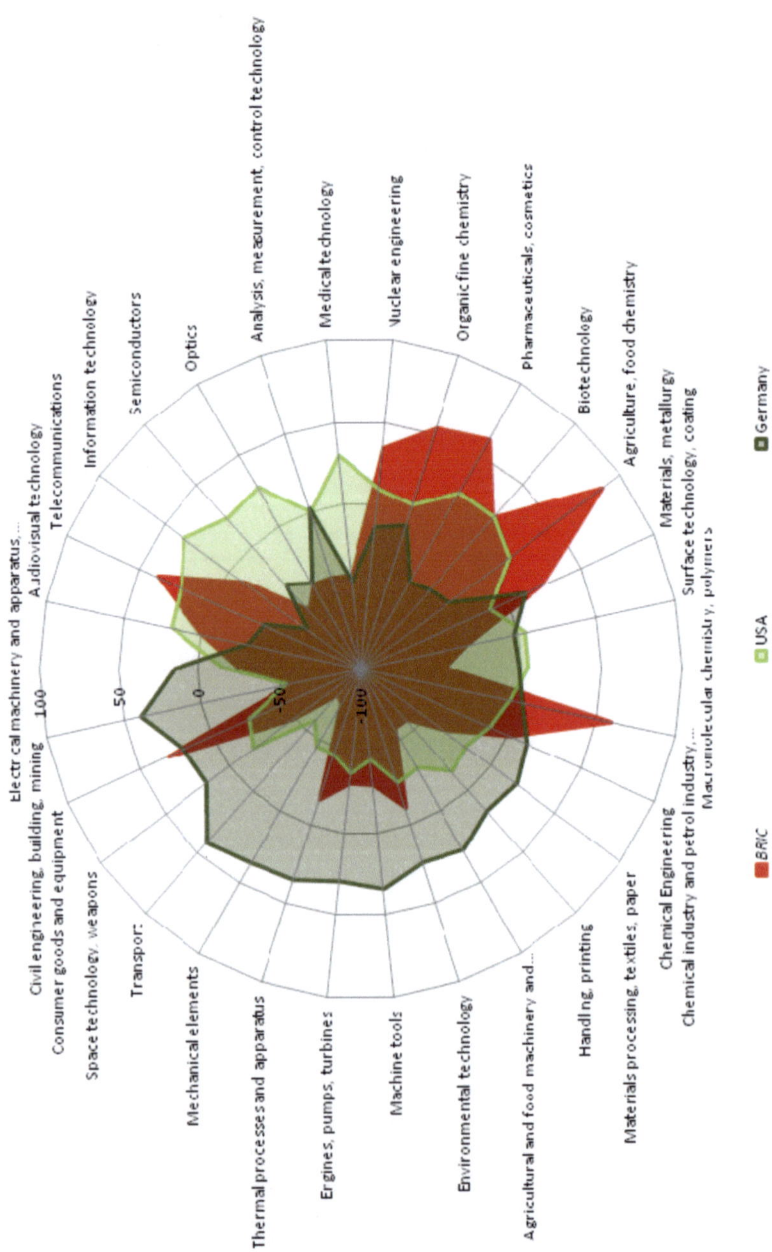

Figure 6-5: RSTA of *BRICs* compared to Germany and the USA[51]

[51] For the detailed list of technological sectors see Appendix.

Regarding relative advantages, Germany and the USA have very different specialisation focuses (see light and dark green graph; correlation coefficient of -0.975). Germany's top five advantages are 'transport', 'civil engineering, building, mining', ‚mechanical elements', 'thermal processes and apparatus' and 'machine tools' and reflect a focus on engineering technologies (see Appendix and Mitusch et al., 2010). Meanwhile, the USA have their focus on 'information technology', 'medical technology', 'optics', 'biotechnology' and 'semiconductors' (see Appendix and Mitusch et al., 2010). The *BRIC*s, as a group, have their focus on 'agriculture, food chemistry', 'pharmaceuticals, cosmetics', 'chemical industry and petrol industry, basic materials chemistry', 'organic fine chemistry' and 'telecommunications'. At a first glance, late-comers are more concentrated in certain sectors and they have their specialisation in other sectors than the *DEUS* countries. These findings are, in fact, on a very general level, but it already underlines that early-mover countries diversify much more than late-comers (see Chapter 7).

Country level

The development of the Brazilian specialisation profile shows a changing structure. This can be seen in Figure 6-6 which illustrates that the technological portfolio of Brazil shifts in some sectors through the time periods. This shifts show that Brazil does not follow a clear strategy. However, the periods have positive correlation coefficients which still show that the shifting is not very dramatic and the technological focus still has a certain way. Looking at each consecutive period, the correlation coefficients are 0.527 (period one to two), 0.707 (two to three), and 0.640[52] (three to four). Even between the first and the last period we can see a positive correlation coefficient of 0.327[53]. The top five sectors are 'agriculture, food chemistry' (sector 13), 'chemical industry and petrol industry, basic materials chemistry' (sector 17), 'materials processing, textiles, paper' (sector 19), 'engines, pumps, turbines' (sector 24) and 'materials, metallurgy' (sector 14) (see Appendix).

[52] All consecutive correlation coefficients are significant at a level of 99% (see Appendix).
[53] This correlation coefficient is significant at a level of 90% (see Appendix).

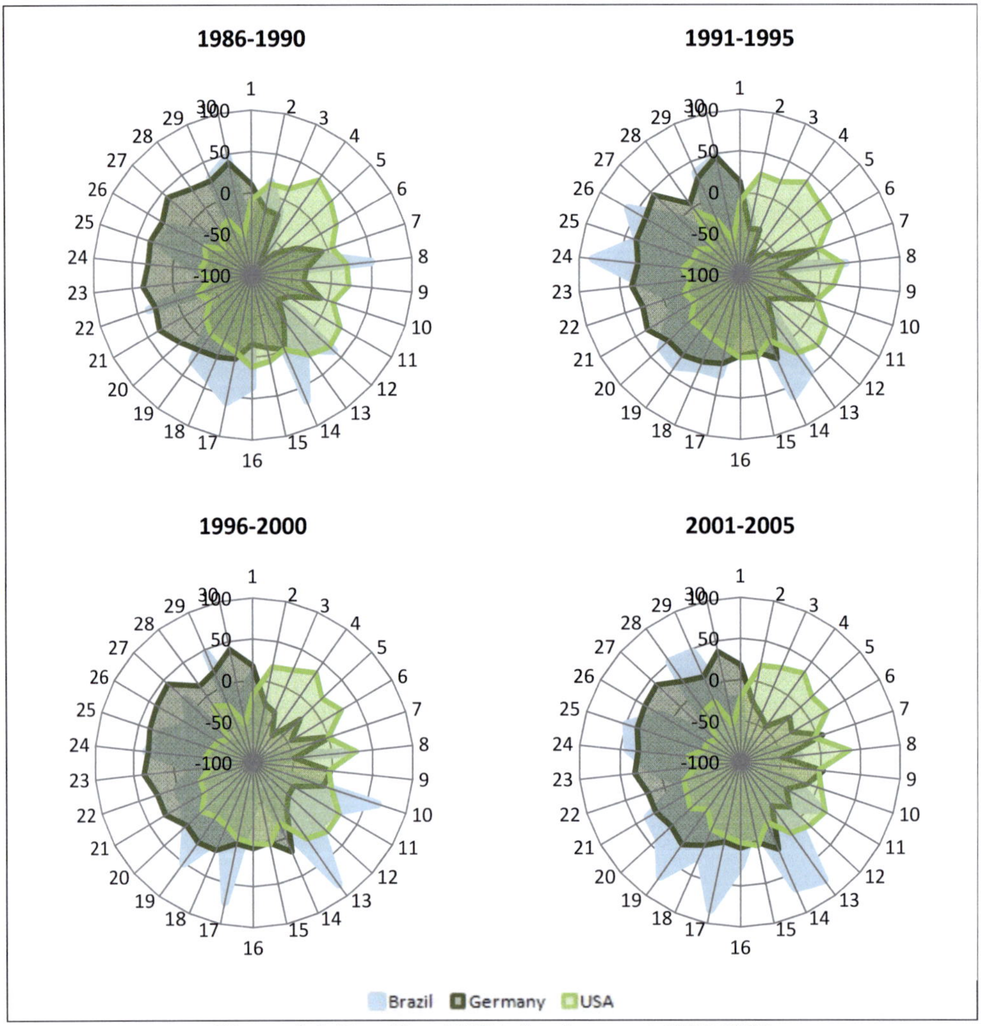

Figure 6-6: Brazilian RSTA development 1986-2005

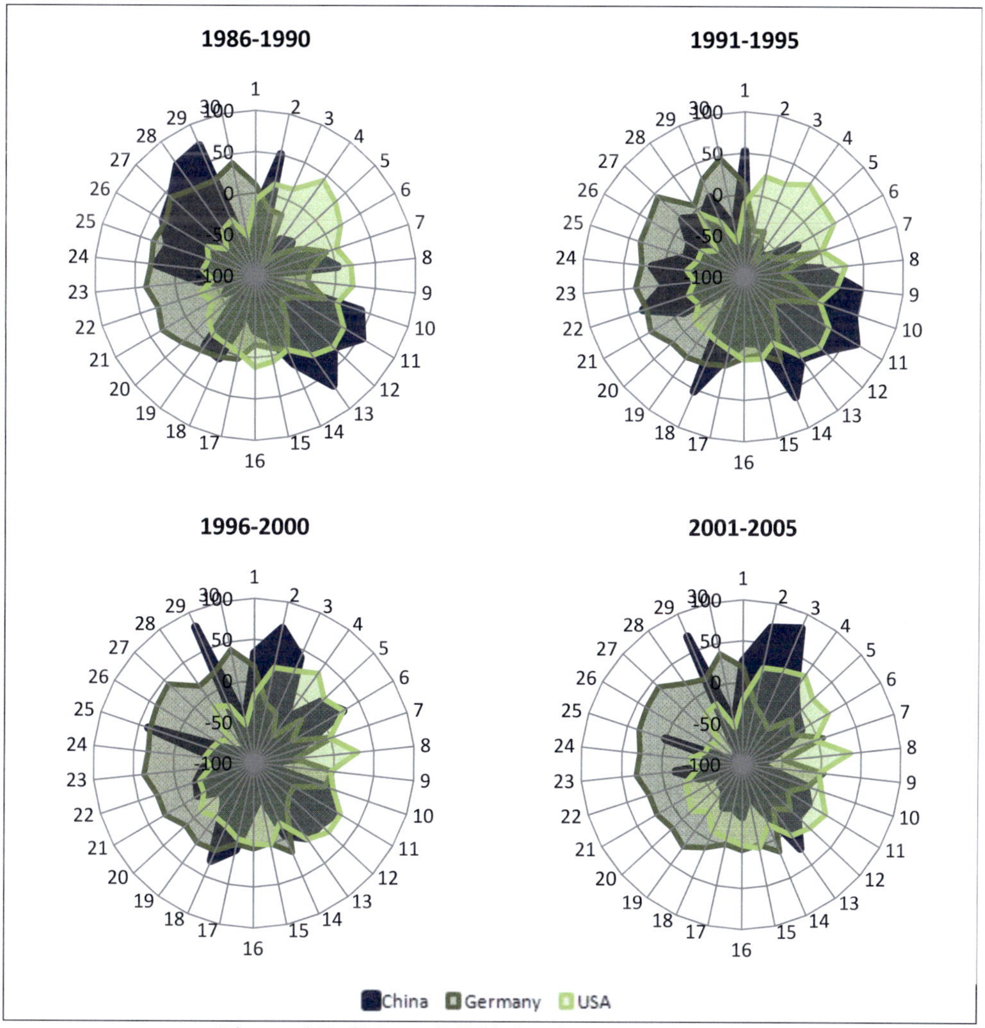

Figure 6-7: Chinese RSTA development 1986-2005

The technological portfolio of China also shows a change in the structure throughout the time periods (see Figure 6-7). The time periods even show lower correlation coefficients with 0.293 (first to second period), 0.069 (second to third) and 0.845 (third to fourth). Hence, China shifts its specialisation during the first two periods, while it established a certain specialisation during the last two periods. The Chinese focus on the sectors of 'telecommunications' (sector 3), 'consumer goods and equipment' (sector 29), 'audiovisual technology' (sector 2), 'electrical machinery and apparatus, electrical energy' (sector 1) and 'agriculture, food chemistry' (sector 13) (see Appendix).

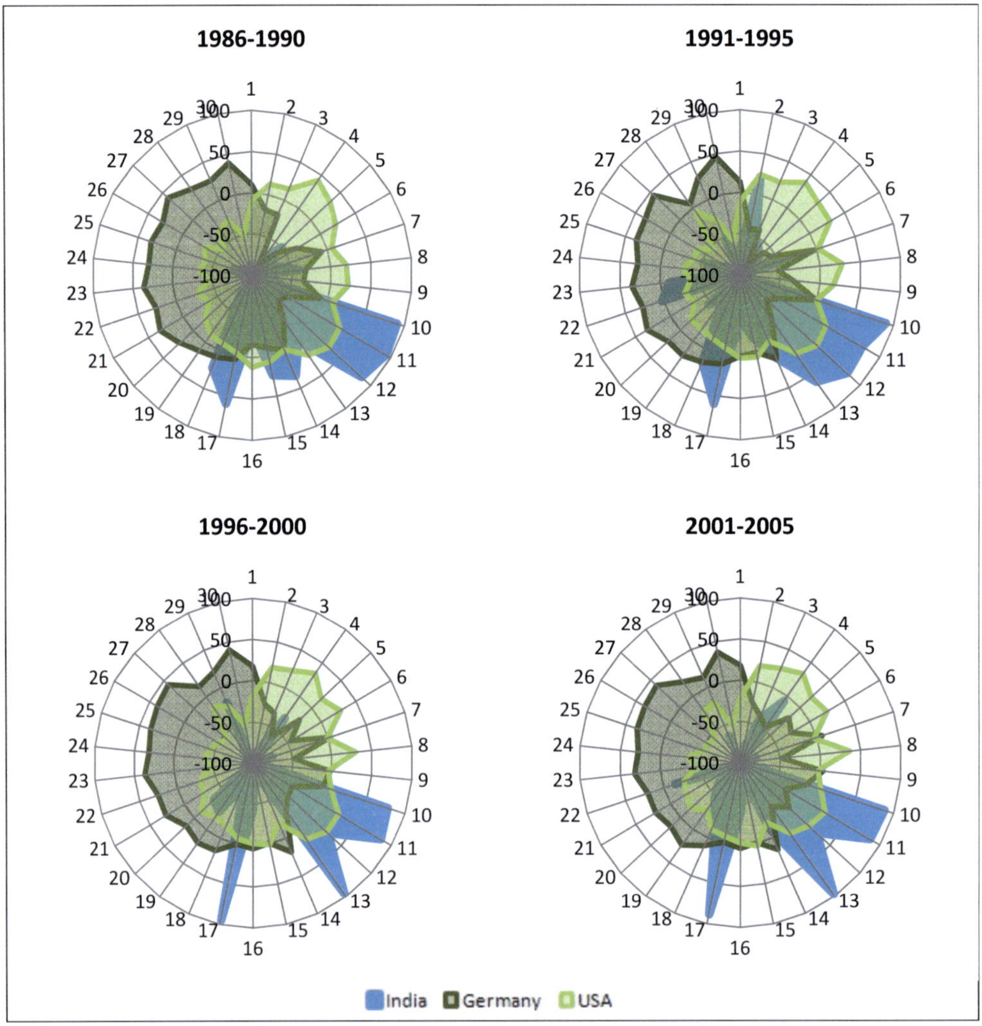

Figure 6-8: Indian RSTA development 1986-2005

The Indian specialisation profile is the most consistent one within the *BRICs*. This finding can be seen in Figure 6-8. The correlation coefficients are 0.805 (first to second period), 0.762 (second to third) and 0.929 (third to fourth). Like the Chinese profile, the Indian one also shows a high correlation between the last two time periods. Even the first and the last period have a correlation coefficient of 0.783. This leads to the assumption that India has a clear strategy and finds its focus in the late 1990s and at the beginning of the new millennium. The most important sectors are ‘agriculture, food chemistry’ (sectors 13), ‘chemical industry and petrol industry, basic materials chemistry’ (sector 17), ‘pharmaceuticals, cosmetics’ (sector 11), ‘organic fine chemistry’ (sector 10) and ‘biotechnology’ (sector 12) (see Appendix).

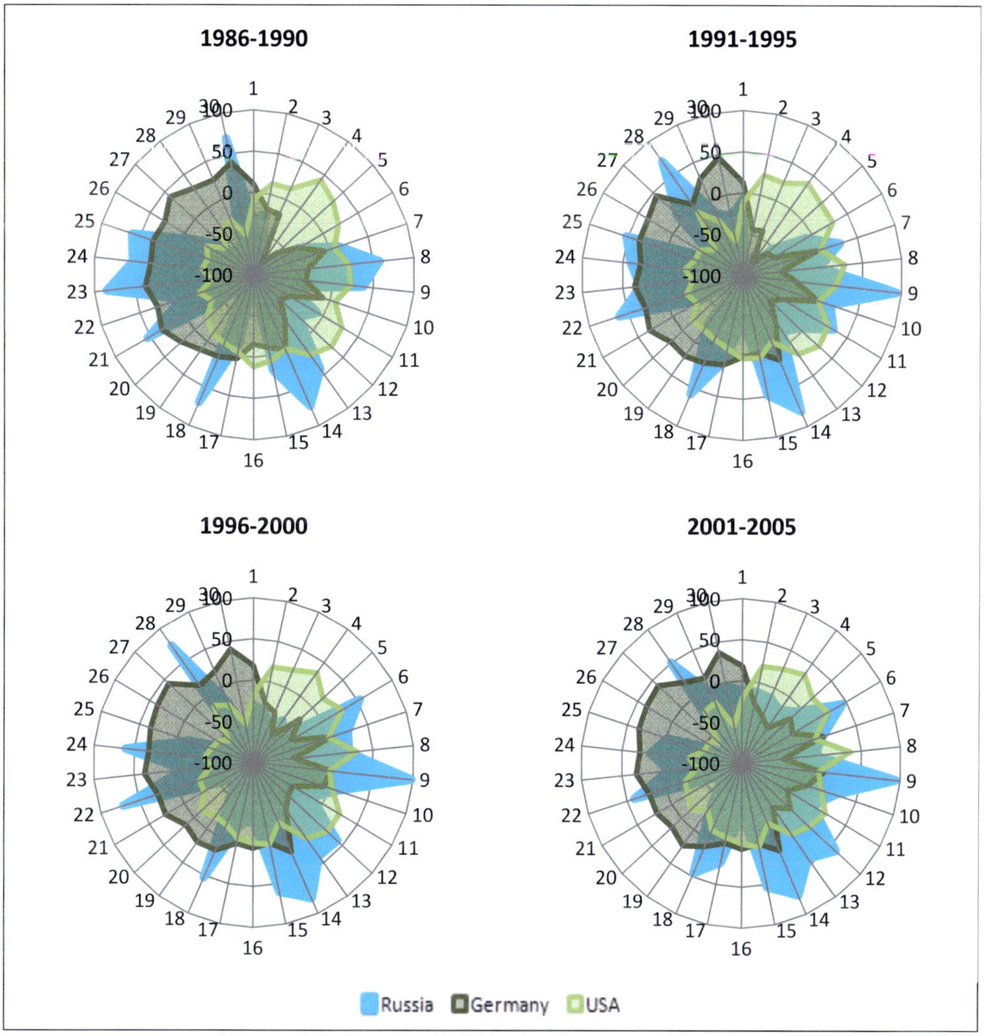

Figure 6-9: Russian RSTA development 1986-2005

For Russia, the development of the profiles shows that their portfolio does not change dramatically. The correlation coefficients rise from 0.528 (first and second period) to 0.758 (second to third) up to 0.895 (third to fourth). Hence, according to the correlation coefficients, they keep their profiles relatively constant. In the Russian technological portfolio, the most important sectors are 'nuclear engineering' (sector 9), 'materials, metallurgy' (sector 14), 'chemical engineering' (sector 18), 'space technology, weapons' (sector 28) and 'environmental technology' (sector 22) (see Appendix).

An examination of the correlation coefficients of the profiles strengthens the first impression that the technological portfolios differ from each other. Table 6-4 summarises the findings for the overall perspective between 1986 and 2005.

1986-2005	*BRIC*	Brazil	China	India	Russia	Germany
DEUS	-0.9136***	-0.3284*	-0.4584**	-0.815***	-0.266	-
Germany	-0.4317**	0.4462**	-0.4606**	-0.4267**	-0.0114	-
USA	0.4271**	-0.4536**	0.4181**	0.403**	0.0527	-0.9745***

Standard errors: *p<0.1, **p<0.05 and ***p<0.01

Table 6-4: RSTA correlation coefficients 1986-2005

Each *BRIC* country has a negative correlation coefficient compared to the *DEUS* group. In this respect, India has the highest negative correlation coefficient. Regarding each *DEUS* country this finding changes. In this case, the Brazilian profile is more like the German one, while the Indian and Chinese profiles are more like the US one. The Russian technology profile is somewhere in between the two early-movers.

	Brazil 96-00	Brazil 01-05	China 96-00	China 01-05	India 96-00	India 01-05	Russia 96-00	Russia 01-05
Germany 86-90	0.338*	0.479***	-0.222	-0.373**	-0.333*	-0.384**	-0.173	-0.316*
Germany 91-95	0.413**	0.545***	-0.243	-0.406**	-0.220	-0.260	-0.192	-0.309*
Germany 96-00	0.251	0.432**	-0.313*	-0.439**	-0.369**	-0.402**	-0.152	-0.262
Germany 01-05	0.187	0.405**	-0.368**	-0.499***	-0.395**	-0.447**	-0.129	-0.239
USA 86-90	-0.299	-0.416**	0.269	0.385**	0.363**	0.420**	0.240	0.369**
USA 91-95	-0.380**	-0.449**	0.260	0.399**	0.282	0.322*	0.277	0.373**
USA 96-00	-0.282	-0.399**	0.324*	0.430**	0.367**	0.398**	0.201	0.303
USA 01-05	-0.303	-0.440**	0.334*	0.429**	0.306*	0.358*	0.213	0.297

Standard errors: *p<0.1, **p<0.05 and ***p<0.01

Table 6-5: RSTA correlation coefficients of different time periods

Comparing the RSTA profile of late-comers and early-movers regarding different time periods, the findings show interesting developments. As the late-comers begin to have rising innovation activities after the middle of the 1990s these two time periods can be seen as a beginning of intensive international innovation activities. Hence, a comparison of the profiles of these two periods to all time periods for the early-movers needs to be conducted.

Although the correlation coefficients are not high, it can be observed that in comparison to Germany the coefficients generally tend to fall. With the exception of Brazil, this means that the coefficients of profiles of late-comers from their last two periods (1996-2000 and 2001-2005) compared with the first two periods of Germany (1986-1990 and 1991-1995) are higher than compared the subsequent two periods of Germany. The correlation coefficients with the USA stand in contrast to the German one. Also, with an exception of Brazil, all other late-comers have closer correlations to the USA in the last two periods. Hence, late-comers tend to develop towards the USA (see Table 6-5).

Biotechnological specialisation

The specialisation portfolio of the biotechnology sector is analysed by means of the different technological sectors interlinked with the biotechnology and also referring to the IPC classifications and *OST/INPI/ISI Concordance* (see also Subsection 6.3.1). As mentioned before the ranking of weighted count of technology sector leads to a very similar profile for the examined countries. The similarity in the profiles is also mirrored by the high correlation coefficients between the biotechnological sectors of the late-comers, as well as of Germany and the USA when the whole ranking is used (see Table 6-6 and Appendix). All countries show a high correlation compared to the US biotechnology profile. Hence, for a clear statement for the analysis of technological niche strategies within the sector of biotechnology an indicator, such as the RSTA, is also needed.

USA	*BRIC*	Brazil	China	India	Russia	Germany
1986-2005	0.9678***	0.9731***	0.9949***	0.9643***	0.9739***	0.9874***

Standard errors: *p<0.1, **p<0.05 and ***p<0.01

Table 6-6: Correlation coefficient of technological sectors occupied by biotechnology patents 1986-2005

Figure 6-10 shows the inner biotechnological specialisation. As not all countries occupy all technological sectors (see Appendix), it can be probably assumed that some technological sectors of the late-comers have weak specialisations or even a specialisation value of -100. This refers to the relative small amount of biotechnology patents compared to the USA and Germany.

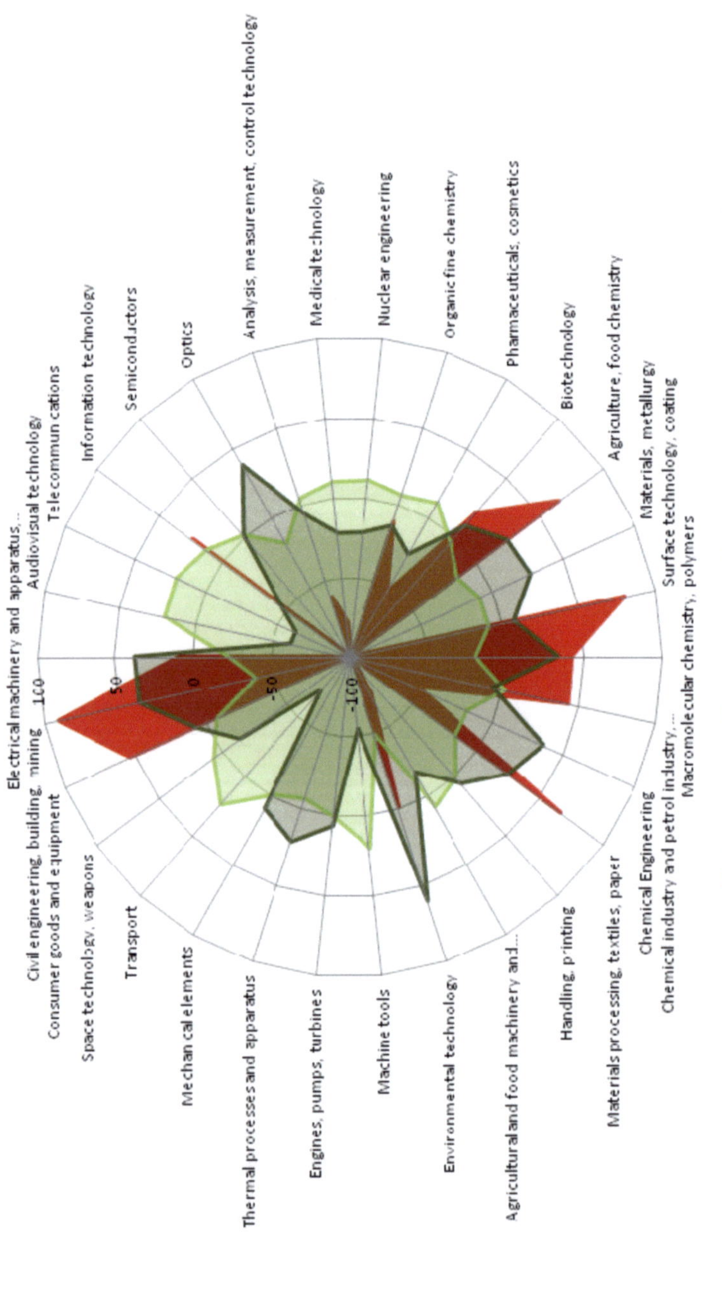

Figure 6-10: Biotechnology RSTA of *BRICs* compared to Germany and the USA

The USA is a biotechnological early-mover and has the most persistent specialisation profile (light green line). The consistent profile mainly refers to the fact that the USA is accountable for the major part of the biotechnology patents and diversification effects of early-movers (see Chapter 7). Findings for the USA which are of interests are not positive specialisations, but negative ones. The most under-specialised sectors[54] are 'environmental technology' (sector 22), 'civil engineering, building and mining' (sector 30), 'electrical machinery, apparatus and energy' (sector 1), 'macromolecular chemistry and polymers' (sector 16), 'chemical engineering' (sector 18) and 'optics' (sector 6). In turn, Germany's 'environmental technology' (sector 22), 'civil engineering, building and mining' (sector 30) and 'electrical machinery, apparatus and energy' (sector 1) sectors, but also the field of 'optics' (sector 6) are highly represented in its biotechnology sector. The following presentation of the late-comers comprises not all outstanding specialisations, but their outstanding sectors where they are different from the USA.

Country level

The development of the RSTA of the Brazilian biotechnology sector shows that Brazil first has its focus on 'agriculture and food chemistry' (sector 13) and 'organic fine chemistry' (sector 10). The specialisation on sector 10 does not last until the third and fourth time period. Besides sector 13, in the third time period, the sectors of 'materials processing, textiles and paper' (sector 19), 'chemical industry, petrol industry and basic materials chemistry' (sector 17) and 'chemical engineering' emerge and become strongly focused by Brazil. Finally, the sector of 'macromolecular chemistry and polymers' (sector 16) becomes a focus of the Brazilian biotechnology. The correlation coefficients of Brazilian specialisation profiles show that their focus is relatively stable. Each consecutive period has a positive coefficient of at least 0.5 (see Appendix). This finding shows persistent niche strategy for Brazil.

[54] The most under-specialised 20%.

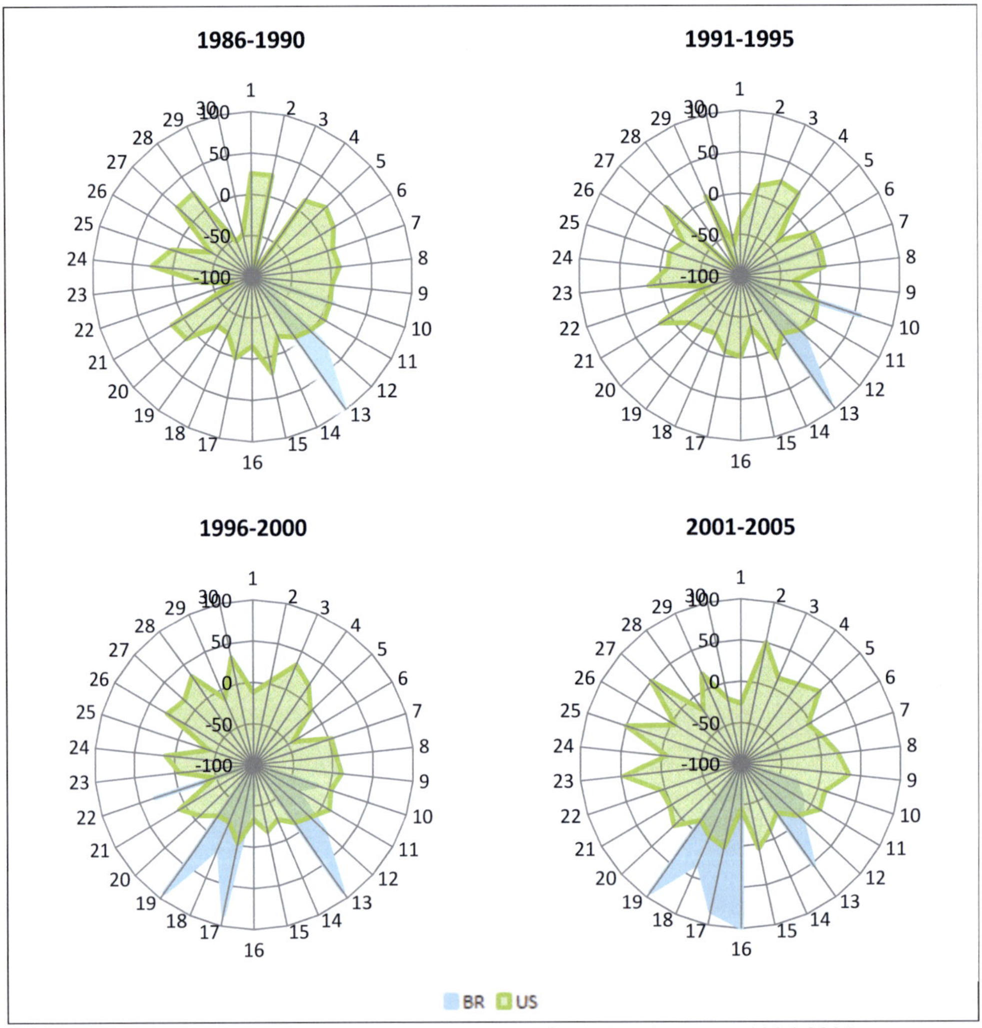

Figure 6-11: Brazilian biotechnology RSTA development 1986-2005

China also starts with a focus on 'agriculture and food chemistry' (sector 13) and 'organic fine chemistry' (sector 10), but also 'agricultural and food machinery apparatus' (sector 21) gain an increasing weight. Interestingly, this specialisation disappears in the second period, but returns in period three and four. In the third period, two sectors just appear one time, namely the sectors of 'semiconductors' and 'surface technology and coating‘. Moreover 'chemical engineering' (sector 18), 'materials processing, textiles and paper' (sector 19) and 'chemical industry, petrol industry and basic materials chemistry' (sector 17) show strong specialisation values (see Figure 6-12).

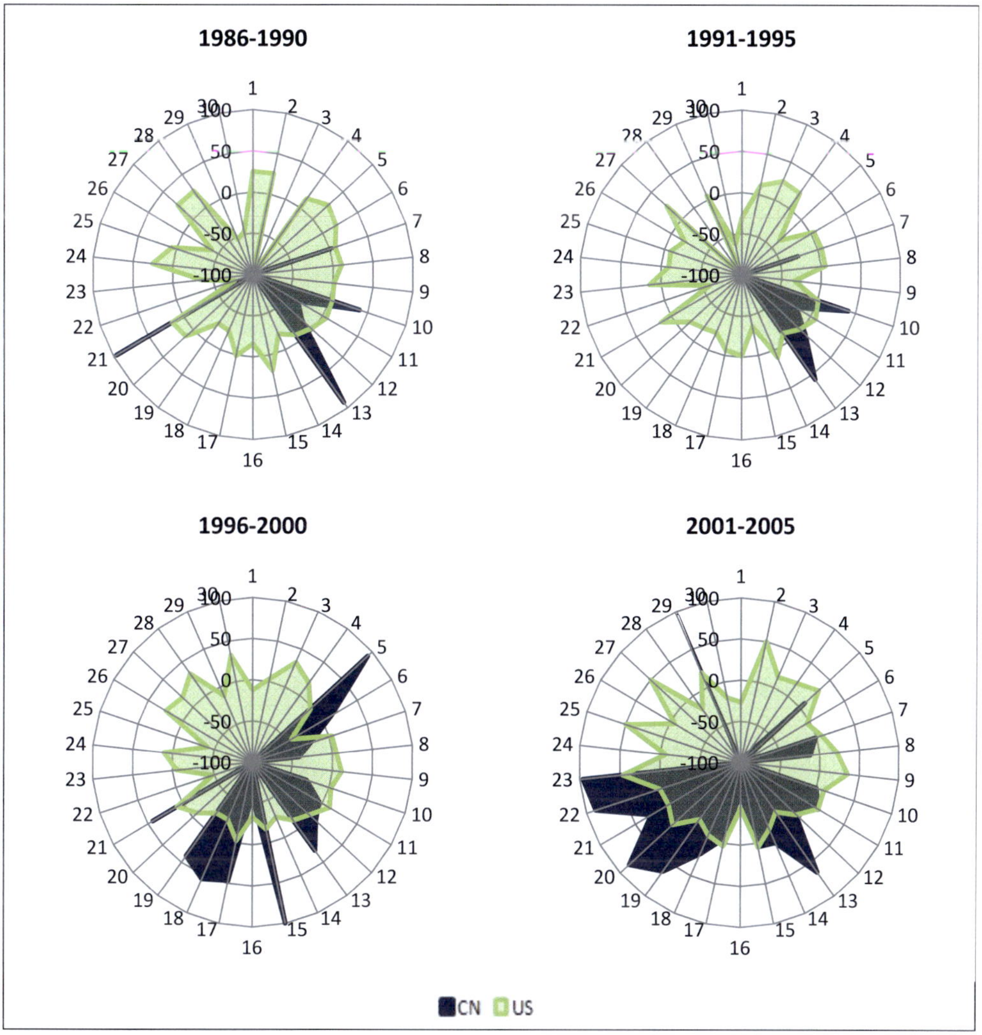

Figure 6-12: Chinese biotechnology RSTA development 1986-2005

With the appearance of some more sectors of focus in the last period, China shows a changing biotechnological profile, while no clear focus on the US biotechnology niches can be stated at a first glance. The correlation coefficients for China show that they still have positive correlation between the periods, but not as high as the Brazilian ones (see Appendix). Hence, they also have a relative clear strategy for the biotechnology sector.

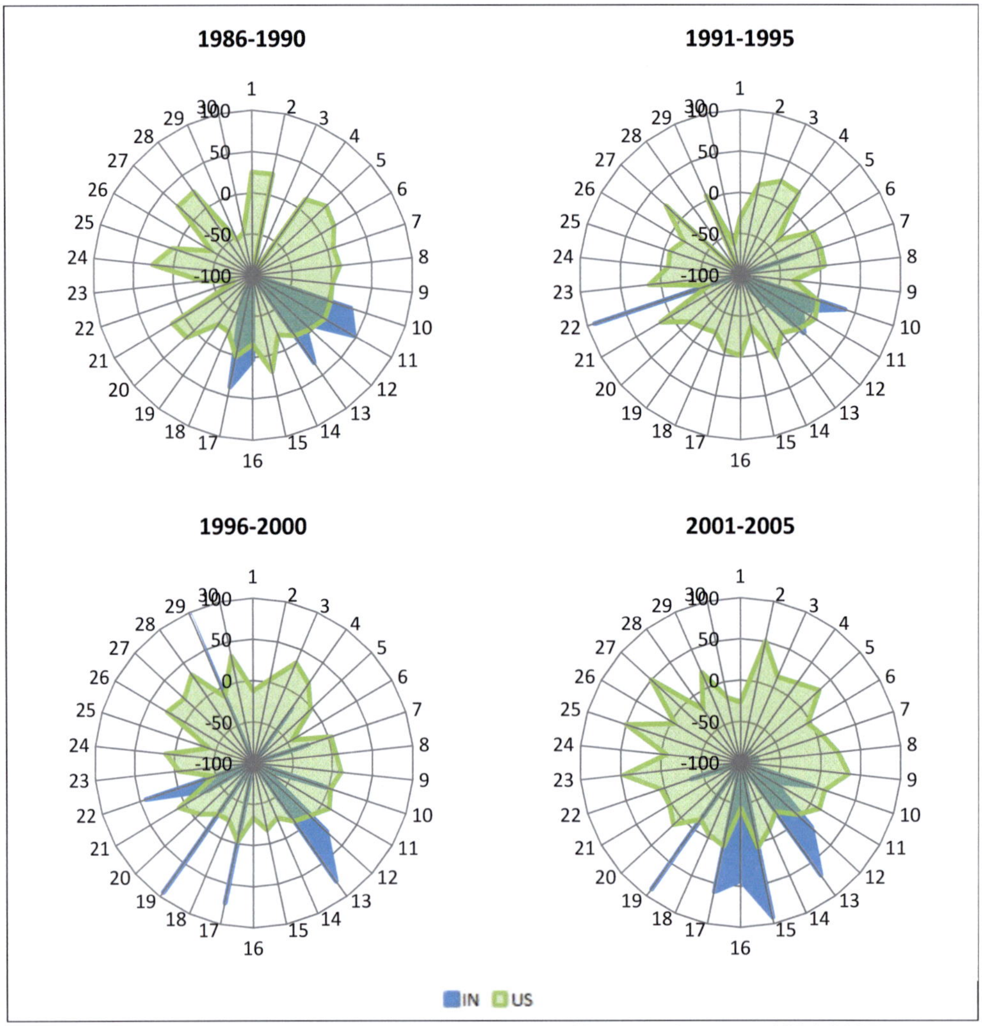

Figure 6-13: Indian biotechnology RSTA development 1986-2005

The Indian biotechnology specialisation profile is more consistent compared to the Chinese one and it shows stronger focuses, but on fewer sectors. The first outstanding specialisation can be found in the second period in the sector of 'environmental technology', where India occupies an under-specialised sector of the USA. This also holds for the third time period in which also strong specialisations can be found for 'agriculture, food chemistry' (sector 13), 'chemical industry, petrol industry and basic materials chemistry' (sector 17), 'materials processing, textiles and paper' (sector 19) and 'consumer goods and equipment' (sector 29). In the fourth period, India also specialises in 'macromolecular chemistry and polymers' (sector 16) which is also an under-specialised sector of the USA.

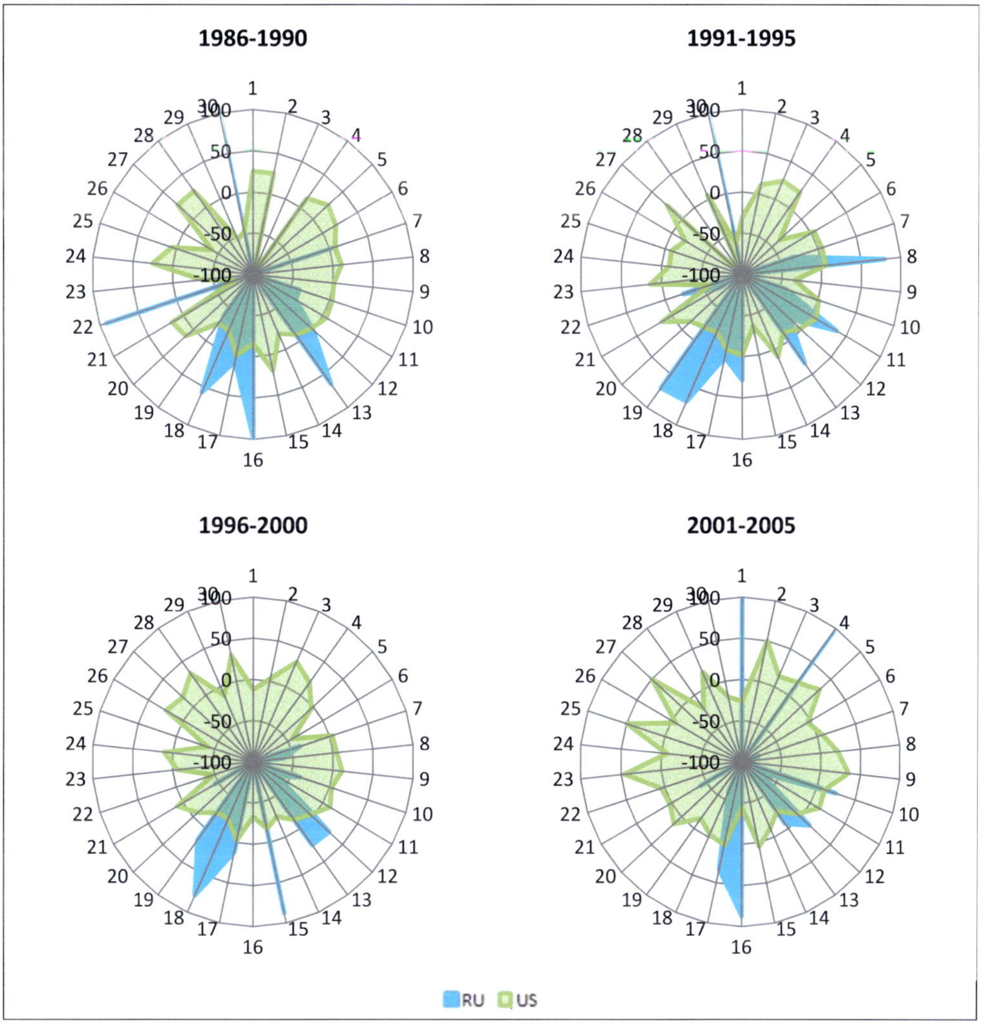

Figure 6-14: Russian biotechnology RSTA development 1986-2005

For Russia, the development also shows patterns of occupation of niches. However, the profile changes in the course of time. In the first period, interesting specialisations are in the field of 'macromolecular chemistry and polymers' (sector 16), 'chemical engineering' (sector 18), 'environmental technology' (sector 22) and 'civil engineering, building and mining' (sector 30). With the last two sectors, Russia occupies under-specialised fields of the US biotechnology. For the second period, the most interesting specialisation is on sector 18 and 30, as well as in the sector of 'materials processing, textiles and paper' (sector 19). All other Russian specialisation focuses are not US niches. In period three and four, Russia shows an outstanding specialisation for sector 18 and 19 (three), as well as for sector 16 and sector of 'electrical machinery, apparatus and electrical energy' (sector 1).

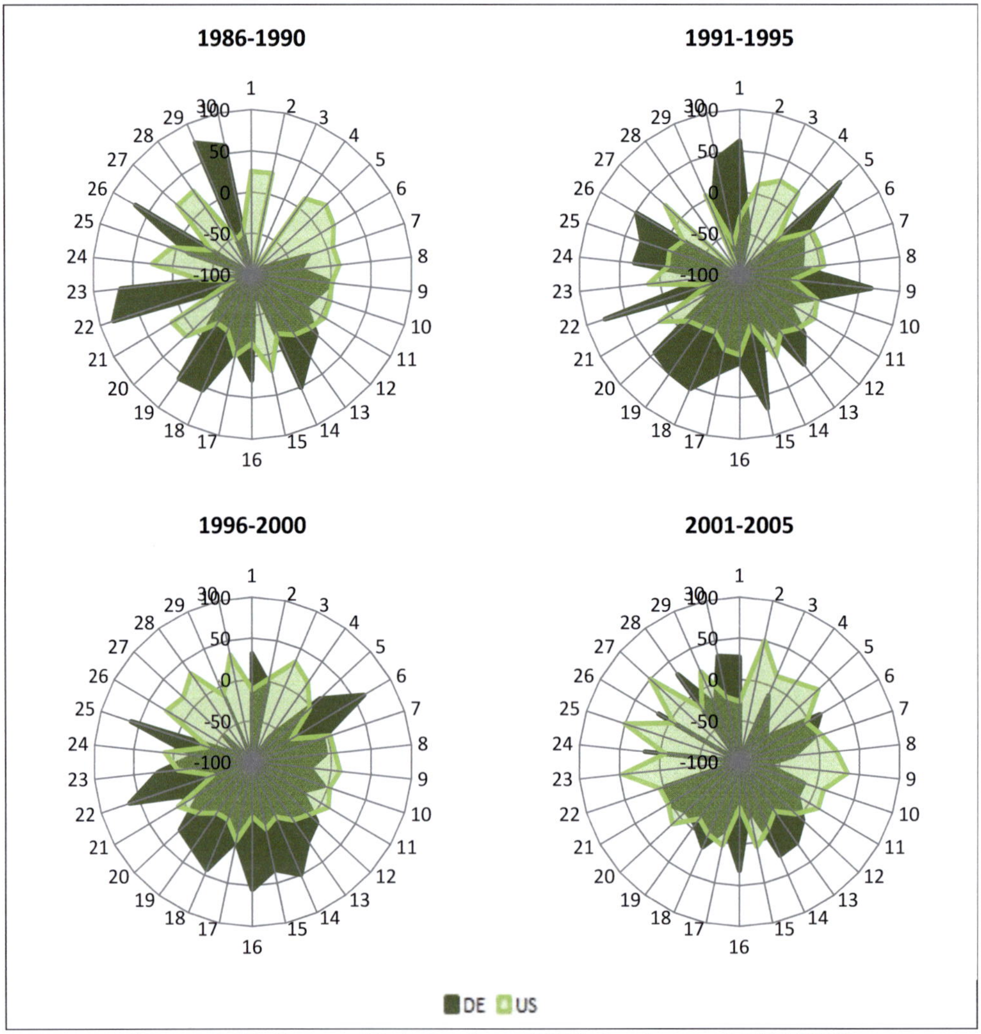

Figure 6-15: German biotechnology RSTA development 1986-2005

The German portfolio shows many occupations of US niches. This can refer to the general different specialisation of the whole country and the higher amount of patent applications compared to the other four late-comers (see Subsection 6.3.1). The most outstanding finding is the sector of 'environmental technology' (sector 22) which is highly specialised in Germany for the first three periods. This can also originate from the general German specialisation in this sector. However, this sector is the only one which has permanent specialisation focus in Germany. Interestingly, the niche occupation of Germany decreases in the course of time. While in periods one and two many of such niche occupations can be found, for instance the sectors of 'mechanical elements' and 'consumer goods and equipment' in period one and 'semiconductors' and 'surface technology and coating' in period two, these focuses decrease. Period three differs from the first two time periods; here, the focus lies more on the specialisation of 'optics' and 'thermal processes and apparatus'. In the fourth period, no clear specialisation can be found.

According to the correlation coefficients, the technological portfolio within the sector of biotechnology in Germany does not correlate with the US one. Brazil, India and Russia show significant correlation coefficients in the last time period which also show a negative correlation to the US biotechnology.

USA	*BRIC*	Brazil	China	India	Russia	Germany
1986-1990	-0.2866	0.0248	0.1390	0.0466	-0.3680	-0.6336***
1991-1995	-0.2579	0.1071	0.1328	-0.0981	-0.1369	-0.4721***
1996-2000	-0.2946	-0.3195	-0.2553	-0.2160	-0.2016	-0.9581***
2001-2005	-0.4697***	-0.4644***	-0.0057	-0.3974**	-0.4053**	-0.9394***

Standard errors: *p<0.1, **p<0.05 and ***p<0.01

Table 6-7: RSTA correlation coefficients of the biotechnology sector 1986-2005

Among the late-comers, the Chinese biotechnology sector still has the closest correlation coefficients to the USA, although it has a very low correlation coefficient of below 0.14. Moreover, if just the last period is considered, every late-comer has correlation coefficients of less than 0.01 which means that they do not have very similar biotechnology IPC profiles compared to the USA (see Table 6-7). A specialisation profile which is close to the US one would lead to higher correlation coefficients. As the biotechnology portfolio of the US stands for the early-mover in this sector, a different profile implicates a strategy different from the mainstream. Hence, the findings of the RSTA analysis reflect that the late-comers in the biotechnology sector tend to occupy niches. Especially the German portfolio is very different compared to the USA.

USA	Germany 1996-2000	Germany 2001-2005	Brazil 2001-2005	China 2001-2005	India 2001-2005	Russia 2001-2005
1991-1995	0.0965	-0.3442*	0.0551	0.0512	-0.0652	0.1748
1996-2000	-0.9581***	-0.0258	-0.2756	-0.3930**	-0.3085*	-0.0633
2001-2005	-0.0491	-0.9394***	-0.4644***	-0.0057	-0.3974**	-0.4053**

Standard errors: *p<0.1, **p<0.05 and ***p<0.01

Table 6-8: RSTA correlation coefficients of the biotechnology sector of different time periods

According to the correlation coefficients of the comparison between different time periods, it can be stated that in general the similarity is still low. The correlation even decreases in the course of time for most of the late-comer countries. As niches change over time and technological niches in previous time periods may not exist in later time periods this finding implicates some interesting results. First, with the exception of China, the technological profile in phase when late-comers have notable biotechnological activities is more similar to the early stages of the US. Take for instance Germany 1996-2000 compared with the USA 1991-1995 (correlation coefficient of 0.0965) and the correlation coefficient of the two countries in the same period (-0.9581). Second, late-comers occupy current niches. Their portfolios in comparison to early-movers in the same period are more different than to earlier periods.

6.4. Discussion of late-comer niches

The *Cosine Index* for Germany and the USA shows similarities between these two countries, as the values are both high. This implicates that both countries cover many similar fields of technologies and have patent applications in all sectors. This also holds for the inner technology profile of the biotechnology sector. In the last case, the high similarity occurs because of the identification of the biotechnology patents itself. The identification of a certain specialisation within a country needs to be interpreted with the RSTA. The examination of the technological profiles of the late-comers, Germany and the USA, shows that Germany and the USA cover a broad field of technological sectors. According to the *OST/INPI/ISI Concordance,* Germany has its technological focuses on 'transport', 'civil engineering, building and mining', ,mechanical elements', 'thermal processes and apparatus' and 'machine tools' which are classic German strengths in engineering sectors. This also mirrors industrial specialisation which is measured for instance, by export numbers (see Mitusch et al., 2010). The top technological sectors of the USA are 'information technology', 'medical technology', 'optics', 'biotechnology' and 'semiconductors'. This shows that the USA focus on emerging technologies (see Mitusch et al., 2010). Comparing the two profiles by means of the RSTA, it can be stated that they have different focuses. Hence, they cover different fields and are specialised in different sectors. The RSTA and the correlation between the USA and Germany in this sector are significantly low (see Subsection 6.3.1). Sectors with a high specialisation in the German biotechnology sector are 'environmental technology' (sector 22), 'civil engineering, building and mining' (sector 30) and 'electrical machinery and apparatus and electrical energy' (sector 1), but also the field of 'optics' (sector 6). Sector 1, sector 22 and sector 30 are general strengths of the German technology profile what is a reason for the specialisation in these sectors within the German biotechnology sector. The specialisation of the German biotechnology sector in 'optics' occurs from the biotechnology cluster in Jena where strong linkages between the optical industry and the biotechnology sector can be found (see Fornahl and Tran, 2009). In this case, it is also interesting to observe that specialisation in optics comes up after 1995 when the BMBF decided to support this biotechnology cluster[55]. Hence, political intervention into the biotechnology sector in Germany seems to be fruitful.

Brazil

Brazil on a general level does not show clear focuses on niches. According to the findings of the similarity values (*Cosine Index*), Brazil develops towards the German technology profile, while its similarity with the USA has no clear trend. Regarding the specialisation topic its technology profile (RSTA) correlates with the German one, but not with the US one. However, an examination of the biotechnology sector shows that within this sector a trend of niche occupation is traceable.

Outstanding specialisations in Brazil are 'agriculture, food chemistry' (sector 13), 'chemical industry and petrol industry, basic materials chemistry' (sector 17), 'materials processing, textiles and paper' (sector 19), 'engines, pumps and turbines' (sector 24) and 'materials and metallurgy' (sector 14). Hence, the technological strength of Brazil reflects also the industrial structure of the country, as the biggest Brazilian companies, for instance Petrobas, Vale and CSN-Cia Siderurgica (see Forbes, 2010), are from these sectors. According to the examinations of the different time periods, its profile correlates with each other, but do not have a certain focus as found by the last periods of the Asian late-comers. This may be caused by the relatively loose governmental innovation targets (Lattimore and Kowalski, 2008).

In the field of biotechnology, an interesting focus in Brazil lies on 'macromolecular chemistry and polymers' (sector 16). Although Brazil has other specialisation areas, this is a focus on a US biotechnology sector which is not specialised and furthermore, the biotechnology sectors of Brazil, especially in the last period, do not correlate with the US biotechnology sector.

China

For China, it can be generally stated that the Chinese similarities are clearly different from the Brazilian ones. China moves towards the US profile, while its similarity to Germany decreases. It has a focus which is more correlated with the USA and less with Germany. Regarding the biotechnology sector, a similarity to the USA can be observed, but it is still on a very low level, especially in the last period (-0.0057).

[55] Jena is one of four German biotechnology clusters to receive governmental support after the *BioRegio* contest (see BMBF, 1996).

Outstanding focuses are on the sectors of ‘telecommunications’ (sector 3), ‘consumer goods and equipment’ (sector 29), ‘audiovisual technology’ (sector 2), ‘electrical machinery, apparatus and electrical energy’ (sector 1) and ‘agriculture and food chemistry’ (sector 13). The first three periods still have changing profiles, as the correlation coefficients are just at a level of 0.293 and 0.069. However, the last two periods are highly correlated with each other (0.845). So, with the rise of Chinese innovation activities, it also becomes more clearly specialised (see Chapter 4). This may be caused by the clearer governmental targets of its innovation activities (MOST, 2008).

Within the biotechnology sector, China shows a changing biotechnological profile and no clear focus on US biotechnology niches.

India

India has the strongest characteristics of niche strategies. This can be observed for the general technology profile and the biotechnology one. The Indian *Cosine Index* shows the strongest differences to the USA, as well as to Germany, which leads to the conclusion that India successfully stands out regarding the innovation activities of the early-movers.

These findings are also confirmed by the RSTA. The Indian specialisation profile is the most persistent one within the *BRIC*s. Correlation coefficients between the periods are all very high (correlation coefficients: 0.805, 0.762 and 0.929). Like the Chinese profile, the Indian one also shows a high correlation between the last two time periods. In the Indian case, the most important sectors are ‘agriculture, food chemistry’ (sectors 13), ‘chemical industry and petrol industry, basic materials chemistry’ (sector 17), ‘pharmaceuticals, cosmetics’ (sector 11), ‘organic fine chemistry’ (sector 10) and ‘biotechnology’ (sector 12). The strong specialisation comes from a clearer focus on innovation and technology policy and the governmental push towards a knowledge-based economy (Ministry of Science & Technology India, 2007 and Kowalski et al., 2008).

As one of the specialisation strengths of India, its biotechnology sector also has a very consistent profile and it shows stronger focuses on less sectors. Furthermore, Indian biotechnology specialisation occupies niches, for instance, the sector of ‘environmental technology’ (sector 22) and ‘macromolecular chemistry and polymers’ (sector 16). This is also confirmed by the correlation coefficients.

Russia

Russian innovation activities tend to occupy niches. This can also be stated for the general assumption and the biotechnology sector. The Russian similarity examination delivers findings which are different compared to the other late-comers, as it develops towards Germany and the USA. Hence, Russia's technology portfolio is situated between both early-movers.

Regarding the RSTA, the development of the profiles shows that the portfolio does not change dramatically and also becomes more consistent (correlation coefficients: 0.528, 0.758 and 0.895). In the Russian technological portfolio, the most important sectors are 'nuclear engineering' (sector 9), 'materials and metallurgy' (sector 14), 'chemical engineering' (sector 18), 'space technology and weapons' (sector 28) and 'environmental technology' (sector 22). Some of these sectors confirm the export strengths of Russia (see Tarr, 2008). The position between the early-movers is also presented by the correlation coefficients of the Russian RSTA which shows no clear correlation either with Germany or the USA.

In the biotechnology sector the development of specialisation also shows patterns of occupation of niches, for instance, in the field of 'environmental technology' (sector 22), 'civil engineering, building and mining' (sector 30).

In general, late-comers show tendencies to niche strategies. These tendencies are clearer within the biotechnology sector. Reasons for such focuses within a sector are the clearer distinction of other competitors on firm level and would need further analysis which is not the focus of this thesis. National innovation activities and strategies are more likely to be long-run strategies, such as five year plans (see Ministry of Science & Technology India, 2007 and MOST, 2008), but the occupation of niches needs flexible adjustments of strategies. Therefore, it is even more interesting that niche strategies can also be examined on a national level.

7. Technology portfolio and technological diversification

The next two chapters consist of the second analytical block concerning a second phase of technological development of late-comers (see Section 4.4). The topic of these two chapters can be summarised as efforts to establish a competitive innovation system within the international technological competition. The first examination deals with aspects of technological diversification as technological late-comers should broaden their technological portfolio for a more robust knowledge base. The second examination, therefore, examines the national innovation networks within these late-comer countries (see Chapter 8). The remainder of this chapter is structured similar to the preceding ones. Section 7.1 discusses the term technological diversification and the existing literature which tackles the topic of diversification in regard to technology and innovation. Afterwards, Section 7.2 introduces the methods used to measure technological diversification, while Section 7.3 presents the empirical analysis of technological diversification of late-comers and their development. Finally, a discussion of the findings is given in Section 7.4.

7.1. Reasons for technological diversification

The topic of diversification in economic studies is discussed on firm, regional and national level. All views on this term have different backgrounds and research interests, as they have different levels of aggregation.

In early works, diversification on the firm level is separated into market and product diversification (Ansoff, 1957). These two kinds of diversification are considered by strategic management decisions to influence firm development and growth. According to this classification, market diversification covers exploitation of different markets, concerning groups of consumers. Product diversification describes the variety of product lines. In this case, diversification stands for activities in different product and/or industrial sectors. Nowadays, large multinational enterprises follow this kind of diversification strategies. Certainly, these two kinds of diversification are not clearly distinct from each other, and exploitation of a new market often goes in line with exploitation of new product sectors.

Studies of regional and national diversifications consider other kinds of diversification than the firm level, because regions and nations do not have to satisfy consumers or certain markets. These two views rather look at industrial diversifications which means that they try to contain a variety of industries to generate successful growth or be resilient against shocks (Boschma and Iammarion, 2009). An important work with a specific view on cities is contributed by Jacobs (1969). She argues that a certain degree of diversification is important for a region. If regions are too concentrated in certain industries, they tend to develop towards a so-called lock-in. Then they are trapped in their specialisation and are much more vulnerable to external political or economic shocks, as happened in Detroit after the collapse of the US automotive industry.

Besides market, product and industrial perspectives, diversification is, in addition, discussed with a technological background. It is also the one which is addressed by all three levels as there can be technological diversification within a firm, a region and a nation. As the technological consideration is also the issue of this chapter, further discussion of scientific work on diversification deals with the technological one.

Technological diversification

Empirical work on technological diversification mostly investigates R&D activities, such as diversification of human capital, and diversification of patent applications, such as the technological sectors in which these applications are applied for. They look at the topic of technological diversification at the two moments when new innovations are developed and when innovations appear.

Regarding the analysis of technological diversification based on R&D, Leten et al. (2007) argue that diversification can influence firm development and performance positively, but the degree of diversification should not be distended. Nowadays the work on different technologies needs many specialists and coordination of their work generates extremely high costs (see also Section 2.1). A positive relationship between technological diversification and success of firms is also stated by Gambardella and Torrisi (1998). They illustrate this relationship employing patent data to measure technological diversification. Thereby, success is measured by profit generated by the firms. Moreover, other researchers state that diversification is a sign of a learning process and a quality indicator for products. World-class companies diversify over time, and hence, technological diversification is a strategic decision which has to be considered, if the performance of a company has to be improved (Argyres, 1996, Zander, 1997, Breschi et al., 2003, and Lin et al., 2006).

The positive effects of technological diversification on the firm level are also partly observed on a regional and national level, but Cantwell and Vertova (2004) express that the field of studies in terms of national technological diversification is still under-developed. In their work on technological diversification on the national level, they show that technological diversification implies learning processes. Countries which diversify their technological basis also develop successfully in terms of technological outputs (measured by patent data). Garcia-Vega (2006) even illustrates an influence of technological diversification to innovativeness on a national level and explains that national innovation output is related to a broad technological diversification. This positive effect is even strengthened by the fact that technological diversification helps to overcome external shocks, and thus, strengthen endogenous growth Koren and Tenreyro (2005). Jacobs (1969) argues the same effect, as aforementioned, on a regional level. In contrast, it is also argued that diversification does not have to be positive. It is also argued that persistent have positive effects on regions. Marshallian externalities, for instance, refer to positive external effects of specialised players within a region (Marshall, 1890). He stated that co-existence of specialised players within a region profit from the each other as they generate external effects, such as knowledge spillover. Moreover, Porter (1984, p. 67) also argues that competition strategies are divided into diversification, cost leadership and specialisation. Additionally, he stated that a persistent focus on niches and specialisations in a well-defined regional market can be a successful firm strategy (Porter, 1999, pp. 77). Nevertheless, for the national technological perspective diversification implies learning process and it reflects the construction of absorptive capabilities.

Derived from theoretical background and the findings of the previous chapters (see Chapter 2 to Chapter 6) the hypothesis that technological late-comers certainly enter the technological competition undiversified can be formulated. However, they should try to diversify in order to establish international competitiveness. This topic also follows the analysis of the hypothesis in Chapter 6, where it is argued that late-comers start into technological competition with niche strategies. Subsequently this indicates that a further step in the development of a competitive innovation-based economy is the diversification of a profound technology portfolio.

Hypothesis 3: Technological early-movers have more technological experience than late-comers. Due to their broader knowledge base, they can generate a broader scope of innovations. For a competitive innovation-based economy late-comers have to diversify their technological portfolio. Thus, after the phase of entry into the international technology competition technological late-comers develop towards early-movers in respect of technological.

To test this hypothesis, the degree of technological diversification of the late-comers is compared to the degree of the diversification of the early-movers. Additionally, the development of these diversification degrees is analysed for an investigation whether late-comers develop towards more diversification or not.

7.2. Measuring technological diversification

To analyse diversification, the empirical examination of this thesis builds upon two indicators of specialisation, namely the *Herfindahl-Hirschman-Index* (HHI), also known as the *Herfindahl-Index*, and the *Krugman-Specialisation-Index* (KSI). These indicators are commonly used for diversification analysis. This twofold approach is used as the present two views on the topic of diversification, because the *HHI* represents an absolute measurement of diversification and the *KSI* a relative one.

Herfindahl-Hirschman-Index

The *Herfindahl-Hirschmann-Index* generally measures absolute industrial concentration of certain regions and markets and uses, for instance, regional employment data, market shares etc. It, therefore, employs the sum of squared employment shares of each industry located in a region to measure the degree of industrial concentration in the regions (Traistaru and Iara, 2002). Moreover, the *HHI* reflects market structures to express market power of major players. In such cases, the *HHI* is calculated using market shares (Rhoades, 1995 and Stavins, 2001). Despite of these initial applications of the *HHI*, it becomes commonly known as an indicator of technological specialisation and diversification. The *HHI* in terms of technology can be calculated using shares of patent data referring to their technological sectors[56].

$$HHI_k = \sum_{i=1}^{N} (\frac{p_{ik}}{P_k})^2 \qquad (7\text{-}1)$$

Term 7-1 shows the *HHI* of a given region, country or sector *k*, while p_{ik} stands for the amount of patents in sector *i* of this region, country or sector *k*. P_k stands for the total amount of patents. This calculation is also possible for inner sectoral analysis, for instance, the biotechnology sector. In this case p_{ik} stands for a technological sub-sector and P_k for the total amount of patents of the examined sector. By using values which represent shares, the results of the *HHI* are between (0; 1]. To illustrate diversification aspects different conversions of the given term are introduced. Term 7-2 is one of the most frequently used conversions (Hall, 2002 and Garcia-Vega, 2006).

$$DIV_k = 1 - HHI_k \qquad (7\text{-}2)$$

[56] See also *OST/INPI/ISI Concordance*, Subsection 3.2.2.

Hence, the degree of diversification (*DIV*) is calculated by the inversion of the co-domain[57] and a *DIV* value close to 1 represents a highly diversified region, country or sector, and a value close to 0 represents a highly concentrated one. For the analysis of technological late-comers, this means that their technological profile should turn from a relative concentration (see Chapter 6) to diversification.

Krugman-Specialisation-Index

The *Krugman-Specialisation-Index* compares specialisation structures of two groups, countries etc., and is therefore a relative measurement of concentration and diversification. It is first used to compare industrial structures between the USA and Europe (Krugman, 1991a and Traistaru and Iara, 2002). As the empirical analysis of this dissertation thesis compares late-comers with early-movers, the *KSI* delivers the possibility to weigh these two groups against each other, as well as the four late-comer countries in comparison to Germany and the USA. In this respect, the *KSI* is calculated as follows:

$$KSI_k = \sum_{i=1}^{N} \left| \frac{p_{ik}}{P_k} - \frac{p_i}{P} \right| \qquad (7\text{-}3)$$

Term 7-3 shows the *KSI* for a given region, country or sector *k*. The variable p_{ik}, again, stands for the amount of patents in sector *i* of a region, country or sector *k,* and P_k stands for the total amount of patents in *k*. The two variables p_i and *P* represent the reference group which, in general, is the total amount of patents in the world (p_i) in sector *i* and the absolute total numbers of patents (*P*). As the fraction $\frac{p_i}{P}$ represents a reference group, it can also be the share of patents in a benchmark country, such as the case of the US biotechnology sector in this thesis. Thus, a *KSI* value close to 0 represents a close technological structure between the two compared regions, countries or sectors, and with a maximum value of 2, the *KSI* represents a totally different technological structure (Traistaru and Iara, 2002).

7.3. Diversification efforts of late-comers

The examination of technological diversification is organised in this subchapter divided into absolute technological diversification referring to the *DIV* index and relative diversification referring to the *KSI*. The absolute diversification comprises the

[57] Other works suggest a conversion, such as (Lin et al., 2006 and Leten et al, 2007):

$$DIV = \sqrt{1 - HHI} \quad \text{and} \quad DIV = \frac{1}{HHI}$$

group of *BRIC* and *DEUS* countries, as well as each country, late-comer and early-mover itself. The exploration of the *KSI* relates to the national level of the group of *DEUS* countries, as a reference for the relative measurement. For the biotechnological sector the reference benchmark is given by the USA.

7.3.1. Absolute technological diversification

The findings of the *DIV* index deliver evidence for a development which is, in fact, already assumed. First of all, diversification values of the early-movers are stable from 1986 to 2005 with a slightly decreasing trend for the USA. The German and the US *DIV* values have a mean value of 0.96 (DE) and 0.95 (US) which represent a relatively high technological diversification for both countries (see Figure 7-1). This finding delivers two results. First, technological early-movers have a stable degree of diversification. This verifies, for instance, the results of Cantwell and Vertova (2004) which shows that large countries (referring to their technological activities) also diversify much more than smaller ones. Second, this leads to the result that the growth of patent applications does not influence the diversification dramatically, even though the number of German and US patent applications rise substantially over the period under observation. This neither decreases nor increases the level of diversification.

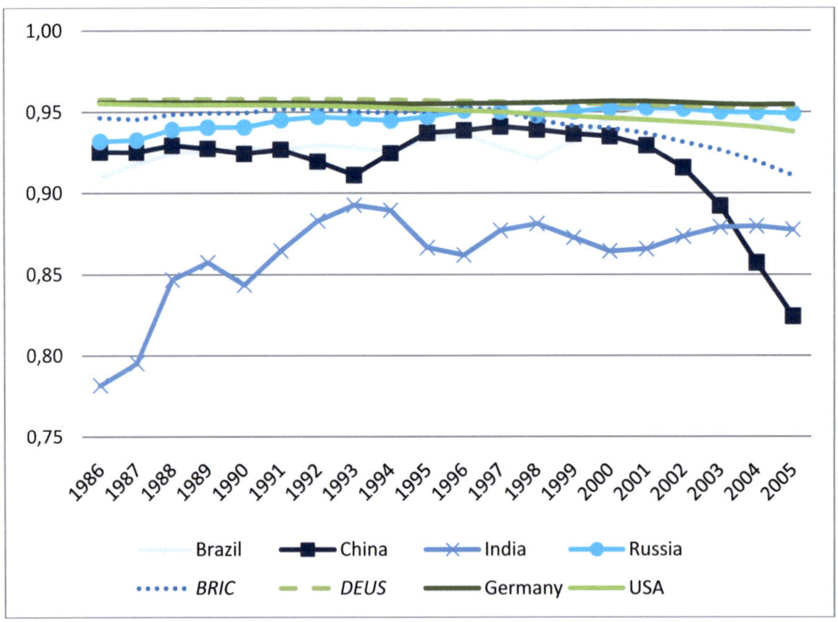

Figure 7-1: *DIV* of late-comers and early-movers 1986-2005

The exploration of the diversification values of late-comer countries shows different developments. In general, all four late-comers do not have such stable diversifications values. Within the group of late-comers, the development paths of all four countries also differ from each other. Brazil and Russia mainly have a rising trend over the twenty years. This underlines the general assumption that technological late-comers also need to develop towards diversified technological activities. One distinction in the diversifications of the last two countries can be detected. While Russia already starts with the highest *DIV* value within the group of 0.93 and rises to 0.95, Brazil starts with 0.91 and rises to 0.94. Both countries finally have *DIV* values quite close to the ones of the early-movers. In the case of Russia, the strong diversification may be a legacy of the impact of the former Soviet Union (see also Section 4.3), where the corner-stones for such activities were given by the *NIS* driven by the competition with the USA. This technological competition with the USA drove the Soviet technological diversification process. The development of Brazil, however, is more interesting. The findings of this chapter reflect findings of the last chapter concerning the examination of the niche strategies, where Brazil also does not show clear specialisation profiles. India has the most concentrated technological activities. Its *DIV* value starts at a relatively low level of 0.78[58]. Even though the diversification spreads within the first years, it holds its level after the first ten years at 0.87, which is still relatively low compared to the other late-comers and especially to the control group of the early-movers. This development approves the niche occupation of India at the beginning of their innovation. China, however, has a converse development, as it is the only country where the diversification values imply that it does not diversify. This results, however, needs cautious interpretation. The examination of the niche occupation shows that China has a focus on some few technological sectors within the last years, such as ‘Telecommunications’, ‘Consuming goods and equipment’, ‘Information technology’ and ’Electrical machinery, apparatus and energy’ (see Subsection 6.3.2). With the intensely rising number of patent applications in these sectors in the last years, in particular, in the sector of ‘Telecommunications’ (see Section 4.2), China obviously exhibits a stronger concentration tendency in its technological activities. This leads to lower *DIV* values. This concentration on specific technologies can be seen in Figure 7-2 where the total amounts of patent applications in the 30 technology sectors are depicted for China. It can be observed that China’s patent applications stay in the same sectors (‘Telecommunications’, ‘Consumer goods and equipment’, ‘Electrical machinery, apparatus and energy’, ‘Information technology’ and ‘Pharmaceuticals and cosmetics’) over the four periods. Especially ‘Telecommunications’, ‘Information technology’ and ‘Consumer goods and

[58] In general the *HHI* has values which are close to the upper border. Commonly the values are between 0.9 and 1.

equipment' are sectors in which Chinese has emerging MNEs, such as Huawei and Haier.

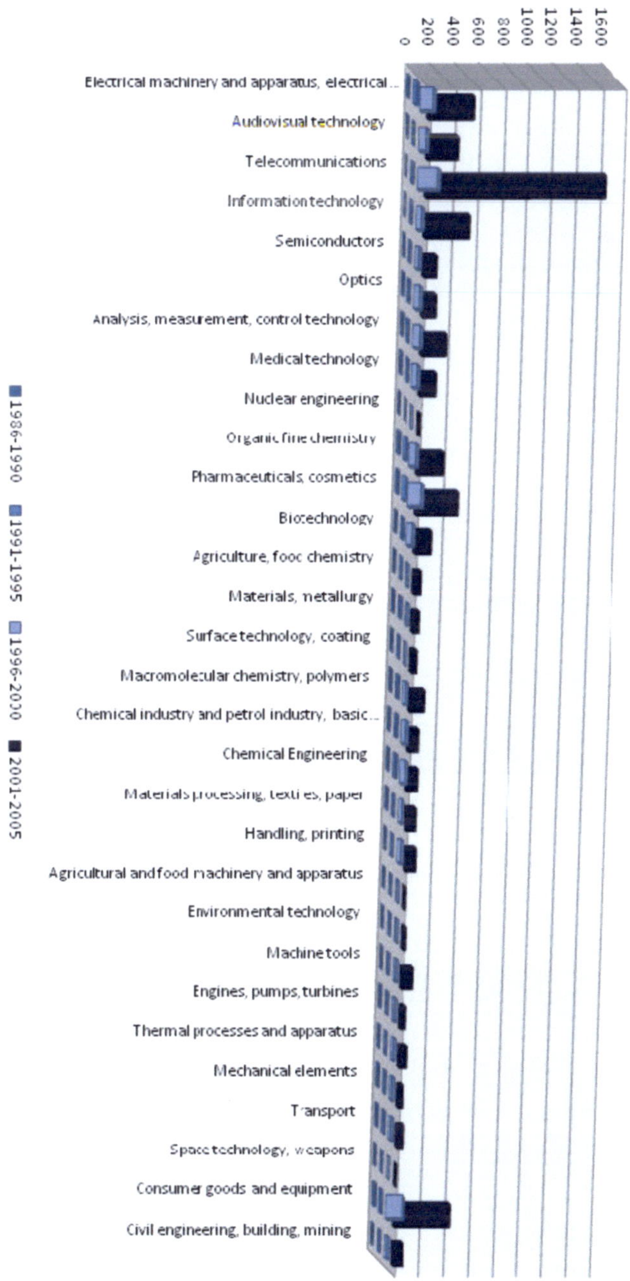

Figure 7-2: Chinese patent application classified in technological sectors[59]

[59] For the detailed list of technological sectors see Appendix.

Compared to established global players, e.g. Siemens and Samsung, Chinese MNEs still have fewer fields of activities according to their technologies and, hence, have specialised fields of technological activities. Hence, this leads to a lower degree of diversification, although the patent numbers rise. Moreover, diversification can also be caused by activities of many different specialised enterprises. The diversity of their activities in certain specialisations also leads to a higher national technology diversification. In cases of smaller innovation systems, such as the case of technological late-comers, the specialisation and diversification of major players have a more important impact on the national diversification.

All	Obs.	Mean	Std.Dev.	*DEUS*	Brazil	Russia	India	China
BRIC	20	0.94	0.0026	5.19*				
DEUS	20	0.96	0.0004		9.25*	7.22*	14.69*	5.83*
Germany	20	0.96	0.0001		9.13*	7.09*	14.63*	5.75*
USA	20	0.95	0.0012		6.16*	2.03*	13.46*	4.75*
Brazil	20	0.93	0.0026					
Russia	20	0.95	0.0014					
India	20	0.86	0.0064					
China	20	0.92	0.0065					

Standard errors: *p<0.05

Table 7-1: t-test of *DIV*

A statistical test of the hypothesis delivers evidence for a higher diversification of early-movers within the last twenty years (see Table 7-1). All four late-comers have diversification values which are significant different to the ones of the early-movers. In particular, the Indian diversification has a high t-value compared to the *DEUS* group, Germany and the USA. These values stand for a high significant difference of all early-movers to India.

All	Obs.	Mean	Std.Dev.	*DEUS*	Brazil	Russia	India	China
BRIC	10	0.94	0.0043	5.21*				
DEUS	10	0.96	0.0001		5.51*	15.73*	38.21*	3.65*
Germany	10	0.96	0.0001		4.86*	11.01*	37.23*	3.48*
USA	10	0.95	0.0003		4.31*	6.11*	36.09*	3.34*
Brazil	10	0.94	0.0033					
Russia	10	0.95	0.0005					
India	10	0.87	0.0022					
China	10	0.91	0.0128					

Standard errors: *p<0.05

Table 7-2: t-test of *DIV* in different time periods

These significant differences still hold, if the first ten years of the late-comers are withdrawn from the statistical test and the second ten years are compared with the first ten years of the early-movers (see Table 7-2). Even Brazil and Russia are still significantly different from the early-movers, although the first impression of Figure 7-1 implies a different notion. These findings stand for a still forthcoming progress of technological diversification in all late-comer countries.

Absolute technological diversification of the biotechnology sector

The *DIV* values of biotechnology are on a lower level than the *DIV* values of the national analysis. This is caused by a fewer number of technology sectors which are related to the sector of biotechnology. Five of the 29 sectors, namely 'Pharmaceuticals and cosmetics', 'Organic fine chemistry', 'Analysis, measurement and control technology', 'Agriculture and food chemistry' and 'Chemical engineering', already cover over 90% of the technologies which are related to the biotechnology. Moreover, the inner diversification is also dominated by the classification of the biotechnology sector itself (see Section 6.3). The *DIV* values of the USA are at a level of about 0.7 until the beginning of the new millennium and decrease in 2003, 2004 and 2005 down to 0.5 (see Figure 7-3).

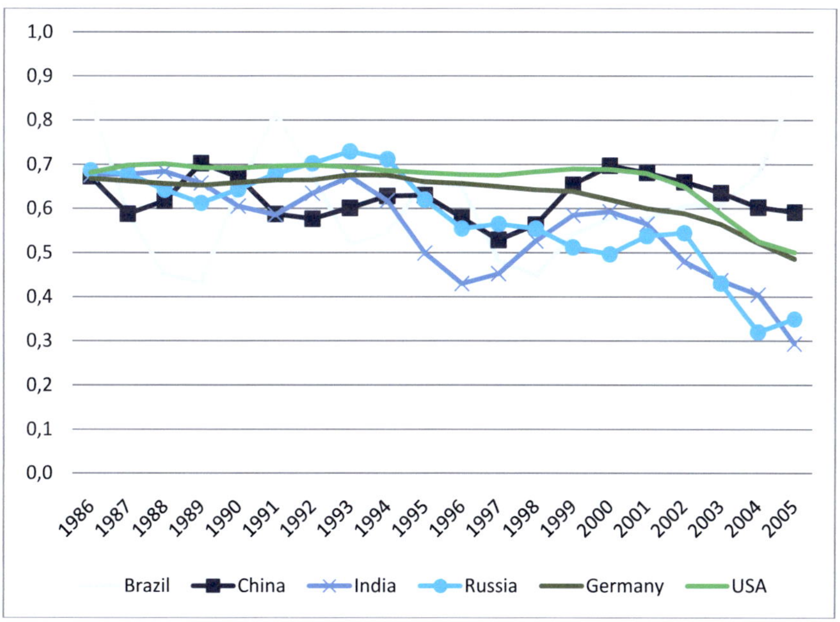

Figure 7-3: *DIV* of the biotechnology sector of late-comers and early-movers 1986-2005

The German diversification of the biotechnology sector develops similar to the US one. Its diversification values are slightly below the US ones between 1986 and 2005, at a level of about 0.65. However, the decreasing trend of the diversification already starts at the second half of the 1990s and goes down to 0.5 in 2005. This trend is, insofar, an interesting finding, as the German biotechnology industry tries to push towards the biotechnology world class players, such as the USA or the UK (see Figure 7-3). Public support helped clusters and, in particular, supported of new entries, such as start-ups and spin-offs. Thus, a more diversified biotechnology sector or, at least, a rising diversified sector would have been expected.

In the case of the four other countries, the *DIV* indexes are unstable over the twenty years. The technological diversification of Brazil is the most alternating one (see Figure 7-3). One reason is the low number of patents, where even some much diversified patents already have a critical influence on the *DIV* value. China, India and Russia also have unstable diversification values, but do not vary as strong as the Brazilian one. While China holds it level between 0.5 and 0.7 in the course of the twenty years, the diversification of the Indian and Russian biotechnology decreases from almost 0.7 down to 0.3 in India and to 0.35 in Russia.

Thus, the first impression does not give clear evidence of diversified biotechnological activities in Brazil, and even a contrary development for India and Russia. China is the only *BRIC* country which has a roughly similar diversification level which can be compared to the US biotechnological sector, but it is, however, not as steady as the US one. The German biotechnology sector is similar to the US one, and is still slightly less diversified over the twenty years. Especially the German-US difference needs a statistical test to give an answer whether they are significantly different to each other or not.

Biotechnology	Obs.	Mean	Std.Dev.	Brazil	Russia	India	China	Germany
USA	20	0.66	0.1286	1.71*[60]	2.96*	3.99*	2.42*	1.94*
Brazil	20	0.61	0.0283					
Russia	20	0.58	0.0259					
India	20	0.55	0.0244					
China	20	0.62	0.0107					
Germany	20	0.63	0.0118					

Standard errors: *p<0.05

Table 7-3: t-test of *DIV* of the biotechnology sector between the USA and late-comers

[60] A significant difference can be accepted in the cases of Brazil and Germany as the limit of the t-value is lower, if the degree of freedom is higher. In this case the degree of freedom is high enough (> 25) to give these values significance.

The test statistics to the whole period shows that all t-values are significant. This leads to the interpretation that all biotechnological late-comer countries are less diversified compared to the USA. However, the t-values are not as clear as the t-values provided by the analysis on the national level. This finding is influenced by the fact that one specific sector is analysed and the technological classifications of these patents are highly influenced by the classification of the biotechnology itself. Hence, the *DIV* values needs to have a lower level, as the calculation of this values already has a certain focus on some fewer technologies. Nevertheless, the *DIV* values of the late-comers and Germany differ from the USA which leads to the result that the process of diversification within this science and knowledge intensive technology is still ongoing. The general decreasing value of technological diversification can be referred to the decreasing numbers of patent application in these years, especially in the sector of biotechnology (see Section 4.4).

Biotechnology	Obs.	Mean	Std.Dev.	Brazil	Russia	India	China	Germany
USA	5	0.69	0.0032	0.39	5.48*	5.71*	3.34*	7.20*
Brazil	5	0.67	0.0552					
Russia	5	0.69	0.0032					
India	5	0.44	0.0446					
China	5	0.63	0.0169					
Germany	5	0.64	0.0062					

Standard errors: *p<0.05

Table 7-4: t-test of *DIV* of the biotechnology sector between the USA and late-comers in different time periods

For the examination of different time periods, the comparison of countries is, once again, separated into three different periods. The beginning of the 1990s of the USA is compared with the end of the 1990s of Germany and the beginning of the new millennium of the late-comer countries. The same approach as it is used in the previous chapters. In this case, it can be observed that the late-comer countries also have different diversification levels, even when the beginning of their technological activities is not considered. The only exception is Brazil which is not significantly different to the US biotechnology sector. This does not mirror the result of the biotechnology specialisation profiles of Chapter 6. Both findings implicate that Brazil begins to diversify, but do not spread its diversification activities into the sectors where the USA is highly represented. All other late-comers, however, are different to the USA what exhibits that they are still not in the stadium of the USA at the beginning of its high rising biotechnological activities.

7.3.2. Relative technological diversification

The last subsection delivered evidence for an ongoing diversification process of the technological late-comer countries. For both time perspectives of the comparison, namely the comparison of the whole period of time and a consideration of different stages of the technological development, almost all differences are significant. Therefore, absolute differences between the technological diversification levels imply that the examined late-comers still have to diversify. This subsection cross-checks these findings with a relative measurement of diversification, namely the *Krugman-Specialisation-Index* (*KSI*).

On a national level, the *KSI* delivers the relative diversification of each country with reference to the whole group of all six countries. Figure 7-4 shows the development of each country, as well as the two groups of countries, in respect to their *KSI*. It is observable that both early-movers are very close to benchmark. Thereby, the *KSI* of the USA indicates the strongest diversification, while the German *KSI* is just slightly above the one of the USA until the last two years. Hence, both early-movers are also close to each other and still relatively close.

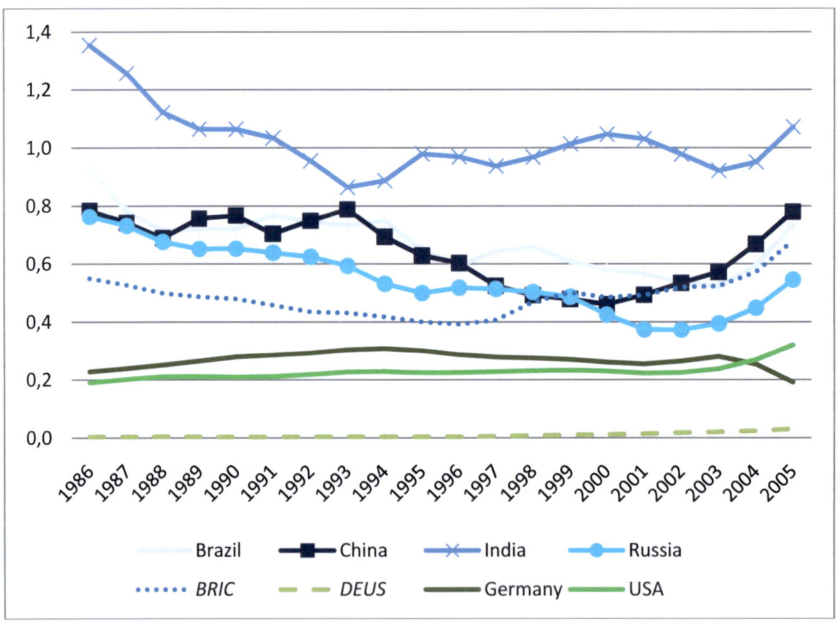

Figure 7-4: *KSI* of late-comers and early-movers compared to the whole group 1986-2005

The relative measurement of diversification draws a notable development for the late-comer countries. All late-comer countries move towards the diversification level of the benchmark group. India follows this trend until the mid-1990s when it begins to stay at a level between 0.8 and 1.0. Brazil, China and Russia even develop closer to the general diversification level. This trend lasts until 2000 for China and even 2001 and 2003 for Russia and Brazil (see Figure 7-4). Hence, the diversification efforts of the late-comer countries, according to a relative measurement, have much clearer characteristics of a convergence towards the early-movers. The last years shows increasing *KSI* values for all countries except for Germany. This is mainly caused by the development of the comparison group. Although the development of the *KSI* in the last years of the examination turns to a lesser relative technological diversification, the efforts until the last years are evident.

All	Obs.	Mean	Std.Dev.	*DEUS*	Brazil	Russia	India	China
BRIC	20	0.50	0.05	49.80*				
DEUS	20	0.00	0.00		37.69*	20.54*	38.51*	5.43*
Brazil	20	0.77	0.09					
Russia	20	0.59	0.13					
India	20	0.98	0.11					
China	20	0.03	0.02					

Standard errors: *p<0.05

Table 7-5: t-test of *KSI*

All	Obs.	Mean	Std.Dev.	*DEUS*	Brazil	Russia	India	China
BRIC	10	0.50	0.08	19.54*				
DEUS	10	0.00	0.00		30.40*	22.71*	62.99*	17.79*
Brazil	10	0.60	0.06					
Russia	10	0.46	0.06					
India	10	0.99	0.05					
China	10	0.56	0.10					

Standard errors: *p<0.05

Table 7-6: t-test of *KSI* in different time periods

The findings of a statistical test for the *KSI* values compared to a total fit with an *KSI* value of 0.0 however reflects that the late-comer countries still are significant different to the *DEUS* group (see Table 7-5). This is not just true for the whole period, but also if different time periods are considered (see Table 7-6). Hence, this findings also implies that late-comers are developing towards early-movers, but do still not have reached their point of relative diversification.

Relative technological diversification of the biotechnological sector

Within the biotechnological sector this trend of convergence is much clearer. The biotechnological *KSI* is calculated with reference to the USA and gives additional evidence for the efforts towards a broader diversification of the *BRIC* countries and Germany (see Figure 7-5). Although the *KSI* values are, again, unsteady, this development is observable for all four countries.

Brazil, once again, has the most unsteady *KSI* values which are similar to the development of the *DIV* index. A clearer decreasing trend, however, is observable for China, India and Russia. China has this decreasing development for nearly all years, as it starts with 0.74 in 1986 and goes down to 0.20 in 2002. From 2003 to 2005, it rises up again to 0.34. This rising is also observed for the national technological diversification and can be influenced by the same effects (see Subsection 7.3.1). India and Russia also have declining *KSI* values which imply that they also move towards a more diversified biotechnology portfolio and towards the USA. Their diversification processes, however, are also unsteady. India's *KSI* declines from 1986 to 1993. From 1993 until 1996, it turns to an upwards trend. Russia has two of such upward exceptions, namely from 1990 to 1995 and from 1998 to 2000. At least the first rising period bears external effects, as it can be the result of the collapse of the Soviet Union. At that point in time, innovation activities in Russia suffered in general which also influenced the diversification activities.

Germany already starts with a relative close diversification compared to the USA (about 0.2) and holds this level until the beginning of the new millennium where it also makes a closer step towards the US biotechnology sector. In 2005, it has a *KSI* of 0.14 (see Appendix). Germany's relatively diversified biotechnology sector relates to its strong patent numbers. However, the trend towards the USA implies a further step towards the biotechnological early-mover. The German efforts to strengthen its biotechnology sector seem to be fruitful.

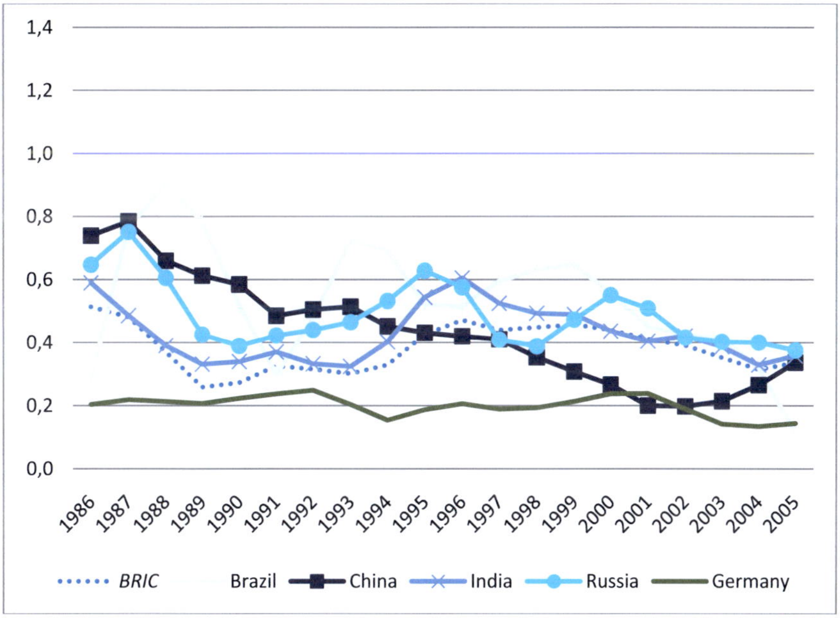

Figure 7-5: *KSI* of the biotechnology sector of late-comers and Germany compared to the USA 1986-2005

The *KSI* developments of the biotechnology sector are also checked with a t-test. The benchmark which is used for this test is the value of a perfect match (0.00) to the early-mover (the USA). Once again, this test shows that the differences of the late-comers in the biotechnology sector are evident. Even Germany has a high t-value what implies that the biotechnology sector of Germany is not as diversified as the USA (see Table 7-7). This finding is also verified by the examination of the different time periods of the late-comers (see Table 7-8). Hence, once again, the still developing and emerging process of the late-comers is emphasised by the findings of this statistical test.

Biotechnology	Obs.	Mean	Std.Dev.	Brazil	Russia	India	China	Germany
USA	20	0.00	0.00	12.23*	20.78*	21.43*	11.15*	26.57*
Brazil	20	0.53	0.19					
Russia	20	0.49	0.11					
India	20	0.43	0.09					
China	20	0.44	0.18					
Germany	20	0.20	0.03					

Standard errors: *p<0.05

Table 7-7: t-test of *KSI* of the biotechnology sector between the USA and late-comers

Biotechnology	Obs.	Mean	Std.Dev.	Brazil	Russia	India	China	Germany
USA	5	0.00	0.00	5.57*	18.26*	23.11*	9.18*	8.60*
Brazil	5	0.34	0.14					
Russia	5	0.42	0.05					
India	5	0.38	0.04					
China	5	0.24	0.06					
Germany	5	0.21	0.02					

Standard errors: *p<0.05

Table 7-8: t-test of *KSI* of the biotechnology sector between the USA and late-comers in different time periods

The analysis of the *KSI* on the sectoral level delivers evidence of the convergence of the late-comer's diversification in this sector. Hence, governmental efforts seem to be successful, because Asian countries stated that biotechnology clearly is a governmental supported sector (see MOST, 2008 and Ministry of Science & Technology India, 2007). Similar efforts can be found in Germany (see BMBF, 1996) which also leads to a decreasing trend, although the German biotechnology sector just diversifies slightly. Russia and Brazil, however, also tend to diversify over the years, but do not have the same clear trend of the other technological late-comers.

7.4. Implications of technological diversification of late-comers

In general, the findings of this chapter imply technological diversification efforts within the late-comer countries. This is basically indicated by the absolute measurement based on the *DIV* index, but in particular by the relative measurement based on the *KSI* index. Thus, the empirical analysis of this chapter delivers the following interim conclusions for each late-comer country.

Brazil

In Brazil, the diversification patterns are more obvious on a national level. The *DIV* index reflects Brazil's diversification efforts. However, its diversification is still significantly different compared to the early-movers, even if the first years, where innovation activities within the late-comer countries were still low, are dropped. Regarding the relative measurement, a general trend of diversification towards the group of early-movers can be observed, but it also demonstrates that the level of the early-movers has not been reached yet. Hence, on the national level, Brazil tends to diversify. In fact, this is an effect of the initial innovation activities and still low numbers of patents. Thus, regarding the underlying hypothesis, the analysis can be confirmed and Brazil is still not in the phase of an established innovation system.

However, the hypothesis of Chapter 6 is strengthened and the status as a developing innovation system can be confirmed.

The biotechnological sector in Brazil is the most blurry one according to its diversification development. The development is very unsteady regarding absolute and relative measurements. Although a light trend to a more diversified biotechnological sector is indicated by both indicators, the hypothesis of this chapter cannot be affirmed clearly for the Brazilian biotechnology sector.

Hence, based on the illustration of the diversification efforts and effects, it can be stated for Brazil that it is still not at the stage of the early-movers in 2005. Although clear diversification efforts on the national level already exist, in fact, the biotechnology sector is still on a very low level according to their patent application numbers. This is, for example, influenced by the lacking political efforts within this sector (see Chapter 4).

China

China has the most unclear patterns of national diversification during the last years of the examined period of time. While in the first years a stagnating *DIV* value is indicated, the last years have a strong falling *DIV* value. As aforementioned, this can be referred to rising activities of upcoming MNEs in China (see Section 7.3.1) and needs a more detailed exploration. Nevertheless, the statistical test shows that China also has a significant different diversification level as the two early-movers and, thus, is also still on the course to a more diversified innovation system regarding its technological output.

On the sectoral level, the findings for China are different. Although the differences in the diversification of the biotechnology sector are still given, a more converging trend towards the USA is apparent. The *KSI* index visualises this development, showing that over the twenty years a convergence to the USA cannot be denied. Hence, political efforts, in particular those efforts that address science and technology, can push certain sectors of the so-called transformation economies. The central government is able to use its financial opportunities to lead the innovation system into certain directions.

To sum up; the hypothesis can also be confirmed for China, as it shows that this country still needs to diversify. Once again, this also strengthens the hypothesis that China is still in the stage of a developing innovation system. The results of the biotechnology sector, however, reflect positive effects of political intervention. As decision makers in this country knows about positive effects of knowledge and technology, it is just a matter of time that it also begins to diversify in other sectors and, hence, broaden the focus of the whole *NIS*.

India

India's diversification is the least developed one. Its diversification values on a national level, measured by absolute and relative indicators, are still on a low level. Although the *DIV* and the *KSI* show that India diversifies in absolute and relative manners rapidly between 1986 and 1994, this increasing trend does not hold for the whole period of time. The technological diversification even decreases after 1994 and stagnates at the end of the 1990s until 2005. This stagnation can result from different effects. First, India's decision makers want to focus on so-called future technologies which are assumed to drive future economic development (see Mitusch et al., 2010). This leads to an exploration of such industries, for instance, pharmaceuticals, chemicals, biotechnology etc., especially in the late 1980s and the beginning of the 1990s (see Chapter 6.3.2). For the development process of the innovation systems, this strategy also is the most feasible one. Nevertheless, India has to improve its strategy as it needs to diversify to establish itself within the technological competition.

On a sectoral level, India also shows that the political influences in an emerging and developing economy play an important role. While the *DIV* analysis does not reflect the diversification process of India's biotechnology sector, the *KSI* shows a diversification trend towards the US biotechnology sector very well. Such a development also implies that promising diversification processes in certain sectors are detectable. As biotechnology is also a long-run core issue of India's science and technology policy, the diversification trend and, hence, the establishment of this sector is in process.

Thus, India's diversification process is also in development and has to improve yet. The analysis of this chapter reveals that it has a strong focus on certain sectors and needs to leave this specialisation, if it wants to establish itself in the global technology competition. However, on a biotechnological level, it delivers evidence that a diversification on certain sectors is already detectable. Hence, similar to China, the diversification process seems to be in progress and points to the promising direction.

Russia

The diversification of Russia profits from the technological efforts of the former Soviet Union. *DIV* and *KSI* deliver the highest degree of diversification on a national level among the late-comer group. In particular, the *DIV* values may imply a relatively well developed technological diversification. However, this is not confirmed by the statistical test which shows that the Russian diversification is still not on the same level as the ones of the early-movers. The *KSI* also delivers the still existing differences in the Russian diversification patterns compared to the early-movers. In fact, the external effect of the fall of the former Soviet Union has its impact on the diversification. Moreover, further diversification efforts can be shown after the fall of the Soviet Union. If Russia successfully deals with this external shock, it can positively use the technological legacy of the former Soviet science and technology efforts.

The Soviet legacy on a national level turns out to be a disadvantage of the Russian biotechnology sector. This refers to the status of biotechnology as a young technology. Diversification patterns in the biotechnology sector are, in fact, increasing for both, absolute and relative points of view. This development may be the result of the lack of stately leaded science and technology policies in certain developing sectors (see Saltykov, 2007). It is of Russia's interest to change these missing efforts, if it wants to catch-up with the early-movers.

Hence, Russia has advantages in its technological diversification and still profits from the diversification of the former Soviet Union. Though it has to deal with external shocks, it still needs to push its diversification efforts. Furthermore, Russia needs to strengthen its efforts in the so-called emerging technologies (see Mitusch et al., 2010). On a national level, Russia's technological diversification is the most developed one, but has not reached the level of the early-movers and, therefore, the hypothesis can also be confirmed

General remarks

In general, the four technological late-comers still show under-diversified technological activities and more efforts towards a broader diversification would be meaningful. However, they are on the right way and have in many regards also the right circumstances, although every late-comer has to deal with different problems. Brazil, in this respect, has to develop innovation activities in general and pushes its technological output. China and, in particular, India need to push their diversification as they already have strongly increasing innovation activities. Finally, Russia has to learn to profit from its national strengths and put its efforts in new emerging technologies.

8. International technology networks

This chapter deals with networking activities within the *National Innovation Systems* of technological late-comers, as well as their international linkages. Here, innovation networks of the biotechnology sector of the four late-comer countries, Germany and the USA are analysed by means of *Social Network Analysis* (SNA). As the analysis on micro-level consists of a huge number of players a limitation to this sector is needed. Even the restriction on one sector delivered tens of thousands of players which needed to be cleaned manually. *SNA* is originally used in sociology to map and measure relationships and information or resource flows between individuals. The network analysis conducted in this thesis, therefore, gives further insights into the topic of innovation activities of technological late-comers on the micro level. The analysis employs applicant and inventor data and delivers a picture of the connections between major players of this sector for all of the six countries. This chapter deals with two different hypotheses which shed light on these two perspectives, namely the applicant and inventor networks. Once again, the restriction on the biotechnology sector is explained in detail in Section 8.2 and refers to the huge amount of data which needs to be harmonized.

The structure of this chapter sticks to the proceeding of the former chapters. Thus, it begins with the rationale of innovation networks and summarises the state of the art in the field of *SNA* and innovation activities (see Section 8.1). Section 8.2 explains the theory and method of the *SNA*. It contains definitions and explanations of specific terms concerning network analysis and, in particular, important measurements and indices for the examination, such as *centrality* and *betweenness*. The subsequent Section 8.3 summarises the findings of the empirical work on the late-comer networks. Finally, Section 8.4 discusses and concludes the findings of the preceding section. Once again, each late-comer country is discussed and compared to the early-movers.

8.1. Networking and innovation activities

Social networks, as well as business networks, are said to have certain effects on the participants of a network. Customers and suppliers, for instance, interact more frequently with each other, if they already know each other. Such interactions between more than two participants can be considered as a network. In recent years social networking also becomes one of the latest hypes in the worldwide web. Social network services, such as *Facebook* and *Twitter*, enjoy great popularity and connect millions of people with each other. However, interactions between the private participants of such networks do not follow commercial intention, but informal and personal ones. One advantage of such networks can be seen in the flow of information between the participants. One other advantage can be collaborations which emerge from personal relationships. In scientific considerations, social networks are already analysed over many years (see, for instance, Wasserman and Faust, 1994, Scott, 2000 and Powell et al., 2005). The research questions of such analyses often tackle discussions of effects of networking activities, for instance, information flows between participants, or the emergence of such networks, for instance, in certain regions, sectors or countries. In fact, these are just two discussed topics in the field of *SNA*. However, the increased information flows between densely connected network partners are one main subject of studies in innovation networks.

8.1.1. Innovation networks

With regard to innovation analysis, network analyses are mainly conducted for two different kinds of networks. The first kind of networks is based upon applicants and inventors. The second kind of networks is so-called citation networks dealing with patent citations, as well as citations of scientific publications. No matter what kind of networks are analysed, one main reason for networking activities is the increasing complexity of new technologies and the necessity for joint efforts and development of these new technologies (see Hagedoorn, 1993). By collaborations agents possessing different but ideally complementary knowledge stocks are linked together with the effect that new knowledge is generated based upon mutual learning processes. Networks, therefore, can have positive effects on the economy as they foster knowledge transfer and knowledge diffusion. Nevertheless, fixed networks also can lead to lock-ins.

Empirical works analysing applicant networks, as well as inventor networks often go along with the topic of innovation systems (see Chapter 2.2). Cantner and Graf (2006) argue that innovation systems, in particular, *Regional Innovation Systems* depend on an efficient network of innovation players, such as firms, research institutes, public organisations and private inventors (see also Ter Wal and Boschma, 2009). Advantages of geographic proximity do not work, if applicants within a region do not interact together, for instance, by the exchange of employees or joint R&D activities. In particular, analyses in the topic of regional networks focus on the crucial role of certain kinds of players in a *RIS*, such as major research institutes and gatekeepers (see Breschi and Lissoni, 2003, Giuri and Mariani, 2008, Graf and Henning, 2009, Graf, 2010, and Miguélez and Moreno, 2010). Similar analyses with different spatial focuses deal with international and national networks analysing broader networks within a *National Innovation System* and importance on cross-border collaborations (see Guellec and van Pottelsberghe de la Potterie, 2001, Montobbio and Sterzi, 2008, Meyborg, 2010 and Mitusch et al., 2010). Moreover, sectoral networks (*Sectoral Innovation Systems*) of specific sectors, and in particular, the biotechnology sector are analysed (see Hagedoorn, 1993, Baum et al., 2000, Powell et al., 2005,

Laforgia and Lissoni, 2009, Fornahl, Tran and Haller, 2008, Ter Wal, 2009 and Haller, 2009). As citation networks play a minor role in the analysis of this chapter they are not described in detail and the remainder of this subsection gives an explanation of the role of technological late-comers in the global technology network. Additionally, the hypotheses of this chapter are generated.

Innovation networks and technological late-comers

The discussion of innovation networks tackles the discussion of late-comers from different perspectives. To analyse the establishment of technological late-comers in the global technology competition, this chapter deals with two different hypotheses which are motivated as follows.

As aforementioned, development of new technologies becomes more and more complex. Applicants look for new sources of knowledge. This fact holds for established applicants, but especially for emergent applicants. The higher dependency on external knowledge is also confirmed by the analysis of Chapter 5 by illustrating through patent citation analysis that late-comers do use more external knowledge to develop their technologies. In this respect, Baum et al. (2000) argue that new firms entering a market often have a lack of resources, especially in the field of R&D. They have to collaborate with other applicants to compensate this short-coming. As innovation systems of technological late-comers do not have enough resources, such as human capital, R&D etc., at the beginning of their innovation activities, collaboration partners have to be recruited abroad. This leads to the first hypothesis:

Hypothesis 4a: Late-comers have fewer resources, such as human capital, for the generation of new knowledge and technologies. They need more external knowledge at the beginning of their innovation activities and, have, therefore, more linkages to external sources.

The first hypothesis tackles, in a certain way, also the question about entry strategies and their difficulties. Nevertheless, the analysis to this hypothesis in this chapter deals with network activities of the late-comer countries during the establishment of late-comer countries. As Graf and Henning (2009) show for regions and Ter Wal and Boschma (2009) also confirm for sectors, it is crucial that innovation networks create certain structures with central firms and research institutes which are the core of a network. Leading countries have such structures with important core players and a periphery of smaller firms (see Mitusch et al., 2010). Hence, late-comer countries should develop towards network structures of such early-movers. This leads to the second hypothesis:

Hypothesis 4b: Innovation networks of late-comers develop towards early-movers with regard to their network characteristics and the role of major players. Major players become more central and gain importance.

To test both hypotheses the tools of the *Social Network Analysis* are used. Especially, the second analysis needs the measures of the *SNA* to locate and compare the players regarding their role and importance. Therefore, the next section gives a brief summary of the *SNA*.

8.2. Analysis of innovation activities and *Social Network Analysis*

8.2.1. Basic concepts and terminology

The basic concepts which are used in this thesis refer to the methods and applications introduced by Wasserman and Faust (1994). According to these two authors, a network is defined as players (also denoted as actors) and their social relationship, respectively linkages to each other (also called ties). Thereby, the nodes are the actors of the network, while ties are relationships between these actors. Such relationships can be measured for different structures. Some works on network analysis draw connections between actors, if these actors just know each other. Information of such relationships is collected by conducting interviews and surveys of actors (e.g. see Hagedoorn, 1993). Other works rely on data derived from databases in which industrial co-operations between firms and public institutes are recorded (e.g. see Powell et al., 2005). In general, a network always shows actors within a certain frame (spatial, sectoral etc.) and their interactions. Moreover, network analysis examines these interactions and the effects of such networks[61].

For the introduction of the *SNA* some formal and theoretical concepts need to be discussed based on mathematical considerations. To visualise a network, the *SNA* refers to the basic mathematical structures of Graph Theory. The basic set defining a network, as aforementioned, consists of a set of nodes (actors) and a set of ties (relationships, respectively linkages). Figure 8-1 shows a simple example of a network. It is an example of a disconnected graph, as there is one node which is not connected to at least one of the other nodes (node 9).

[61] More examples for empirical work on this topic see Wasserman and Faust (1994, pp. 3-68) and Coulon (2005).

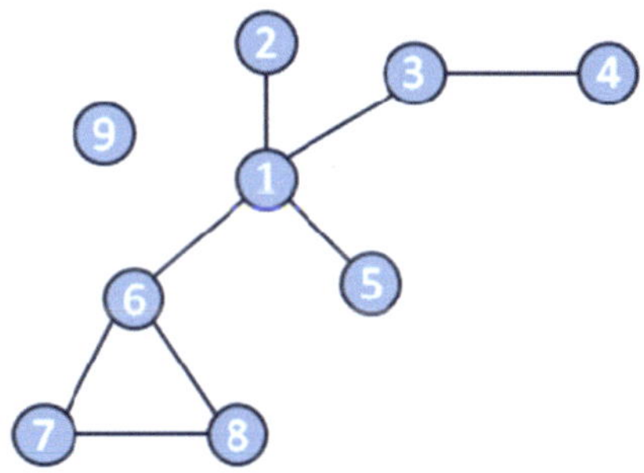

Figure 8-1: Example for a simple disconnected graph

The nodes which are presented in the example play different roles (see Figure 8-1). Node 1 demonstrates situated in the centre and has the most connections and is at a first glance more important for the network than the other nodes. In contrary, node 9 is disconnected and therefore plays a minor role in the network. However, besides the pure description and visual evaluation, approved tools have to be used. For such sophisticated description and statistical analysis, the empirical work of this chapter refers to the *SNA*. For this reason the next subsection introduces these methods and discusses briefly specific network structures.

8.2.2. Network measurement concepts

In smaller networks, such as the example given in Figure 8-1, the importance of certain nodes is obvious. However, such evaluations of networks and actors with a huge amount of nodes are not a straight-forward process. Therefore, certain *SNA* tools and measures are introduced. Simple concepts are based on the counting of nodes and linkages.

General network measures: **degree *and* density**

The total number of linkages connected to node n_i is the *degree* of this node and it is denoted by $d(n_i)$. The co-domain of the *degree* is between zero, if the node is isolated and has no connections to any other node, and $g - 1$, if it is completely connected to all other nodes in the network. In this case, g is number of nodes in the underlying network. Nodes with a higher *degree* have more connections and also seem to have a more important role. However, this interpretation of relevancies of certain nodes can be misleading as nodes with smaller *degrees* can also play crucial roles in a network, if they are connected to important components with some few ties. This would, for instance, underestimate the role of gate-keepers (see Section 8.1). Similar to the *degree* of a node a simple measure exists for the network structure. The *density* of a network measures the number of connections within a network L divided by the maximum number of possible linkages $g * (g-1)/2$. The *density* starts with a value of zero, if all nodes are isolated and reaches to the upper limit of *1*. It is calculated as follows:

$$D = \frac{L}{g * (g-1)/2} = \frac{2 * L}{g * (g-1)} \quad (8\text{-}1)$$

Figure 8-2 presents a completely connected network where all nodes are connected with each other. All nodes have a *degree* $d(n_i) = 4$ and the network has a *density* $D_2 = 1$.

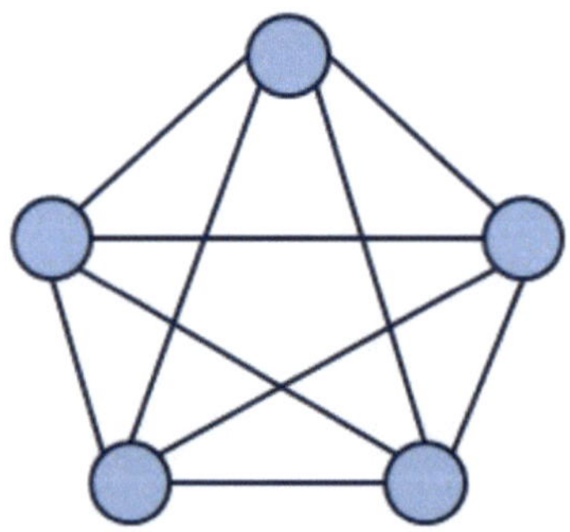

Figure 8-2: Completely connected network

This example shows that *degree* and *density* can deliver useful measures, however, they are not comparable to each other, if different networks are analysed. Node 1 of the network given in Figure 8-1 has also a *density* $d(n_1) = 4$, but has a more crucial role for its network compared to all the other nodes in Figure 8-2. The *density* of the first network has a value of $D_1 = 0.222$. While *density* still reflects some comparable values between the two networks, the *degree* of the networks does not mirror the right level of importance of each node. This importance needs to be exploited by some more sophisticated measures. The following summary of these network measures refers to the work of Wasserman and Faust (1994, Chapter 5, pp. 169-215) and Haller (2009, pp. 124-130).

Actor level measures

The first measure on the actor level is the *degree centrality* which normalises pure *degree*. The *degree centrality* reflexes rather a role of a node by dividing the existing linkages through the numbers of existing nodes. It is calculated as follows:

Degree centrality:

$$C_D(n_i) = \frac{d(n_i)}{g-1} \tag{8-2}$$

The actors with the most links still have the highest *degree centrality*. This value, however, also considers the size of a network. Therefore, it is also possible to compare nodes of different networks as differences of the networks, such as amount of nodes, are considered.

Betweenness centrality stands for the frequencies how often a node is in on the shortest path between two other nodes. The number of shortest paths between two nodes *j* and *k*, also called the geodesics, is denoted as g_{jk}. While the number of geodesics where the node n_i is involved is denoted as $g_{jk}(n_i)$. *Betweenness centrality* is calculated with the following term:

Betweenness centrality:

$$C_B(n_i) = \sum_{i=1}^{N} \frac{g_{jk}(n_i)}{g_{jk}} \tag{8-3}$$

A node with a high value of *betweenness centrality* also stands for actors which are in the shortest line of information, thus can accumulate more knowledge or even block the flow of knowledge.

Network level measures

Besides actor level measures, there are also network level measures to measure the network structure. By these measures the networks structure as a whole can be analysed and different networks can be compared to each other. The first measure is the *network centralization*[62] which focuses on the *centrality* values of the actors. It can be considered as a method to reveal equalities among network actors and is calculated as follows:

Network centralization:

$$C_N = \frac{\sum_{i=1}^{g}(c_{max} - c_i)}{max\{\sum_{i=1}^{g}(c_{max} - c_i)\}} \tag{8-4}$$

Network centralization values range between zero and 1. To calculate the *network centralization,* the *centrality* of each node *i* and the maximum *centrality* are used. They are denoted as c_i and c_{max}. If C_N has a value near zero, the network has very equal actors which can appear, for instance, in a *cycle network.* In contrary, a network with a very central actor, for instance star networks, has *network centralization* values near to the maximum of 1 (see Figure 8-3).

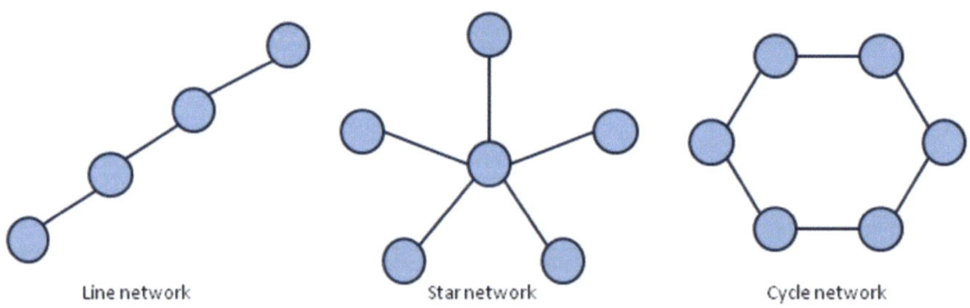

Figure 8-3: Sample for special networks

The second network level measure is the *degree centralization* which is based on the *degree* values of the actors. The term of the *degree centralization* follows a similar approach as the network *centralization.* It also sums up all differences between the maximum *degree centrality* (c_D^{max}) of a network and all other *degree centrality* values of each node ($c_D(n_i)$):

[62] Note: Actor level measures are denoted as *centrality* values, while *centralization* values stand for network level measures.

Degree centralization:

$$C_D^N = \frac{\sum_{i=1}^{g}(c_D^{max} - c_D(n_i))}{(g-1)(g-2)} \tag{8-5}$$

The third network structure measure refers to the *betweenness centralities* of the nodes. It also refers to the differences between maximum *betweenness centrality* (C_B^{max}) and the *betweenness centrality* of each node ($c_B(n_i)$).

Betweenness centralization:

$$C_B^N = \frac{2 * \sum_{i=1}^{g}(c_B^{max} - c_B(n_i))}{(g-1)^2(g-2)} \tag{8-6}$$

Apparently, higher values of *degree centralization* and *betweenness centralization* means that many nodes have *degree centrality* and *betweenness centrality* values close to the maximum. Thus, such networks have structures where nodes are well connected to each other and the network is relatively balanced. The other way round, networks with higher values have some important nodes which are central.

8.2.3. Composition of late-comer networks

To test the hypotheses of this Chapter the network measures have to be brought together with the research questions. For this reason, existing studies are discussed and linked with the measures employed in for the analysis of this Chapter.

The analysis of the late-comer networks employs patent data. According to the graph theory actors are represented by applicants or inventors and the relationship between them. The empirical examination of this work, therefore, follows the different works on this topic, drawing two different kinds of networks, namely applicant-applicant networks and inventor-inventor networks (see e.g. Guellec and van Pottelsberghe de la Potterie, 2001, Montobbio and Sterzi, 2008, Ter Wal, 2009 and Ter Wal and Boschma, 2009). Applicant-applicant networks are constructed, looking at patent applicants of patents from late-comer countries, as well as the early-movers. A connection between two actors is existent, if two applicants are on the same patent. This first step draws relationships, especially for important firms and institutes of the late-comer regions. It sheds light on the structure of applicants within the late-comer countries and, in particular, their external linkages. This question tackles the first hypothesis of this Chapter (Hypothesis 4a). However, this approach bears shortcomings, as patent applicants do not often have joint applications. The reason is the legal status of patents and their ownership. Especially cross-border collaborations inherit problems, if patent applicants apply for patents together. To deal with this problem, the second hypothesis (Hypothesis 4b) is analysed with inventor-inventor networks, where two inventors are connected to each other, if they appear on one patent. These networks are used to analyse the network measures and the development of late-comer innovation networks. It needs to be mentioned that innovation networks based on patent data also uses different approaches to draw networks. Cantner and Graf (2006), for instance, also use patent data to draw regional networks for the *Regional Innovation System* of Jena in Germany. In their work applicants are linked with each other, when they have one inventor in common (applicant-inventor approach). The link of applicants in such cases is represented by a mobile inventor who transfers his knowledge between the applicants during the collaboration of these applicants. Moreover, knowledge is also transferred, when an inventor moves from one applicant to another one. This approach delivers most meaningful insights into a local innovation system. It is, however, not useful for the investigation of wider national and international innovation networks, because most inventors which appear on patents with different applicants are not necessarily working for both applicants (see Arora et. al., 2001, Giuri and Mariani, 2005 and Ter Wal and Boschma, 2009). Such multiple-applicant inventorships appear when inventions are sold from one firm to another one. The inventers, however, still belongs to the selling firm and never worked for the firm which buys the invention. The probability of applicant collaborations, therefore, is reasonable if applicants are in close geographic approximations.

8.3. Late-comers in the global biotechnology network

After the introduction and definitions of methods of the *SNA*, as well as the explanation of the networks which are constructed for this thesis, this section firstly presents some descriptive statistics delivering evidence for the amount of external linkages of the late-comer countries (see Subsection 8.3.1). Second, the roles of the top applicants in the national applicant network, also named applicants network, are compared by employing a statistical test (see Subsection 8.3.2). Last, the structures of the inventor networks of the late-comer countries are compared to the inventor networks of the early-movers (see Subsection 8.3.3).

8.3.1. Country level networks of the biotechnology sector

The examination of the international linkages of the late-comer countries shows that foreign collaborations play a major role for the late-comer countries at the beginning. Table 8-1 shows the numbers of foreign collaborations and the share to the total numbers of collaborations. The mean values of the percentage of international linkages (see, for instance, *Brazil (%)* in Table 8-1) for all late-comer countries are higher compared to the ones of Germany and the USA (see Table 8-1). However, this refers to the low numbers of collaborations of the late-comers. In particular, Brazil and Russia have a very low level of collaboration activity and also a high level of foreign collaborations. In contrary, the Asian countries show increasing numbers of general applicant collaborations, especially in the last period.

	1986-1990	1991-1995	1996-2000	2001-2005	Mean
Brazil (total)	2.00	1.00	3.00	3.67	***2.42***
Brazil (%)	100.00	100.00	50.00	40.74	***72.69***
China (total)	1.00	1.00	2.00	8.67	***3.17***
China (%)	100.00	50.00	28.57	22.31	***50.22***
India (total)	-	1.00	30.67	18.00	***16.56***
India (%)	-	100.00	83.64	50.00	***77.88***
Russia (total)	1.50	8.00	5.00	3.39	***4.47***
Russia (%)	50.00	100.00	100.00	73.01	***80.75***
Germany (total)	44.00	94.80	110.77	226.67	***119.06***
Germany (%)	50.57	56.95	31.71	52.12	***47.84***
USA (total)	59.87	119.10	269.99	207.69	***164.16***
USA (%)	19.60	17.82	24.30	29.75	***22.87***

Table 8-1: Numbers and share of collaborations with foreign applicants

The development of the share of foreign collaborations shows different developments within the group of late-comer countries (see Figure 8-4). While almost all late-comer countries experience a decreasing trend in the share of foreign collaborations (Brazil from 100.00% down to 40.74%, India from 100.00% down to 50.00%, and China from 100.00% down to 22.31%), Russia sees a different trend. Russia's share of external linkages rises after the first period and remained at a level of 100.00% for two periods. In the last period it decreases down to 73.01%. This finding also indicates the unsteady time after the collapse of the Soviet Union. However, these findings have to be analysed with care, as the late-comers have small numbers of collaborations.

Germany has a more steady development. While the total numbers of foreign collaborations rise, the share is steadily at a level of 50.00%. Only the time period 1996-2000 has low numbers of foreign collaborations. This development can result from the *BioRegio* contest in the mid-1990s where the Germany supported the regional German biotechnology clusters and local collaborations also received governmental funding (see Fornahl and Tran, 2009).

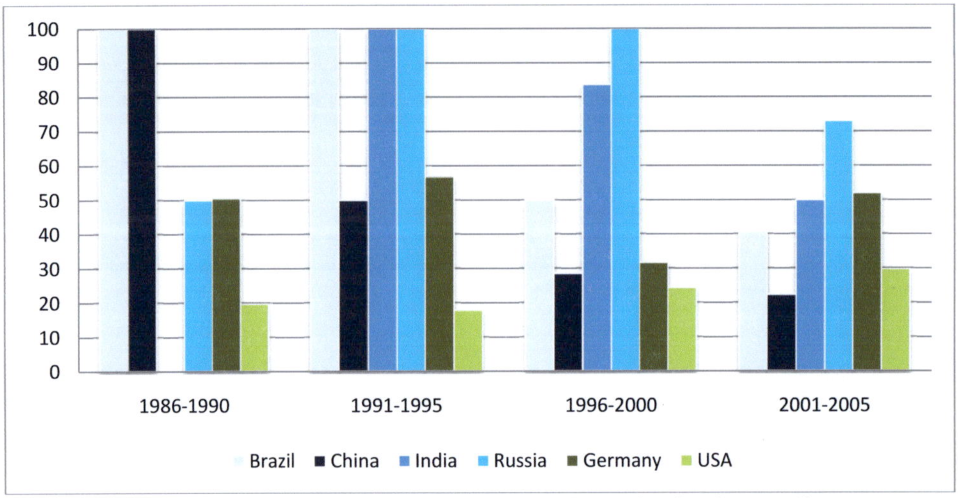

Figure 8-4: Development of shares collaborations with foreign applicants

The USA, however, has the lowest level of foreign collaborations. This finding strengthens some findings of the other chapters of this work. First, the USA has many inner-country collaborations. This finding indicates that most of the applicants look for collaboration partners in their own country. The increasing numbers and share of foreign collaborations indicate that foreign biotechnology knowledge becomes more and more important. Even the USA uses this foreign source of knowledge (see Figure 8-4).

8.3.2. Collaboration of applicants in late-comer countries

The analysis of the innovation structure in this work consists of an analysis on actor level and an analysis on network level. While the analysis on network level is presented in the next section, this section deals with the analysis of the applicant network on actor level. Top players of the late-comer countries are compared to top players of the early-movers by means of *degree centrality* and *betweenness centrality*. As an efficient *NIS* needs a core of established applicants (see Mitusch et al., 2010), the examination on the micro level in this thesis focuses on this core of applicants.

Table 8-2 summarises the top ten players of the biotechnology sector of each analysed country and their numbers of applications over all years.

Brazil		China	
9	Fundacao Oswaldo Cruz (Fiocruz)	24	Tsinghua University
8	Fundacao de Amparo a Pesquisa do Estado de Sao Paulo	22	CapitalBio Corporation
6	Universidade Federal de Minas Gerais-Ufmg	10	The Chinese University of Hong Kong
5	PHB Industrial S.A.	8	Shanghai Institute of Biochemistry Chinese Academy
4	Petroleo Brasileiro S.A. Petrobras	6	Guangdong Center for Disease Control and Prevention
4	Universidade Federal do Rio de Janeiro	6	Hong Kong DNA Chips Limited
3	EMBRAPA-Empresa Brasileira De Pesquisa Agropecuaria	6	Beijing University
2	Alellyx S.A.	6	Yu, Long
2	Biobras S.A.	5	Oakville Hong Kong Co., Limited
2	Biolab Sanus Farmaceutica Ltd.	4	Yang Sheng Tang Company. Ltd.
India		**Russia**	
118	Council of Scientific & Industrial Research	12	Frank, Ludmila
48	Hindustan Lever Limited	12	Markova, Svetlana
22	Avesta Gengraine Technologies Pvt, Ltd	12	Vysotski, Eugene
12	Biocon Limited	9	Institute of Protein Research
11	Reliance Life Sciences Pvt, Ltd.	8	Dorokhov, Yurii
9	Ranbaxy Laboratories Limited	8	Ivanov, Peter
7	National Institute of Immunology	6	Atabekov, Joseph
6	All India Institute of Medical Sciences	6	Bonch-Osmolovskaya, Elizaveta
6	Nicholas Piramal India Limited	6	Institut Molekulyarnoi Biologii
6	Ramakrishna, Nirogi, Venkata, Satya	6	Skulachev, Maxim
Germany		**USA**	
1450	Bayer AG	1027	Merck & Co. Inc.
925	BASF AG	788	Regents of the University of California
597	Max Planck Society	610	Genentech Inc.
597	Degussa AG	570	Human Genome Sciences
404	Genencor International GmbH	556	Inctye Genomics, Inc.
402	Aventis Behring GmbH	511	Government of the US, Department of Health and Human Services
349	Schering AG	453	Pfizer Inc.
344	Hoechst AG	451	Du Pont Pharmaceuticals Company
265	Chiron Behring GmbH & Co.	380	Abbott Biotech. Inc.
229	Epigenomics AG	344	Becton Dickinson and Company

Table 8-2: Top applicants of the biotechnology sector and numbers of applications 1986-2005

Structure and characteristics of top applicants

The top applicants of the US and Germany are predominantly *MNE*s. In Germany, the only exception in the top ten is the *Max Planck Society* which ranks third in the German biotechnology sector. The US biotechnology sector is also dominated by *MNE*s with two exceptions; the *Regents of the University of California* and the *Department of Health and Human Services* which represents the government of the US. The biotechnology sector in these two countries is driven by enterprises and some strong research institutes.

For the late-comer countries the applicants show a different structure. Brazil has a mixture of research institutes and enterprises, but as the top numbers of applications range from nine patents down to two, a clear picture is not given for Brazil. China has dominant universities in their biotechnology sector which are well represented in their top list of applicants. Interestingly, there is also a private person who appears in the Chinese biotechnology top list. Top applicants are the *Tsinghua University* and the *CapitalBio Corporation*. India also has a mixture of research institutes which is similar to the Brazilian biotechnology sector. In India, there is one outstanding applicant, namely the *Council of Scientific & Industrial Research*. Also remarkable numbers of applications are filed by *Hindustan Lever Limited*. However, the Russian biotechnology sector delivers the most interesting findings of the late-comer countries. With exception of two research institutes, all other top applicants are private persons. These findings show that the innovation systems of the late-comer countries, except for Russia, are still mainly driven by public institutes, such as research institutes and universities. The innovation system and its drivers, therefore, are still at a stage where governmental efforts are necessary and important. Russia, however, shows that the biotechnology sector is mainly driven by private persons. It can be assumed that these persons have a biotechnological background and they work, for instance, as researchers. This assumption can be made, as biotechnology is a knowledge-intensive technology and private persons do not have the research infrastructure to develop new technologies by their own. The Russian top list discovers a problem in the Russian innovation system which is also discussed in the previous chapters. Innovations are still not directed and planed by the government and this short-coming can lead to further problems of the innovation system.

Collaboration of applicants

The list of top applicants shows that late-comer applicants just have few outstanding applicants. These outstanding applicants also play major roles in the network of applicants. Figure 8-5 shows the collaboration networks of the late-comer countries from 2001 to 2005. Compared to these networks, Figure 8-6 shows the networks of Germany and the USA from 1991 to 1995 (DE1 and US1) and from 2001 to 2005

(DE2 and US2). Obviously, Germany and the USA have networks where applicants are much more linked and connected to each other. The size of the nodes stands for the numbers of patents each applicant jointly applied for. The code of the nodes also shows the countries of the applicants. The Brazilian figure, for instance (see BR in Figure 8-5), has one co-application with two applicants. This collaboration between the applicants BR-16631 and BE-3317 shows collaboration between a Brazilian and a Belgian applicant. The number on the tie (in this case *1*) shows the amount of collaborations. As an example for multiple collaborations the Chinese network (see CN in Figure 8-5) has two applicants with 18 co-applications. The applicants CN-16459 and CN-2607 work together on more than one patent. The bubble with the Chinese applicants at the right side of the last example represents just few patent applications with multiple applicants.

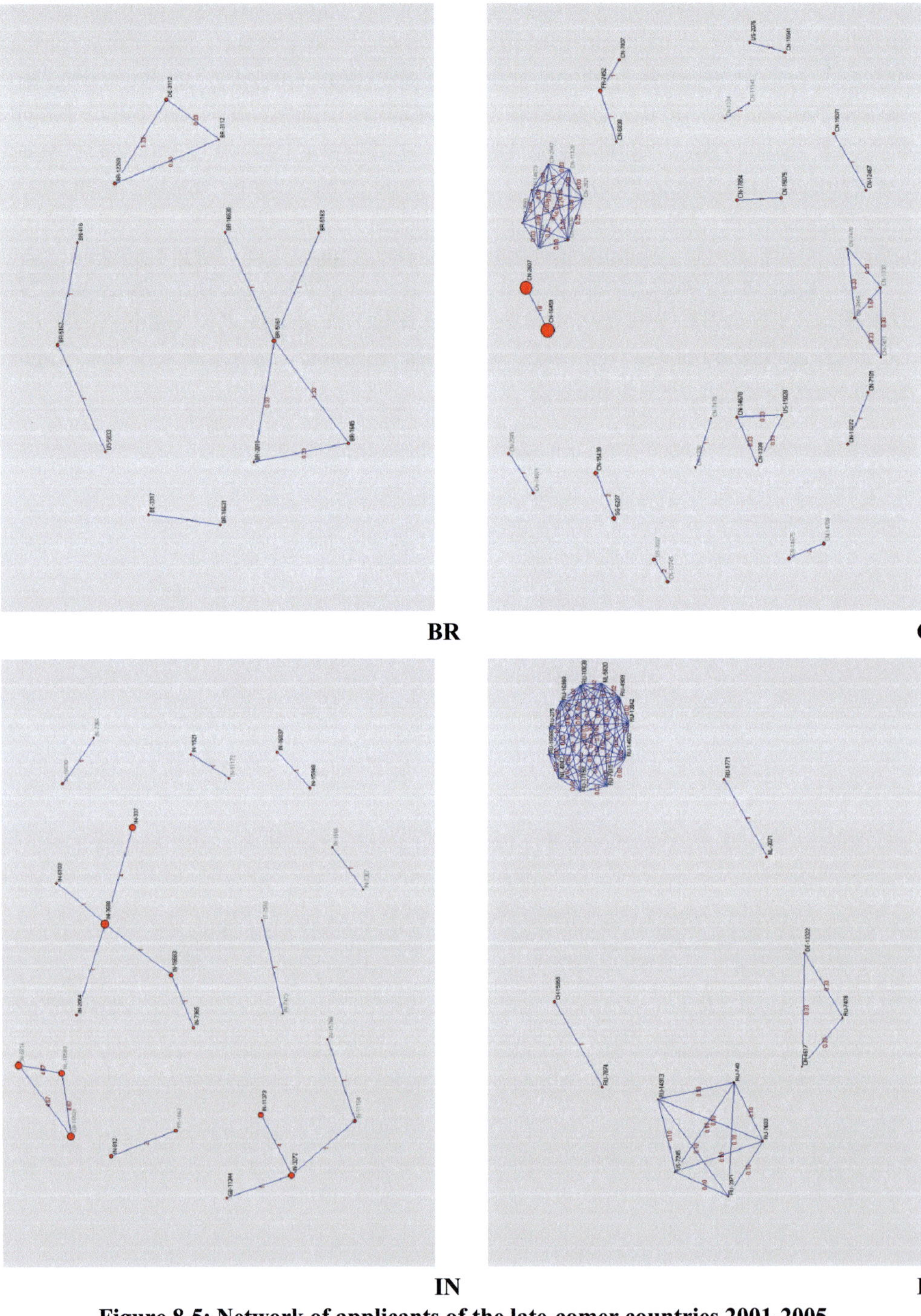

BR CN IN RU

Figure 8-5: Network of applicants of the late-comer countries 2001-2005

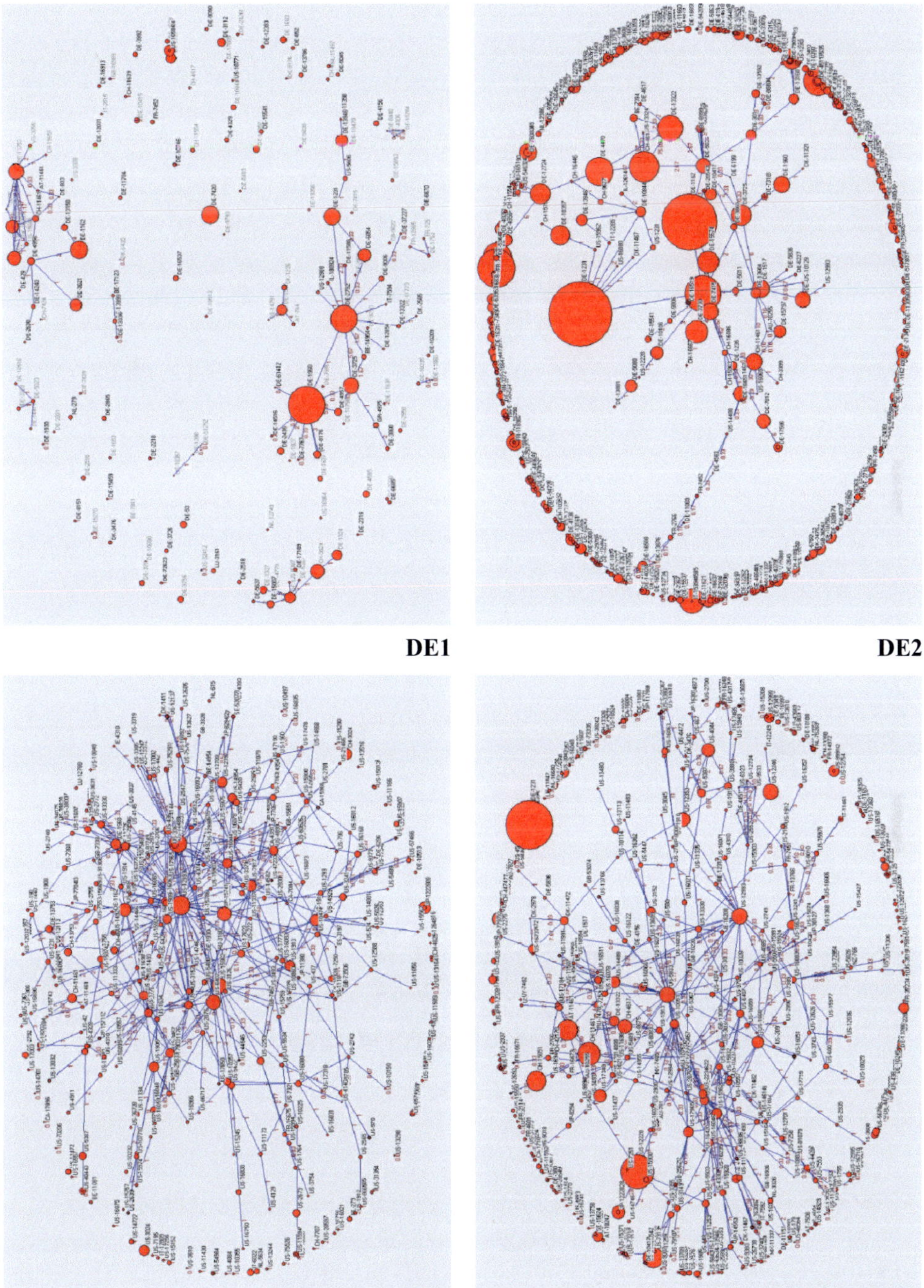

Figure 8-6: Network of applicants of the early-movers 1991-1995 (1) and 2001-2005 (2)

Compared to the networks of the US biotechnology sector, the applicants of the late-comer networks are still very loosely connected. This even holds for the last time period (see Figure 8-5). It is also observable that most applicants of the late-comers are just involved in a few numbers of collaborations, and just some applicants collaborate more than once at all. Germany and the USA have different pictures as they also have more established innovation systems. In particular, the USA has a well-connected core of main applicants and a less-connected periphery with smaller applicants regarding the numbers of patent applications. In this respect, it can be observed that Germany's biotechnology sector profits from related sectors and the major players of these sectors, for instance, the chemical sectors and *MNE*s, such as BASF and Bayer. However, the German biotechnology sector has still many smaller players at the periphery of the sectoral innovation network, while the USA has a much more connected biotechnology sector (see Figure 8-6). This finding strengthens their role as biotechnological leader in the world.

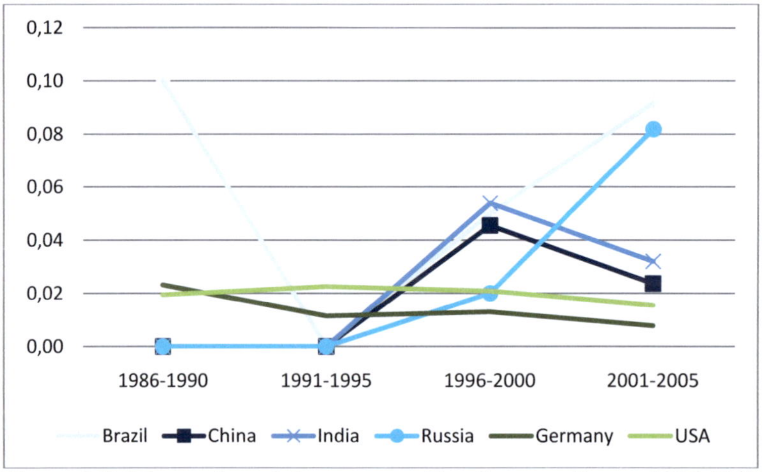

Figure 8-7: Mean value of *degree centrality* of top applicants 1986-2005

Regarding the characteristics of the top applicants, the analysis shows that the development of *degree centrality* of this players are much more stable in the USA, as well as in Germany, compared to the late-comer countries (see Figure 8-7). However, within the small national networks, the domestic top players develop to major actors and the mean value of these players increase. The development of Brazil and Russia has to be treated with care as they show low levels of networking activities.

USA	Brazil	China	India	Russia
1986-1990	3.25*	0.95	2.38*	20.55*
1991-1995	3.93*	-0.69	1.91*	6.14*
1996-2000	4.41*	-0.68	2.13*	5.27
2001-2005	3.07*	1.20	2.64*	17.64*

Standard errors: *p<0.05

Table 8-3: t-test of late-comer *degree centralities* 2001-2005 to US top applicants

USA	1986-1990	1991-1995	1996-2000	2001-2005
1986-1990	1.37	-0.40	-0.72	-2.29
1991-1995		-0.32	-0.82	-1.77
1996-2000			-1.02	-2.03
2001-2005				-1.22

Standard errors: *p<0.05

Table 8-4: t-test of German *degree centralities* to US top applicants

Table 8-3 and Table 8-4 present the comparisons of *degree centrality* values of the late-comer applicants, as well as the German ones with the USA. The t-values show that the *centrality* and, therefore, the importance of the USA major players in their networks still differ significantly compared to the ones of Brazil, India and Russia. First of all, this means that these countries lack major players in their innovation systems which have many connections to other players. Thus, the connections need to be fostered, as well the generation of stronger major players. This can be done, for instance, by financial support or projects, such as the *BioRegio* in Germany (see Subsection 8.3.1). Especially, Russia lacks these players (see also Table 8-2). Interestingly, China already does not differ significantly from the USA. This finding implicates that major players within the innovation system in China developed well Germany, in comparison to the USA, also has not significant differences in the *degree centrality* examination.

The *betweenness centrality* reveals that the top applicants of the US biotechnology sector still play a much more critical role within their networks compared to all other countries. The mean of the *betweenness centrality* values of the US top applicants are much higher than in the late-comer countries and Germany (see Figure 8-8). This means that they are much more within the shortest path of any player in the innovation network and, thus, they are more important for the network compared to their late-comer counterparts, as well as to the German ones.

With the exception of the Chinese *betweenness centrality* value of the time period 1996-2000, all between values are on a low level. This difference between the biotechnological early-movers and late-comers can also be reflected by the statistical test (see Table 8-5 and Table 8-6).

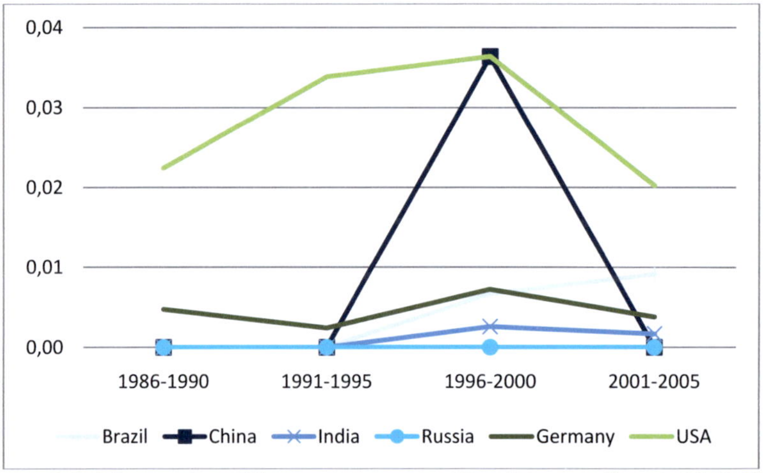

Figure 8-8: Mean value of *betweenness centrality* of top applicants 1986-2005

USA	Brazil	China	India	Russia
1986-1990	1.24	1.64	1.68	1.00
1991-1995	1.91	1.35	1.15	1.29
1996-2000	1.99	1.44	1.29	1.80
2001-2005	1.12	1.04	0.87	1.08

Standard errors: *p<0.05

Table 8-5: t-test of late-comer *betweenness centralities* 2001-2005 to US top applicants

USA	1986-1990	1991-1995	1996-2000	2001-2005
1986-1990	2.92	1.54	1.49	1.72
1991-1995		1.10	1.41	1.72
1996-2000			1.82	1.91
2001-2005				1.29

Standard errors: *p<0.05

Table 8-6: t-test of German *betweenness centralities* to US top applicants

Although these *betweenness centrality* values are not significant, they can show that there is still a difference between the US biotechnology top applicants and the ones of the late-comers and Germany. This is also significantly confirmed by the *degree centrality* values with the exceptions of China and Germany.

To sum up, the analysis of the players shows that the *BRIC* countries have a different structure of applicants compared to the USA. While the biotechnology sector of the USA is mainly driven by *MNE*s, the *BRIC*s still have a mixture of more public and governmental institutes. In Russia, applicants of biotechnology patents are predominantly private persons. According to the different *centrality* measures of these players, *BRIC* applicants also still differ compared to the USA. Only China's top applicants play a role in their countries which is not significantly different to the top applicants of the USA. In contrast to the *BRIC*s, Germany's biotechnology sector profits from the traditional chemistry sector. Large *MNE*s, such as BASF and Bayer, can switch from their main activities to the related biotechnology sector. This advantage is also reflected by the results of this analysis. In fact, German top biotechnology applicants do not have as high *betweenness centrality* values as their US competitors, but they have similar *degree centrality* values. This means that they are in similar central positions, but they are not likely to be within the shortest paths of two nodes.

8.3.3. Inventor networks of late-comer countries

After the examination of the applicant networks, this subsection deals with the characteristics of the inventor networks. This topic focuses on the structure of inventor networks and the evaluation of this network to deliver insights into the diffusion of knowledge within the innovation systems and the sources of their new technologies. Figure 8-9 and Figure 8-10 are examples of inventor networks of the USA and Germany. A clear structure of the network is not distinguishable.

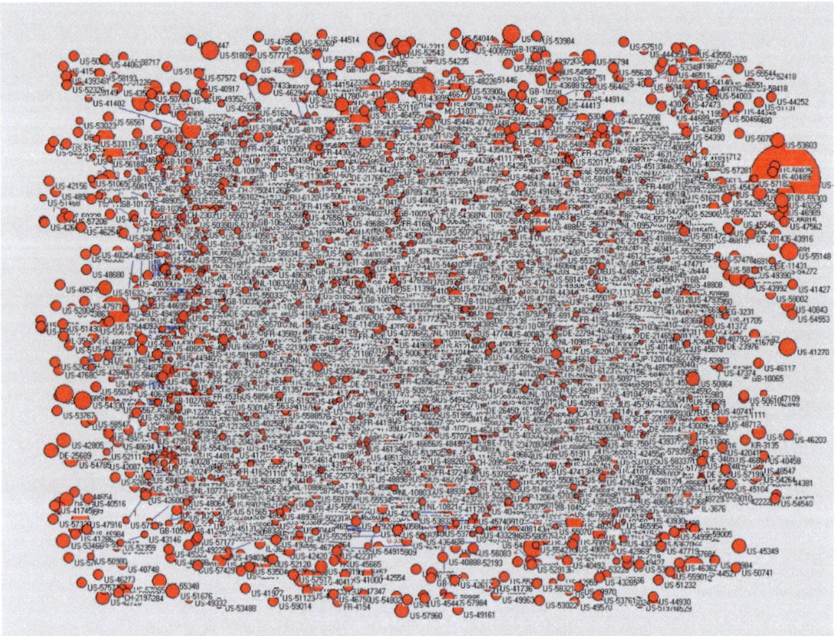

Figure 8-9: US inventor network 2000-2005

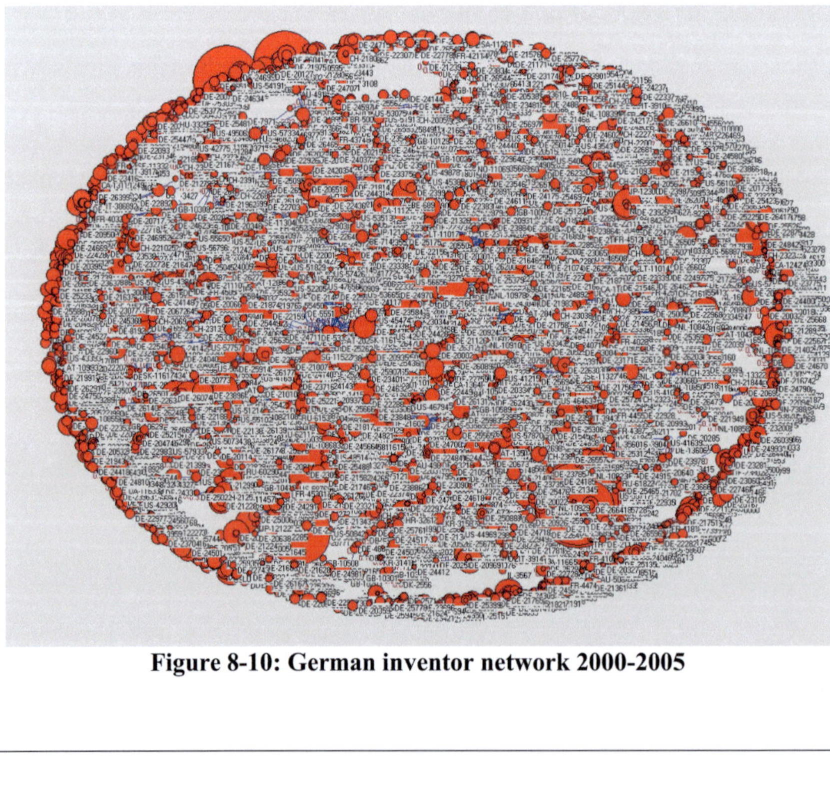

Figure 8-10: German inventor network 2000-2005

Multiple inventors are much more likely to appear on patent applications than multiple applicants. The analysis of the inventor networks comprises much more nodes and ties. Therefore, the examination of such dense inventor networks has to be based on *SNA* measures, such as *density, average degree, degree centralization* and *betweeneess centralization* (see also Subsection 8.2.2).

	Average degree	*Density*	*Degree centralization*	*Betweenness centralization*
Brazil	3.22	0.0963	0.1030	0.0237
China	4.95	0.0511	0.0800	0.0076
India	5.81	0.0469	0.0750	0.0020
Russia	5.57	0.0939	0.1301	0.0341
Germany	4.69	0.0023	0.0131	0.0007
USA	4.97	0.0026	0.0156	0.0006

Table 8-7: Mean values of inventor networks characteristics 2000-2005

	Average degree	*Density*	*Degree centralization*	*Betweenness centralization*
USA 1991	3.67	0.0013	0.0092	0.0001
USA 1992	3.60	0.0012	0.0107	0.0002
Germany 1996	3.62	0.0029	0.0092	0.0003
Germany 1997	4.07	0.0028	0.0118	0.0001

Table 8-8: Inventor networks characteristics for Germany (1996-1997) and the USA (1991-1992)

Table 8-7 and Table 8-8 show the mean of the network characteristics, as well as the network characteristics of the USA of 1991 and 1992 and of Germany of 1996 and 1997. It is observable that the network measures of the late-comers exceed the early-movers in almost all categories. Just the Brazilian *average degree* has a lower level compared to the early-movers. However, network characteristics of the USA and Germany also changed since the beginning and the middle of the 1990s (see Table 8-8). With the exception of the German *density* all values increase. This implies that the biotechnological innovation networks are not only in progress in the late-comer countries, but also the developed ones. The higher levels of *average degree*, *density*, *degree centralization* and *betweenness centralization* in the late-comer countries can refer to the lower level of development, in particular, lower level of absorptive capacities and basic knowledge. Even though inventors in the biotechnology sector in these countries are still rare and they are more likely to have collaboration activities. Another reason is the higher level of public and governmental involvement in this sector. Researchers and inventors in the public sector are more likely to collaborate than researchers and inventors of private companies.

Figure 8-11 illustrates the development of the network characteristics from 2000 up to 2005. This reduction to the last five years needs to be done for a clear harmonisation of the data. The inventor data of these last years already exceeds 85,000 records which are cleaned manually. It shows that USA and Germany experience a stable development while the late-comer countries see quite unstable measures during these years. The development of *density* and *degree centralization* of all late-comers, and *betweenness centralization* of Brazil and Russia highly differs compared to the USA and Germany. However, the *average degree* and the *betweenness centralization* of, in particular, China and India develop towards the level of the *DEUS* countries. This difference between the first three measures and the *average degree* implies that there are components of networks within the networks of the USA and Germany which are separated from each other or just loosely linked to each other. Otherwise, the other measures would also be at similar levels compared to the late-comers. Such components evolve in research co-operations and regional innovation systems (see also Subsection 8.1.1) and can be crucial for the *NIS*. China and India are 'closer' to the early-movers in this respect.

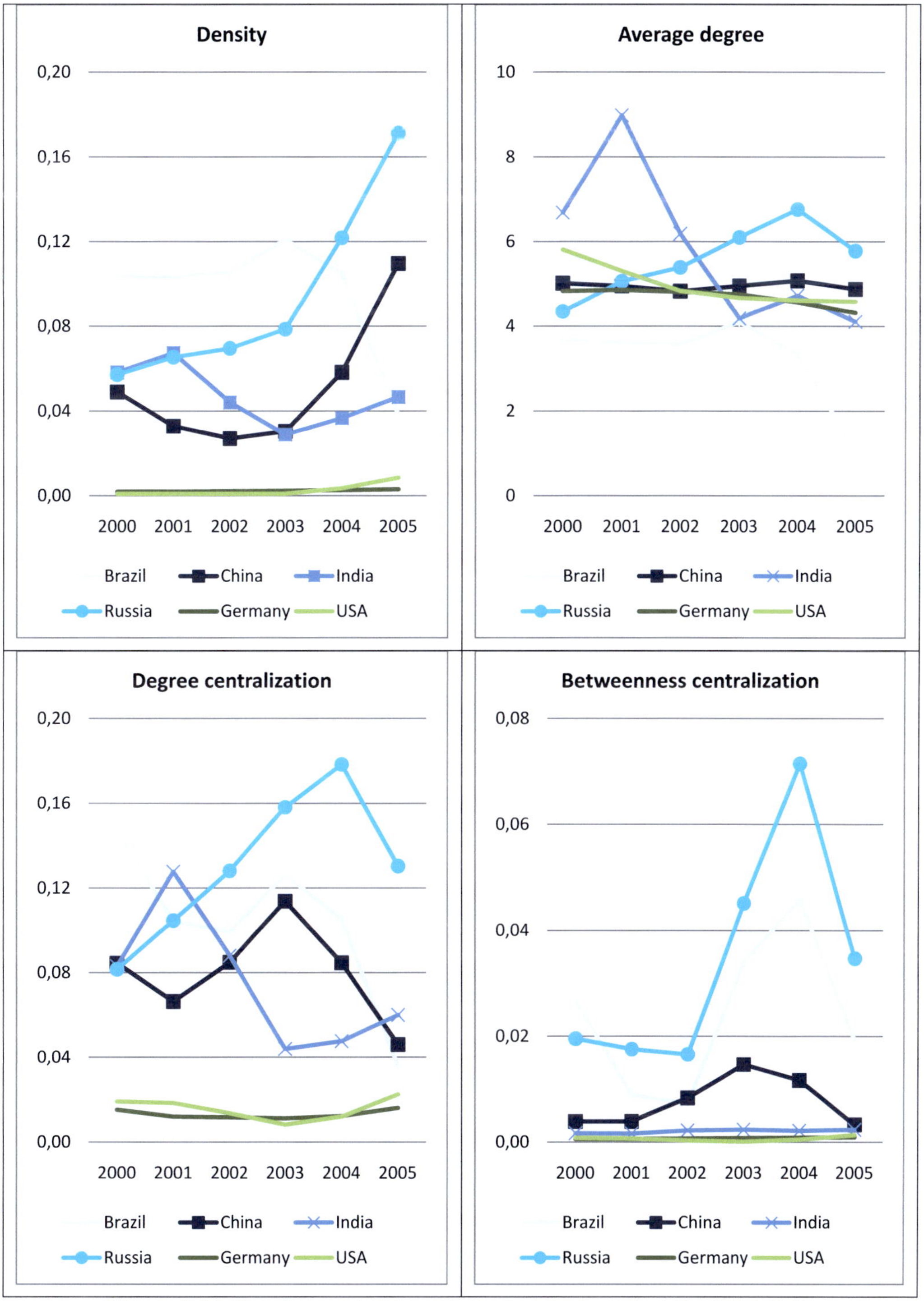

Figure 8-11: Development of inventor network characteristics 2000-2005

Density	Brazil	China	India	Russia	Germany
USA	11.96*	3.06*	3.76*	4.61*	-0.19
Germany	11.93*	2.82*	3.77*	4.34*	
Average degree					
USA	-2.50	-0.07	0.50	0.79	-1.38
Germany	-2.74	2.09*	0.68	1.38	
Degree centralization					
USA	6.09*	3.11*	2.27*	3.81*	-0.89
Germany	6.91*	3.56*	2.19*	4.12*	
Betweenness centralization					
USA	1.96	2.12*	3.36*	1.61	0.43
Germany	1.96	2.22*	5.29*	1.62	

Standard errors: *p<0.05

Table 8-9: t-test for inventor network characteristics

A statistical test of the network measures between 2000 and 2005, however, discovers that the observed development of *betweenness centralization* of China and India is still significantly different in contrast to the USA and Germany (see Table 8-9). While the difference in the values of *density* and *degree centralization* can also be proofed by the statistical test, the other findings regarding average degree and *betweenness centralization* are not definitely unambiguous. For the average degree this result reflects also the 'close' level of average degree between the late-comers and the USA and Germany. The results of the test of *betweenness centralization* are unexpected, as they show that China and India are still different compared to the USA and Germany.

The analysis of the inventor network shows that all late-comer inventor networks are constructed with strong components which are connected loosely with each other, as they have similar average degrees compared to the early-movers, but higher values *degree* and *betweeness centralization.* This result is driven by the structure of applicants in these countries. Although the late-comer inventor networks have higher levels of *density*, *degree centralization* and *betweenness centralization*, the analysis of this work shows that these results are not driven by established networks. It is rather driven by strong substructures. This result also reflects the findings of former works (see e.g. Graf and Henning, 2006). However, the stable development of the Chinese and Indian biotechnology inventor network implies that they are on the way to establish well-functioning knowledge diffusion mechanisms within their countries.

8.4. Role and dynamics of late-comer players in the biotechnology network

The examination of the innovation networks reveals that there are differences in the innovation system of late-comers and early-movers, but also differences within the group of late-comer countries. This section summarises the findings of this chapter and delivers the discussion on the topic of innovation networks.

Germany

As a biotechnological late-comer, Germany's innovation network shows more characteristics of an early-mover status, rather than a late-comer status. Regarding their foreign collaborations, Germany has a higher amount of foreign linkages than the USA. The main players are also *MNE*s which have higher *degree centrality* and *betweenness centrality values*. They do not differ a lot compared to the USA. The inventor network has also similar characteristics compared to the USA. These results show that Germany profit from related sectors, such as the chemistry sector. In particular, network activities profit from existing collaborations between players and actors which already know each other. The German biotechnology sector, although it is regarded as a late-comer, is more likely to have a fast take-off and catch-up process.

Brazil

Brazil is still at the beginning of the establishment of a functioning innovation network in the biotechnology sector. The number of external linkages still appears quite often. However, it needs to be considered that Brazilian biotechnology players have just few linkages. The group of main players are a mixture of firms and public institutes. This reflects the governmental support in this sector. The d*egree centrality* values are still different in contrast to the top players of the USA, but *betweenness centrality* values already changed. This finding results from the stronger division of the US network into sub-structured network components. Top players of Brazil, therefore, are also very likely to be on the shortest paths between certain other actors and players. The inventor network has an unstable development. The most network characteristics are still different compared to the US network. This implicates that the inventor network of the Brazilian biotechnology sector is still not established. Brazil needs to strengthen their biotechnology sector in many respects to deal with this short-coming. In particular, Brazil needs to push their efforts regarding education and training of skilled labour forces to build up more absorptive capacities and basic knowledge.

China

Foreign linkages in the Chinese biotechnology sector at the beginning of the examined time period are also still on a high level. However, China decreases their external knowledge linkages and reaches the level of the USA at the beginning of the new millennium. Top players of this sector in China are mainly public institutes and universities. Hence, the biotechnology sector is still state-driven. The *degree centralities* are already on a high level, but the values of *betweenness centrality* are still very different compared to the top players of the USA. The examination of the inventor network shows that the network structure is still different to the USA. However, the structure is even more stable compared to the other late-comers. These findings implicate that China has still a biotechnology sector which is highly supported by the government. This governmental support also already shows their effects. Surely, the network still needs time to become an efficient innovation network.

India

Compared to China, India has more foreign linkages. Although they decrease, India still has much foreign collaboration. The group of main players are a mixture of firms and public institutes which is different to China where the top innovation leaders are still directly supported by the government. The *degree centralities* of these players are also different to the USA, while *betweenness centralities* are already not significantly different. The Indian inventor network is on a different level compared to the USA, but it is also more stable than the ones of Brazil and Russia. Like the Chinese biotechnology sector, the Indian one still needs time and support to establish an efficient innovation network. An advantage of the Indian network, however, is the more important role of firms within the group of main players. The future development of these firms is crucial for an efficient Indian innovation network.

Russia

The Russian biotechnology sector is the most different one within the group of late-comers. The number of external linkages increased between 1986 and 2000. The high level of foreign linkages did not decrease before the last period. However, similar to Brazil, it needs to be stated that Russia has just only few linkages. The top players of the Russian biotechnology sector are private persons who have different *degree centralities* and *betweenness centralities* compared to the biotechnology sector of the USA. The inventor network also reveals an unstable development. The different development of the external linkages, compared to the other late-comers, can result from the breakdown of the Soviet Union, and the efforts to link them to foreign applicants after the opening of the former Eastern Bloc. Nevertheless, the findings for Russia imply that the biotechnology sector of Russia is a stagnating sector and needs tremendous efforts to catch up with the US one. Besides of the efforts to push the pool of skilled labour and absorptive capacities, as aforementioned for Brazil, Russia even needs to build up a core of strong applicants.

General remarks on the innovation networks

In general, it can be summarised that the *BRIC* countries have a different status regarding the establishment of their biotechnology sectors. Concerning the first hypothesis (Hypothesis 4a) all late-comers show higher amounts of foreign linkages. China is a remarkable exception, as it develops towards the early-movers and also reached the level of the early-movers. Regarding the second hypothesis of this chapter (Hypothesis 4b) the analysis, firstly, shows that the groups of top players in Brazil, China and India are different compared to the USA and Germany. However, China's top players also show an astonishing development towards the early-movers. Second, the inventor networks imply that India and China begin to establish an efficient network. Brazil, in this respect, needs to catch up. The analysis of the Russian biotechnology innovation network reveals that Russia's biotechnology stagnates. Moreover, Russia needs to push their efforts to be able to catch up with the other late-comer countries.

This chapter shows that first efforts to establish efficient innovation systems within the global competition can be detected. Once more, the Asian late-comers reveal their success in pushing their innovation efforts. Within the next step, the late-comer countries are analysed regarding these successful developments. Therefore, the next chapter deals with the topic of late-comers as the source of new technology and the influences on the use of technologies and knowledge which were developed within the late-comer countries.

9. International knowledge flows of late-comers

This Chapter presents the last analysis of this thesis dealing with schemes of success of technological late-comers and their growing role as knowledge sources in the international technology competition (see Section 4.4). It is a description and summary of the work 'BRIC-*Countries as a Source of International Knowledge Flows - A Patent Citation Analysis*' and explains in detail the results of this paper (see Tran, 2009). It addresses the contribution of the *BRIC*s to the global technology network and the influences on knowledge diffusion originating from these countries. Therefore, the analysis consists of two parts. The first part shows that *BRIC* technology is also a source of knowledge for inventions all over the world. Moreover, it is based upon patent forward citations indicating the development of the citation network between 1986 and 2000. The shorter time period is due to restrictions of the forward citation analysis (see Section 9.2). Second, knowledge flows from the *BRIC* countries are analysed by means of a Tobit model to control whether effects such as geographic and technological distance and cultural and language differences hinder knowledge diffusion or not. The focus in this chapter lies on the national efforts of the late-comer countries, and therefore, do not tackle the sector of biotechnology.

The remainder of this Chapter consists of the following parts. Section 9.1 outlines the hypotheses and delivers the rational of the role of late-comers in the international knowledge network. Section 9.2 gives an overview of the methodology of the regression model used to analyse influencing effects on knowledge transfer and spillover. Therefore, in this section, methods for the forward citation analysis are described, as well as the Tobit regression model. The empirical part of the analysis consists of a closer look at the citation links of technological late-comers (see Section 9.3) and the findings of the regression model testing the influences on knowledge transfer (see Section 9.4). Finally, Section 9.5 concludes.

9.1. Exploration of new international sources of knowledge

Emerging economies, such as the *BRIC*s, have been the focus of many economic analyses, but they are rarely considered as sources of knowledge. To establish constant economic development, countries need to build up a knowledge-based economy. Policy makers of the *BRIC*s are also aware of these effects of knowledge on economy. The creation of technology parks and the support of R&D facilities and universities were just a few efforts to strengthen their *NIS* and, in the case of scientific output, these efforts already seem to be fruitful. As previous chapters show, late-comer countries have rising innovation activities and also become visible with regard to international patent activities (see Chapter 4). Krawczyk et al. (2007) address the topic of late-comer knowledge and their relevance within the global technology competition.

By analysing the publication activities it has been shown that especially in Asian countries the scientific publication output experienced strong growth rates. Furthermore, patent activities, in particular from China and India, were not only recorded at national patent offices, but also increasingly at patent offices abroad, such as the EPO. This is also affirmed by the empirical analysis of this work (see Chapter 4). Hence, the *BRIC* countries have begun to build up their own knowledge stock. On the one hand, these efforts boost competitive pressure on the developed countries. On the other hand, the developed countries might, in turn, profit from knowledge flows generated by the *BRIC*s. Moreover, developed countries should not only keep their interest in the economic development of the *BRIC*s, but also observe the development of their knowledge-stock. For the last reason, it is more and more important to understand how knowledge of late-comer countries spreads to other countries.

To understand the effects of knowledge spillover from late-comer countries, traditional views on these spillovers can be considered. The Asian countries, for instance, have a high geographic distance to the developed countries, which might have an influence on the spillover of knowledge. Krugman (1991) and later on Audretsch and Feldman (1996) argued that technology transfer can be influenced by geographic distances. Furthermore, it can also be assumed that language, cultural, and technological differences can hinder technology transfer. In regard to innovation, in general, Boschma (2005) also argued that proximity plays a crucial role. He stated that innovation needs certain levels of proximities and refers to five different dimensions of proximities, namely cognitive, organizational, social, institutional and geographical proximity. In particular, geographical proximities influence innovation activities as it is responsible for spatial externalities. Thus, there is a higher likelihood that developed countries use knowledge generate in Russia compared to the other *BRIC* countries, because Russia has a higher proximity to the developed countries in several dimensions (e.g. geographic distance, language etc.). The research question of this Chapter, therefore, is also separated into two hypotheses. Firstly, as a preliminary examination the first hypothesis is:

Hypothesis 5a: Late-comers develop to a source of international knowledge flows.

Subsequently, the second hypothesis is formulated as an additional analysis to the first examination. It can be stated as follows:

Hypothesis 5b: Influences on knowledge flows originating from these countries are based on geographical and technological closeness, as well as cultural similarities and a close language background.

For the examination of the second hypothesis a Tobit regression model is used. The components of this model are explained in detail in the next section.

9.2. Effects on knowledge transfer and spillover

Patent citation analysis is a proxy for measuring knowledge flows and technological spillover effects. This method is already used for the examination of external knowledge in Chapter 5. In this chapter, it is already explained that knowledge transfer and, in particular, spillover - the unintentional transfer of knowledge from one actor to another - is a key-driver of economic development (Krugman, 1991a).

Carpenter and Narin (1983), Schmoch (1993), and Jaffe et al. (1993) trace knowledge spillovers by analysing the origin of patent citations. In their works, they assumed that inventors are aware of cited patents. So, if they cite a certain patent, they know about the knowledge this patent is based upon. These approaches are validated by a later survey in Jaffe et al. (2000). The researchers showed that patent citations are a "noisy" indicator of knowledge flow which means that most of the inventors who cite another patent really know about the knowledge of the cited patent. All theoretical background of the topic of knowledge transfer is also described in detail in Section 5.2.

Analysing knowledge spillover effects

After the short review of knowledge flow analysis in general, this subsection introduces further examinations of the factors that influence spillovers. As influences on knowledge transfer can be manifold, this analysis contains a Tobit regression model to test different variables as well as their role in citation rates. Thus, the citation rate between two countries can be explained by using four distance values. Similar distances were also used by Bascavusoglu (2007) who analysed the effects on transfer of knowledge in emerging economies to other parts of the world. The underlying regression developed for our study is written as follows:

$$Cit_{ij} = \beta_0 + \beta_1 d_{geo,ij} + \beta_2 d_{tech,ij} + \beta_3 d_{lang,ij} + \beta_4 d_{cult,ij} + \sum_{ctry}^{BRIC} (\beta_{ctry}\, dum_{ctry}) + \varepsilon \quad (9\text{-}1)$$

As the knowledge flows from late-comer countries to other countries are explained in this model, the explained variable is the rate of patent citations denoted with Cit_{ij}. It stands for the citation of a patent from country *i* by a patent from country *j*. In this study patents from country *i* stands appear for the four *BRIC* countries, while patents from country *j* can originate all over the world. For the regression, a Tobit model was chosen, as all variables are non-negative and all explanatory variables are normalised. The explanatory variables are defined as follows.

First, the geographical distance between two countries $d_{geo,ij}$ is considered. The value $d_{geo,ij}$ is the normalised distance between the centres of two countries. It is calculated with the real distance $d_{geo-real,ij}$ and standardised between 0.0 and 1.0. It is denoted as:

$$d_{geo,ij} = (1 - \frac{d_{geo-real,ij}}{20{,}000\ km}) \tag{9-2}$$

A value of ‘1.0’ stands for countries which are close to each other and ‘0.0’ otherwise.

The second measure, $d_{tech,ij}$, represents the technological distance between two countries and is also used in Chapter 6 and is denoted as:

$$d_{tech,ij} = \frac{\sum_{n=1}^{N} p_{in} * p_{jn}}{\sqrt{\sum_{n=1}^{N} p_{in}^2 * \sum_{n=1}^{N} p_{jn}^2}} \tag{9-3}$$

The calculation of $d_{tech,ij}$ is taken from an approach used by Jaffe (1986). Two countries are determined to be quite similar regarding their technological progress if they have many patent applications in the same sector. Proximity, denoted $d_{tech} \approx 1.0$, refers here to technological similarity.

The third and fourth variables are variables to check the importance of language similarities and cultural bonding. Therefore two countries have $d_{lang,ij} = 1$, if their official language[63] is the same. Moreover, the cultural proximity $d_{cult,ij} = 1$ is defined by Huntington (1996), who categorised all cultures into different groups. According to this, two countries are culturally close to each other if they belong to the same group.

To increase model fit, it is also enriched by four control variables representing the four *BRIC* countries. In the regression model they are denoted as:

$$\sum_{ctry}^{BRIC} (\beta_{ctry}\, dum_{ctry}) \tag{9-4}$$

Lastly, for the analysis of knowledge transfer, forward citations are used. When conducting a forward citation analysis, one has to deal with a so-called 'time advance' of older patents. Since patents filed in 1986 have 20 years to receive citations and patents filed in the year 2000 just have five years, special consideration for this imbalance needs to be taken into account. Thus, a time window of five years after the patent application is used. This time window is also used by Trajtenberg (1990) who shows that citation numbers decline after five years. Hence, the findings of this chapter cover the time period between 1986 and 2000. This overall period is again separated into four periods to consider the development of the late-comers.

9.3. International knowledge flows of late-comer countries

First, general findings of the forward citations of late-comer patents are compared to the citation values of the overall citation values of all EPO and WIPO patents (see Table 9-1). The mean values of these patent citations range between 0.66 and 1.05 with relatively stable numbers, but a negative trend. In contrast, the late-comers have mean values with large differences. On the one hand, Brazil and Russia remain below the mean values of the EPO/WIPO until the last time period. On the other hand, China surpasses the values of the international benchmark for several times. In the majority of the cases, Indian patents are cited more often, and only in the first period, forward citation rates of these patents are below the global average.

An additional examination of each year shows that forward citations of patents with Indian involvement have mean values ranging between 0.60 and 2.11. They are cited twice as often as Brazilian ones (0.31 – 1.32). Chinese patents follow the negative trend of the world and begin with a mean value of 1.57, even decreasing to

[63] Source: CEPII (2006)

0.54 over time. Russian patents are cited least. Maximum numbers, on the other hand, increase over the 15 years. Hence, the quality level of certain patents of the late-comer countries seems to increase. Furthermore, there are international patents generated with *BRIC* involvement which are of importance regarding the invention of new technology.

		1986-1989	1990-1993	1994-1997	1998-2000
Brazil	mean	0.84	0.69	0.69	0.76
	max	9	18	24	22
China	mean	1.45	1.05	0.70	0.77
	max	16	16	24	28
India	mean	0.82	1.49	1.27	1.73
	max	9	18	30	48
Russia	mean	0.61	0.82	0.85	0.71
	max	18	16	26	52
EPO/WIPO	mean	1.05	1.02	0.91	0.66
	max	101	105	94	191

Table 9-1: Aggregate mean value and maximum citation numbers

The general trend illustrates that patents originating from the *BRIC*s, except for China, have increasing citation numbers. Compared to the international benchmark, Brazilian and Russian patent applications remain below the average. The Asian countries have different developments. India develops faster than the average and has outstanding rising citation numbers. In contrary, China's citation rate has a general decreasing trend, but it is almost in all periods above the global average. The observed decreasing trend for the mean values of the EPO/WIPO patents can be influenced by the high growth of international patent applications (see Section 4.2). The higher numbers of patent protection leads also to a higher number of insignificant patents which are also not cited frequently. Regarding this development the increase of the Indian patent citations are even more impressive.

International knowledge citation networks

The major part of the links between the late-comer countries and other countries can be reduced to a set of 25 countries (see Table 9-2). This set of links between countries contains more than 96% of all the links. Thus, further analyses are concentrated on these countries. Most of the links are to the USA and Germany. Both countries together are accountable for over one third of the citation linkages of the late-comer countries.

	Total amount	Share
USA	***1682.38***	***21.78***
Germany	***1018.56***	***13.19***
Great Britain	636.82	8.24
India	***574.36***	***7.44***
Japan	457.33	5.92
France	269.69	3.49
Netherlands	258.41	3.35
Russia	***204.15***	***2.64***
China	***189.35***	***2.45***
Italy	172.83	2.24
Switzerland	110.27	1.43
Belgium	105.96	1.37
Korea	99.11	1.28
Israel	91.67	1.19
Spain	84.13	1.09
Canada	77.60	1.00
Sweden	72.66	0.94
Finland	57.42	0.74
Brazil	***56.94***	***0.74***
Australia	53.63	0.69
Taiwan	45.75	0.59
Austria	41.98	0.54
Hong Kong	40.64	0.53
Denmark	36.10	0.47

Table 9-2: Top linked countries by total count and shares

Beside the international linkages, it is observable that late-comer countries also cite their own patents. Such inner linkages are generally very important. Inner linkages in Brazil account for 7.27 % of all linkages. This means that Brazilian inner linkages occupied forth place compared to all cited patents (see Appendix). These linkages ranked third in Russia (12.90 %) and China (9.87 %). India occupied second place with 14.52 % compared to all other linkages.

Figure 9-1 shows the connectivity between the late-comers and other countries from 1986-1989. The citation networks are separated into continents to give an overall impression of the late-comer connections and to keep the clearness of the network structure. All four countries are connected to 'Europe', 'North America', 'Asia,' and 'Australia and Oceania'. 'South America', however, is just connected to Russia. 'Africa' had no connections at all. Outstanding connections are the 'Russia-North America', 'Russia-Europe' and the 'China-North America' links. Interestingly, there are no connections between the *BRIC*s.

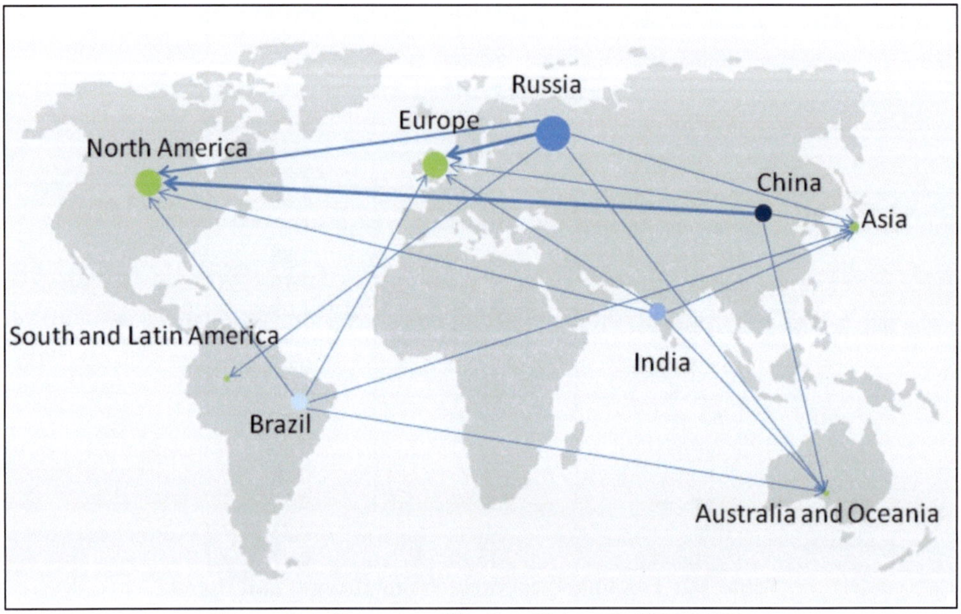

Figure 9-1: Inventor-Citation Network 1986-1989

Time period two and three already shows an increasing trend of the connections (see Figure 9-2, Figure 9-3 and Appendix). Particularly the connections to ‘North America’ and ‘Europe’ increase for all *BRIC*s. ‘Africa’ gain connections to Russia in the second time period and to Brazil in the third time period. Within the group of late-comer countries, Russia plays an important role as all late-comer connections have connections with Russia (Brazil and China in the second time period and Brazil, China and India in the third time period). Moreover, Brazil, China and India do not establish any connections with each other in these two time period.

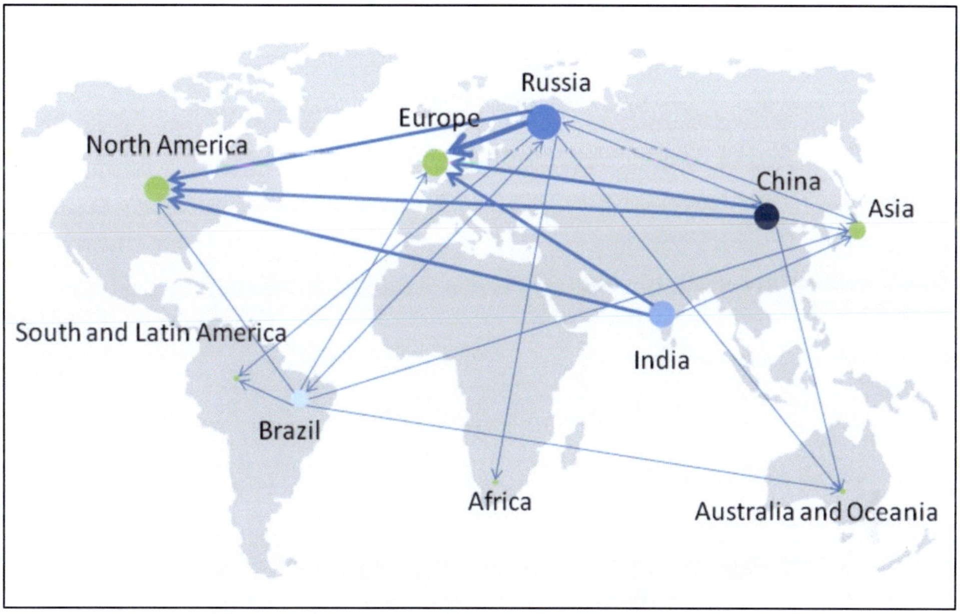

Figure 9-2: Inventor-Citation Network 1990-1993

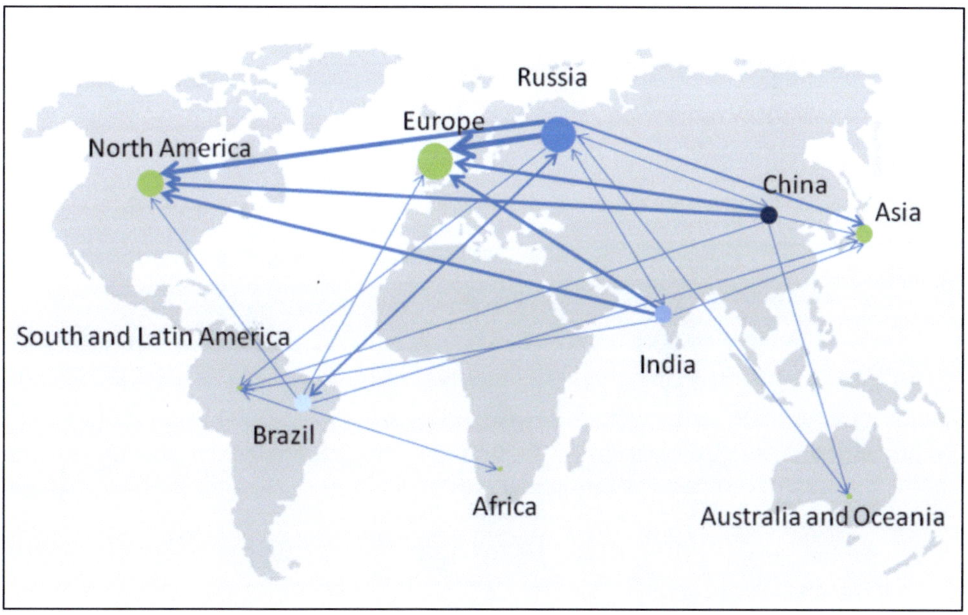

Figure 9-3: Inventor-Citation Network 1994-1997

Compared to the first period, the network of the last period grows dramatically (see Figure 9-4). All four countries are connected to each other and to nearly all parts of the world, except for the missing link between Russia and 'Africa'. India becomes the most connected country with strong connections to 'Europe' and 'North America'. For 'Asia', Indian knowledge also plays an important role. 'Australia and Oceania', 'Africa' and 'South America', however, just play a minor role. This finding holds also for China and Russia, although there are fewer connections than in India. Brazil has by far the least connections, which are mostly to 'Europe', 'North America' and 'Asia'.

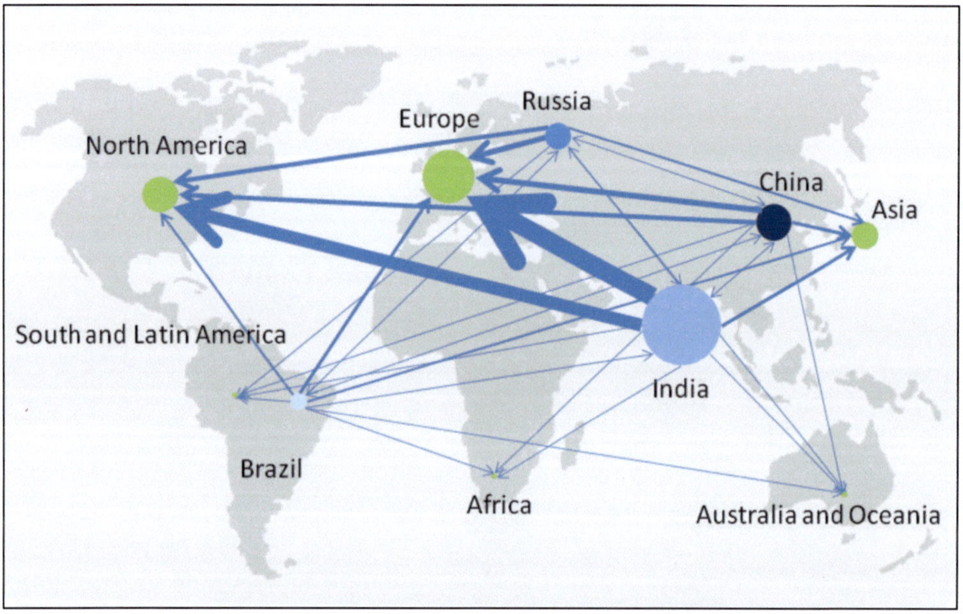

Figure 9-4: Inventor-Citation-Network 1998-2000

Comprising all four periods, the findings show that the late-comers get more and more linked to the rest of the world. 'Europe', 'North America' and 'Asia' are the major users of *BRIC* knowledge. Knowledge flows from these countries became more important. A detailed discussion of the findings for each late-comer country is, once again, given in the last section of this chapter.

9.4. Influences on international knowledge flows of the late-comer countries

The findings of the regression model (see Table 9-3) show that geographical distance and culture do not play an important role in citation activities, i.e., inventive activity using *BRIC* knowledge is not influenced by geographical or cultural differences. But, technological proximity and language differences do influence the transfer of knowledge. Both variables are highly significant. Although a precise statement about the intensity is not possible, one can see that the coefficients are positive and significant. To be exact: this means that technological proximity and common language foster spillover effects. These two influences may help to understand knowledge generated abroad. One reason can be the emerging role of absorptive capacities and related variety. Recent technology needs specialists to develop and it is more important to have a profound base of knowledge to use the current knowledge base (see Section 8.1). Hence, the role of geographic distance is declining, while the role of technological distance gets more important. Furthermore, it is necessary to prove whether these findings also hold for all time periods or not.

Dependent variable: Cit_{ij}	**1986-2000** **model**	**sigma**
d_{geo}	-3.988	
	(3.500)	
d_{tech}	34.85***	
	(3.270)	
d_{lang}	6.093***	
	(2.019)	
d_{cult}	-3.455	
	(2.874)	
dum_{BR}	-3.341**	
	(1.516)	
dum_{RU}	2.693**	
	(1.371)	
dum_{IN}	9.460***	
	(1.633)	
Constant	-27.90***	15.33***
	(3.267)	(0.455)
Observations	1440	1440

Standard errors in parentheses *** p<0.01, ** p<0.05, * p<0.1

Table 9-3: Tobit regression for 1986-2000

For the coefficients of the country controls, it needs to be expressed that country effects are also significant. This means that the citation rates are also influenced by effects of the late-comer countries themselves which are not taken into account in this regression model. These effects can be manifold. One important reason are differences in the levels of innovative activity of these countries. Moreover topics of this thesis discussed in the previous chapters, such as specialisation and diversification patterns (see Chapter 6 and Chapter 7) may also influence citation rates.

Change over time

The separation of the data into different time periods show that the significant effects of the total regression are not persistent over time and that, in particular, the control variables are also just important in the last periods (see Table 9-4).

Dependent variable: Cit_{ij}	1986-1989 model	1986-1989 sigma	1990-1993 Model	1990-1993 sigma	1994-1997 model	1994-1997 sigma	1998-2000 model	1998-2000 sigma
d_{geo}	-1.176		-2.660		-2.695		-15.20*	
	(2.421)		(2.899)		(3.165)		(9.174)	
d_{tech}	14.30***		11.46***		18.61***		39.75***	
	(2.587)		(2.967)		(3.087)		(7.981)	
d_{lang}	2.139		1.715		2.181		18.47***	
	(1.422)		(1.834)		(1.872)		(5.237)	
d_{cult}	-3.484*		-0.0540		0.194		-1.409	
	(2.041)		(2.561)		(2.595)		(7.365)	
dum_{BR}	-0.136		-1.622		-0.178		-12.38***	
	(0.999)		(1.295)		(1.344)		(4.188)	
dum_{RU}	1.085		2.217*		4.542***		0.401	
	(0.910)		(1.168)		(1.224)		(3.711)	
dum_{IN}	2.284*		1.294		2.722*		23.03***	
	(1.218)		(1.364)		(1.474)		(4.423)	
Constant	-11.42***	4.921***	-9.273***	6.442***	-13.76***	7.224***	-19.12**	20.39***
	(2.387)	(0.360)	(2.690)	(0.446)	(2.960)	(0.407)	(8.860)	(1.036)
Observations	384	384	384	384	384	384	288	288

Standard errors in parentheses *** p<0.01, ** p<0.05, * p<0.1

Table 9-4: Tobit regression for citation time periods

The first impression of the effects of geographical and cultural distance is confirmed by the separation of the analysis into different time periods (see Table 9-4). The coefficient of the geographical distance just has a significant negative effect at a level of 90% in the last time period. Cultural distance in this respect has a significant negative effect on the same level in the first period. This means that a closer geographical distance leads to a lower citation rate. Hence, both distances have just a light effect on patent citations and do not play an important role over the whole time period. Both have negative effects on citation rates when significance is detectable. Although this effect is just very low, it implicates that in the first period cultural similarity influences citation rates negatively (-3.484).

On the contrary, it is possible to see an increasing positive effect of technological distance. The coefficients increased from 14.30 to 39.75. These values are also highly significant. Although it is not possible to examine the values of this development over time with a Tobit regression, it is still possible to assume that there is a change of importance within these periods. Hence, technological similarity is getting more and more important.

Regarding the impact of language patterns, an interesting change over time can be seen. A significant positive influence on spillover is only measured during the last period. This implies that language similarities are important for citation rates and, hence, the same language background can improve knowledge spillover. However, this effect can be caused by the high amount of Indian patents and the citations of such patents. Therefore, this may not be the reason of any similar language, but the ability to speak English.

Finally, the control variables show that their effects are also just significant in one period each. Country effects of Brazil and India appear in the last period. The reason can refer to the enormous rise of Asian patents at the end of the 1990s (see Chapter 4). The non-persistent role of the country variables, however, implies that country effects just play an inferior role and do not have a permanent effect on the citation rates, such as the effect of technological distance.

9.5. Acquiring late-comer knowledge

The analysis of the *BRIC* countries shows very different findings for each country. Although all countries had astonishing economic growth rates, they played different roles in the global technology competition. The analysis of knowledge transfer illustrated that the *BRIC*s became more and more connected to all parts of the world. In most cases, 'Europe', 'North America' and 'Asia' have used *BRIC* knowledge. Furthermore, connections within every country were very important. Connections to each other, however, are still very low. For each country the following findings can be summarised.

Brazil

Brazilian patents play a minor role in the global citation network. They have the lowest citation numbers and the connections going out of Brazil are also very low. Most of their connections can be found in links with 'Europe'. Interestingly, the connections with 'Europe' even exceed connections to 'North America' and 'South America', although their geographical distance is much closer than the distance to Europe. One reason can be the high numbers of European subsidiary company and their spin-offs, such as Volkswagen and Bosch.

China

Inventions with Chinese origin are more frequently cited than Brazilian ones, and rates are nearly as high as rates of the EPO/WIPO patents. These citations are first mainly driven by citations of patents from 'North America'. In the last time period, however, the most connections are with 'Europe'. Thus, European inventors profit the most from Chinese knowledge. Again, it is interesting that the most connections are not established with countries and parts of the world which are geographically closer to China. In the case of China, this finding is even more remarkable as two highly innovative countries, namely Japan and Korea, are close neighbours. These two countries do not profit from their geographical closeness. This can be caused by political and historical effects, as Japan and China still have political differences since the Second World War.

India

Indian patent citation activities have a positive development. Except from the first time period, their citation rates are all above the global average. Furthermore, India also profits the most from late-comer patents as they are ranked at the fourth place in ranking of users of late-comer knowledge (see Table 9-2). The most linkages are shared by two parts of the world, namely 'North America' and 'Europe', in the first three periods. It is until the last time period when Indian knowledge becomes more important for 'Europe' than for 'North America'. As language similarities also become very important, this result leads to the implication that English speaking countries profit the most from Indian knowledge. In particular, this effect can also be strengthened by the political backgrounds, such as the Commonwealth membership of India and, therefore, a stronger co-operation and migration of Indian scientists or qualified workers.

Russia

Russian patents, as well as Brazilian ones, also receive lower citation numbers. They even start with the lowest citation rate. This may be caused by political differences between the former Eastern Bloc and the Western countries. However, Russia's strongest linkages are with 'Europe' over almost all time periods. For the first time period, an advantage of geographical closeness appears. This effect may be the reason of the strong knowledge sourcing activities of Europe in general.

Influences on knowledge spillovers

As a general result of the regression model, it is possible to conclude that language similarities, but in particular technological proximity influence the use of *BRIC* knowledge. But, while the importance of technological proximity rises in each period, language influences only play an important role within the last time periods. As aforementioned, this effect may be caused by the strong increase of Indian linkages and, therefore, influenced by linkages of countries with English language backgrounds. However, both important influences refer to the topic of absorptive capacity and it again emphasises the necessity to generate absorptive capacities and strong *NIS*. Culture and geographical distance, however, do not have any important effects on the use of *BRIC* knowledge. In particular, the vanishing of geographical distance is a result of the ongoing globalisation. Moreover, the usage of modern information and communication technology seems to support diffusion of knowledge all over the world.

BRIC application numbers are rising. Their technology pool is growing and they are also gaining importance. In particular, Indian and Chinese technologies gain attention during the last years. However, in some respects, they still lag behind the global level. Especially Russia and Brazil still have to catch up with global technological leaders. India and China, on the other hand, are a pool of technology and can also become more and more important for future knowledge acquisition. The end of the examined period still delivers specialised and concentrated technological profiles for the late-comers (see Chapter 6 and Chapter 7). This also means that spillover effects can still increase with further diversification efforts of these countries.

10. Profiles of ascending late-comers

This chapter is the last step of the analysis of technological late-comers. It does not introduce new empirical analysis and findings. In fact, it gathers the results and findings of all preceding chapters and delivers an overview and discussion on these results. Additionally, an overall picture of the technological catch-up process is drawn to evaluate the catch-up process of the four late-comer countries. Thus, this chapter consists of two parts. First, it summarises results the previous analysis. Moreover, by bringing together the analytical steps, the late-comer countries are classified in order to their stage of technological catch-up (see Subsection 4.4). Hence, each country is discussed in detail. Second, as the Asian late-comer countries have a more successful catch-up than the other two countries, this chapter analyse the general scheme of the catch-up process to show the differences between each late-comer country. Therefore, it highlights the specific characteristics of each country's innovation activity in one scheme (see Section 10.6) and evaluates them in respect of their influence on the technological catch-up process. In particular, it aims on an evaluation of the factors which enables Asian late-comer countries to have an efficient technological catch-up.

The structure of this chapter is composed as follows. The next section introduces some theoretical background to the topic of the ascension of late-comers and the necessity to detect patterns for successful catch-up processes (see Section 10.1). Afterwards, the findings of the late-comers is summarised for each country and discussed in detail. Therefore, each late-comer country is dedicated a section to highlight their specific characteristics (see Section 10.2: Brazil, Section 10.3: China, Section 10.4: India and Section 10.5: Russia). Finally, the results are drawn together in matrix scheme to deliver a brief overview and to evaluate the patterns of the catch-up process (see Section 10.6).

10.1. Learning from patterns of success

In the global competition national economies attempt to push economic growth and development. Well-developed economies try to preserve economic prosperity and wealth, while developing economies try to foster their economic catch-up. In recent years, rising countries, such as the *BRIC* countries, have experienced remarkable economic growth rates which are mainly driven by their exports of consumer goods, raw materials and resources (see Section 4.3). However, these are not the main factors of sustainable development (see Section 2.3), but they are a starting point and can be an important difference for a successful economic catch-up process. The difference between a successful catch-up story and the fail of such process has been the topic of many research works. In particular, these works attempt to identify specific factors for a successful catch-up. It is often stated that for the economic catch-up process it is crucial to drive the constitution of a profound knowledge base and the capability to introduce new technological. In fact, these are the main reasons for the catch-up of Germany in the period between the World Wars and these are also the driving forces for the ascension of Japan after post-war era (Fagerberg and Srholec, 2005). These two countries are just examples for successful economic catch-up processes. Their success stories drive other economies to copy these economic catching-up stories. After their rise, there were other countries which had successful catch-up processes and establish in the global technology competition, such as the Finland, Korea and Taiwan (Hobday et al., 2004 and Fagerberg and Srholec, 2005). Although other factors play important roles in the economic catch-up of developing countries, it is often stated knowledge and technology is the most important factor. It is even named as a 'must' to economical catch-up processes (Fagerberg and Srholec, 2005, p. 69). In these works, however, the development of the technological base and the development of innovation capabilities are not tackled in detail. It is not negligible that the construction of an effective knowledge base and a stable technological pool also runs through a catch-up process, namely the technological catch-up.

Economic catch-up and technological catch-up

Similar to the analyses of economic catch-up processes this chapter aims on a detailed reflection of different factors of technological catch-up. As some late-comers are more successful compared to other late-comers this chapter attempts to shed light on this differences. Zhang (2009), for instance, describes different technological catch-up processes of late-comer firms. Her work shows that certain profiles of catch-up processes of late-comers are more successful on firm-level. Moreover, Altenburg et al. 2008) shows that Asian late-comer countries are also more successful in their catch-up processes than others. However, a profound analysis of the patterns of technological catch-up, as well as the combination of different analytical methods to evaluate these catch-up processes is still missing. This chapter aims to close this gap. For doing so, it brings together all analytical steps of this thesis. The last step of this thesis, therefore, examines the following statement:

Hypothesis 6: Successful technological late-comers follow certain steps in their catch-up process. They develop towards early-movers in respect of technological diversification, centrality, niche strategies and scientific linkages. Hence, successful technological late-comers follow specific patterns of success.

This statement summarises all considerations of the preceding chapters and, therefore, is the main research question for this thesis.

10.2. Brazil: Early stages of innovation activities

Although innovation policy has a long tradition in Brazilian history and many efforts have been made to improve the conditions for innovative activities, the findings of this thesis show that innovation activities are still at an early stage. This also concurs with the work of other researchers who also express that Brazil is still far away from achieving constant economic growth rates through technological progress (Lattimore and Kowalski, 2008).

10.2.1. Abridge of the *Brazilian Innovation System*

Brazilian technology, namely Brazilian patent applications, use external knowledge to a higher extend than new technology generated in the early-mover countries. They cite other patents more than early-movers do, but they do not cite non-patent literature in higher frequency. In fact, that shows that new technology from Brazil still needs more external knowledge, but interestingly, they refer more to technological knowledge than scientific knowledge. Thus, innovation from Brazil is not based on scientific knowledge.

In regard to niche strategies, Brazil does not show clear focuses on niches, on a general level. The similarity values (*Cosine Index*) reflect that Brazil develops towards the German technology profile, while its similarity with the USA has no clear trend. Its technology profile (RSTA) also correlates with the German one and not with the US technology profile. The findings of the same chapter also show that Brazil specialisation sectors are 'agriculture, food chemistry', 'chemical industry and petrol industry, basic materials chemistry', 'materials processing, textiles and paper', 'engines, pumps and turbines' and 'materials and metallurgy'. The technological strength reflects the industrial structure of the country (see Section 4.3).

The analysis of the diversification patterns shows that on national level the diversification of Brazil describes a positive development. The diversification value reflects Brazil's efforts towards are more diversified technology portfolio. Although the diversification is still significantly different compared to the early-movers, a positive trend is observable between 1986 and 2005. The examination of the diversification with the indicator of relative diversification also shows that a general trend of diversification towards the group of early-movers can be observed. Thus, diversification efforts are detectable in Brazil, but it is still not in the phase of an established innovation system.

The examination of the role of Brazilian patents in the global technology network shows that they just play a minor role. They have the lowest citation numbers. Most of their connections can be found in links with 'Europe'. Interestingly, the connections with 'Europe' even exceed connections to 'North America' and 'South America', although their geographical distance is much closer than the distance to Europe.

10.2.2. Biotechnology in Brazil: A neglected knowledge-intensive sector

The use of external knowledge in the Brazilian biotechnology sector is not significantly higher compared to the early-movers. It even shows mean values close to the citation rates of the US biotechnology sector.

The analysis of niche strategies shows that within the Brazilian biotechnology sector a trend of niche occupation is traceable. The focus, hereby, lies on 'macromolecular chemistry and polymers'. Although Brazil has other specialisation areas, this is a focus where the USA has no comparative advantage. Furthermore, it can be stated that the biotechnology sectors of Brazil, especially in the last period, do not correlate with the US one. Hence, the Brazilian biotechnology sector has its technological activities in some niches.

The diversification development of the Brazilian biotechnology sector is very unsteady regarding absolute and relative measurements. Although a light trend to a more diversified biotechnological sector is indicated by both indicators a clear diversification trend is not observable. This is also caused by the low numbers of Brazilian biotechnology patents.

The most important analysis for the biotechnology sector is the analysis of its sectoral network (see Chapter 8). The findings of this analysis illustrates that Brazil is still at the beginning of the construction of a functioning innovation network. External linkages are still very common and Brazilian biotechnology players just have few linkages with each other. The group of main players are a mixture of firms and public institutes. Their *degree centrality* values are still different to top players of the USA, but *betweenness centrality* values already changed. Top players of Brazil, therefore, are also very likely to be on shortest paths between certain other actors and players. Furthermore, the inventor network describes an unstable development. Most of the network characteristics are still different to the US network.

10.2.3. Brazilian initial technological capabilities

All findings indicate that Brazil is still on an initial level in their innovation activities. They cite other patents more frequently than early-movers, but they do not cite more non-patent literature. This indicates that the scientific linkage in Brazil is on a low level. In case of knowledge-intensive technologies, such as the biotechnology, the link to scientific work is essential. Thus, the missing linkages induce that the Brazilian knowledge-base is still not well-developed. This finding is confirmed by the results of the network analysis. Although the main players of the Brazilian biotechnology sectors consist of firms and public institutes, the players in this sector still have most of its linkages with foreign players. This means that the capabilities of Brazilian innovators still need to develop.

Compared to the other late-comer countries Brazil show a weak focus on certain technological specialisations at the beginning of their catch-up process. As aforementioned, Brazil has a long history of innovation policy. This tradition, however, has not enabled Brazil with the experience to concentrate their catch-up process on certain sectors which is more helpful at the beginning of a catch-up process. In contrary, a positive effect is implicated by the diversification efforts at the end of the analysed period. With the rise of patent activities at the end of the 1990s the patent portfolio also diversifies which shows that new innovators on Brazil also spread their innovation activities. At least, this is a positive sign for up-coming innovation activities.

All findings implicates that Brazil needs further innovation policy efforts to strengthen the *NIS*. In particular, it needs to push their efforts regarding education and training of skilled labour forces to build up more absorptive capacities and basic knowledge. This enables Brazil to build up a profound knowledge base and also leads to new national sources of new knowledge. Moreover, the current status of Brazil also implies that a clear focus at this stage would be more useful.

10.3. China: Construction of *a Chinese Innovation System*

The 'working bench' of the world has gained economic and financial power since the opening of its economy in 1978. For more the first twenty years after the opening China has been associated with imitation rather than with innovation. The enduring effort to acquiring new technologies since the beginning of the 1980s pays-off since the beginning of the new millennium. The defined long-term plans, to catch up with the developed countries, already worked out for the initial stage of an efficient innovation system. Technological capabilities of China increase steadily and the output of new technology in certain sectors shows that in global technology competition developed countries has to be aware of Chinese competitors. Export shares of the high-technology sector, for instance, could constantly rise up to 30.6% of the total exports.

10.3.1. Abridge of the *Chinese Innovation System*

Chinese patent applications show that at the beginning of the technological activities the use of external knowledge was higher than in the early-mover countries. This finding holds for citation of patents and non-patent literature. In the course of time a positive development is observable, as this higher use of external knowledge was declining at the end of the examined period. Interestingly, this finding does not hold for the use of non-patent literature what shows that Chinese technology still uses more scientific knowledge. However, a positive development is not deniable. In the mid1980s Chinese technology built on external knowledge, but later on it develops a more independent innovation environment.

The analysis of Chinese niche strategies, it is possible to say that the Chinese specialisation profile moves towards the US one, while its similarity to Germany decreases. Outstanding focuses are on the sectors of 'telecommunications', 'consumer goods and equipment', 'audiovisual technology', 'electrical machinery, apparatus and electrical energy' and 'agriculture and food chemistry'. While China has changing specialisation profiles between 1986 and 1995, it stabilised its focus afterwards and show a clear concentration on consumer goods and electronic devices, such as 'audiovisual technology' and 'electrical machinery and apparatus, electrical energy'. A niche strategy is not clearly observable, although a clear specialisation focus has been established.

The finding of the diversification analysis for China shows that it has the most unclear patterns of national diversification during the last years. While in the first years a stagnating diversification is indicated, the last years have a strong falling diversification. This can be referred to rising activities of upcoming MNEs in China which has still has their main fields of activities, such as *Lenovo* and *Huawei*. The examination also shows that China also has a significant different diversification level as the two early-movers and, thus, is also still on the way to a more diversified innovation system regarding its technological output. Hence, China still needs to diversify.

According to the last analysis of this thesis, it can be stated that Chinese knowledge are more frequently cited than Brazilian ones, and they have citation rates which are comparable with the EPO/WIPO patents. Only in between 1994 and 1997, the citation rates of Chinese patents are below the rates of the global benchmark what show that their patents are highly visible in the global technology competition. These citations are mainly driven by citations of patents from 'North America' in the first time periods and then move towards 'Europe'. Inventors and innovators from Europe profit the most from Chinese knowledge. Interestingly the most connections are not established with countries and parts of the world which are geographically closer to China. Although there are two highly innovative countries which are situated close to China, namely Japan and Korea, the most connections are still with Europe.

10.3.2. Chinese beginning efforts in biotechnology

China's biotechnology sector shows a changing biotechnological profile and no clear focus on US biotechnology niches. However, especially between 2001 and 2005, a similarity to the USA can be observed.

The diversification analysis of the biotechnology sector illustrates a positive development for this knowledge-intensive sector. Although there is still a difference between the diversification levels of China and the USA, a more converging trend towards the USA is apparent. The *KSI* index visualises this development, showing that over the twenty years a convergence to the USA cannot be denied. Political efforts, in particular those efforts that address science and technology, can push certain sectors of the so-called transformation economies.

Regarding the network activities of the Chinese biotechnology the results illustrates that foreign linkages, at the beginning of the examined time period, are still on a high level. In the course of time, China achieves to decreasing their external linkages and reaches the level of the USA. Top players of this sector are mainly public institutes and universities. Hence, the biotechnology sector is still state-driven. The *degree centralities* are already on a high level, but *betweenness centralities* are still very different to top players of the USA. This means, the top players have an important function within their networks, but other players are also interacting with each other. Finally, the examination of the inventor network shows that the network structure is still on a level different to the USA. Hence, the exchange of knowledge within their network is not as efficient as in an early-mover network.

10.3.3. Heading towards an innovation-driven economy

The findings imply that the *Chinese Innovation System* is ascending. Efforts of the central government are fruitful. The construction of an innovation-driven economy, which was the long-run objective, is on the way to become reality. The innovation system describes many positive developments. In particular, the use of external knowledge at the beginning of the catch-up process and the decreasing numbers in the course of time show that innovation capacity is developing. The higher rate of scientific linkages is a positive sign for the use of new scientific knowledge and a well-developed scientific base. This is also indicated by the findings of the network analysis, as the most important players in the Chinese biotechnology are mainly research institutes and universities. In this respect China is much more developed than Brazil.

The results of the niche strategies, however, leave negative impressions on the catch-up process of China. Since the beginning of the catch-up process, no clear focus on certain specialisation niches can be found. Furthermore, the findings of the diversification analysis also do not draw a clear development. In these two cases the central government still needs to push their efforts.

Nevertheless, Chinese technology is highly visible in the global technology competition. This shows that China is already on the right way to establish an innovation-driven economy. In the past, the central government was able to use its financial opportunities of the strong economic growth and led the innovation system into the right direction. The Chinese biotechnology sector reflects these positive effects of political intervention. For sure, China is still not at the same level of the early-movers and there is still a lag to the technological frontier, but it shows aspects of a successful developments. The next steps are some more efforts to occupy technological niches and subsequently more efforts to broaden the technological base. However, the decision-makers in China are aware of the role of knowledge and technology, it is just a matter of time that it also begins to diversify in other sectors and, hence, broaden the focus of the whole *NIS*.

10.4. India: A source of new technological knowledge

According to Intellectual Property Rights (IPR), India is a late-starter compared to countries such as Brazil. After the 1970s the Indian government recognised that they had to strengthen their efforts to push Indian economic development. These efforts are still reflected by current programs of the Ministry of Science & Technology which focus on R&D-intensive sectors, such as 'biotechnology', 'space and nuclear science' (see Section 4.3). However, the development of the *NIS* shows that efforts are worth the endeavours which have been invested over the last decades. Although the *Indian Innovation System* is still developing, examinations reflect that India is on the right way to catch-up with early-mover countries.

10.4.1. Abridge of the *Indian Innovation System*

India's use of external knowledge has the highest level among all late-comers. Indian innovators exploit external knowledge successfully. Furthermore, they do not just use technological knowledge, but also scientific knowledge, which is represented by citations of patents and non-patent literature of Indian patent applications. In contrary to China, the exploitation of external knowledge does not decrease in the course of time. This implicates that India is still exploiting external knowledge sources.

The Indian specialisation focuses illustrates that India has the strongest characteristics of niche strategies among the late-comer countries. This can be observed for the general technology profile and the biotechnology one. The Indian

Cosine Index shows the strongest differences to the USA, as well as to Germany. These findings are also confirmed by the *RSTA*. The Indian specialisation profile is the most persistent one within the *BRICs*. The most strongest sectors of India are 'agriculture, food chemistry', 'chemical industry and petrol industry, basic materials chemistry', 'pharmaceuticals, cosmetics', 'organic fine chemistry' and 'biotechnology'.

As a result of the strong niche occupation, India's diversification is the least developed one. Its diversification values on a national level, measured by absolute and relative indicators, are still under-exploited. Although the *DIV* and the *KSI* show that India diversifies in absolute and relative manners rapidly between 1986 and 1994, this increasing trend just holds for the beginning of the examined time period. The technological diversification even decreases after 1994 and stagnates at the end of the 1990s until 2005. Hence, India's diversification process is also in development and has to improve yet. The analysis reveals that it has a strong focus on certain sectors and needs to leave this specialisation, if it wants to establish within the global technology competition.

Indian patent citation activities have the most impressive development among the late-comers. Except from the first time period, their citation rates are all above the global average. Indian knowledge is highly visible in the global technology competition. The most linkages are shared by two parts of the world, namely 'North America' and 'Europe'. It is until the last time period when Indian knowledge becomes more important for 'Europe' than for 'North America'. As language similarities also become very important, this result leads to the implication that English speaking countries profit the most from Indian knowledge.

10.4.2. Indian biotechnology: a sector on the fast lane

The biotechnology sector in India is already on a mature level. This result is backed by all findings of the preceding chapters. The level of external knowledge, for instance, in this sector is lower than in all other late-comer countries and already reached a level which is similar to the German biotechnology sector. The examination of different time periods also shows that the exploitation of external knowledge is decreasing.

The specialisation profiles show that India's biotechnology sector also has a very consistent profile and it shows stronger focuses on lesser sectors. Its specialisation sectors within the biotechnology occupy niches, for instance, the sector of 'environmental technology' and 'macromolecular chemistry and polymers'.

The diversification analysis does not reflect a consistent process of India's biotechnology sector, but the *KSI* shows that India is very well approaching to the US biotechnology sector. Such development implies that positive diversification processes in this sector is detectable. As biotechnology is also a long-run core issue of India's science and technology policy, the diversification trend and, hence, the establishment of this sector is in process.

India has more foreign linkages than China. Though these linkages are decreasing, India still has comparatively much foreign collaboration. The group of main players are a mixture of firms and public institutes which is different to China where the top innovation leaders are still directly supported by the government. The *degree centralities* of these players are still different to the USA, while *betweenness centralities* are already not significantly different. This leads to the implication that Indian innovators do not play a comparable central role, as they do in the USA. The Indian inventor network is also still on a different level compared to the USA, but it is also more stable than the ones of Brazil and Russia. Like the Chinese biotechnology sector, the Indian one still needs time and political support to establish an efficient innovation network. An advantage of the Indian network is more important role of firms in the group of main players. The future development of these firms is crucial for an efficient Indian innovation network.

10.4.3. A rising innovation power in the global technology competition

Indian innovation activities describe the most impressive development within the group of late-comer countries. The findings of this work show that not only patent numbers are rising. The *Indian Innovation System* has also undergone many important steps within the technological catch-up process. In particular, the use of external knowledge begun with higher rates of citations, but the biotechnology sector in India has already reached the level of the early-movers. Additionally, Indian technology efforts also focused on niche strategies which also helped to accelerate the technological catch-up process. Niche strategies are even observable for the general analysis and on sectoral level for the biotechnology sector.

Despite of the positive development according to the use of external knowledge and occupation of niches, the *Indian Innovation System* needs some further activities concerning diversification and networking. Especially, the diversification activities described a stagnating development. This stagnation can result from different effects. First, India's decision-makers want to focus on so-called future technologies which are assumed to drive future economic development (see Section 7.4). For the initial stage of the technological catch-up process this strategy is also the most feasible one. Nevertheless, India has to improve its strategy as it needs to diversify to establish itself within the technological competition. On a sectoral level this diversification is already visible. The biotechnology sector shows a diversification profile which is developing towards the US biotechnology sector.

According to the results India is improving its innovation capabilities. This is also illustrated by the citation of Indian knowledge also points out that India is becoming a future innovation power. Indian decision-makers have done well in many aspects. For sure, the development of the *Indian Innovation System* has not finished yet, but in some sectors it already reached a competitive level. All findings indicate that India is on the verge to establish an efficient innovation system and an innovation-driven economy.

10.5. Russia: resting on the laurel's of the Soviet legacy

In the late 1980s and the beginning of the 1990s Russia faced tremendous political changes. The transition from the former Soviet Union to the Russian Federation overthrew some established institutional structures. The state-run research and technology activities, once the biggest rival of the USA during the Cold War, were neglected and lost their importance. The Russian government reduced, for instance, the investing into innovation activities and state-controlled innovation efforts at the time of transition to a minimum. Government-funded innovation activities remained at a low level limited by the small public budget (see Section 4.3). Nowadays the main players of the Russia economy are dominated by huge firms from the resources sector.

10.5.1. Abridge of the *Russian Innovation System*

The empirical analysis shows that external knowledge plays no decisive role to Russian innovation in respect of citations of patents. The average of citations of other patents has the lowest level within the whole group of analysis. In contrary, the use of scientific knowledge is on a higher level compared to the early-movers. These findings hold for the whole period of time. A decreasing trend of the use of scientific knowledge is not observable. This indicates that Russia is still exploiting knowledge from scientific works. Its technological innovations rely on a scientific base.

Niche strategy plays a major role in Russian innovation activities. The Russian similarity examination delivers findings which are different compared to the other late-comers, as it develops towards both early-movers. Regarding the RSTA, the development of the specialisation sectors shows that the portfolio does not change dramatically. It even becomes more consistent in the course of time. Russia's specialisation profile has its focus on 'nuclear engineering', 'materials and metallurgy', 'chemical engineering', 'space technology and weapons' and 'environmental technology'.

At first glance, Russia has the highest degree of diversification on a national level among the late-comer group. In particular, the diversification values may imply a relatively well developed technological diversification. The statistical test, however, reveals that the Russian diversification is still not on the same level as the ones of the early-movers. The *KSI* also delivers still existing differences in the Russian diversification patterns compared to the early-movers. Further diversification efforts occur at the beginning of the 1990s after the fall of the Soviet Union.

Russian patents just receive a low rate of patent citation compared to the early-movers, but also to the Asian late-comers. They even start with the lowest citation rate. Thus, the visibility of Russian patents just plays a minor role in the global patent competition. Russia's strongest linkages are with 'Europe' over almost all time periods. For the first time period, an advantage of geographical closeness appears. This effect may be the reason of the strong knowledge sourcing activities of Europe in general.

10.5.2. Russia's biotechnology sector: missing efforts in upcoming technologies

The use of external knowledge in the Russian biotechnology is higher compared to the USA. It shows that Russian biotechnology is still in an early stage of development. This is also reflected by the small numbers of Russian biotechnology patent applications.

The Russian biotechnology sector develops a profile of certain specialisation and shows patterns of occupation of niches. Outstanding specialisations are, for instance, in the fields of 'environmental technology' and 'civil engineering, building and mining'. These few specialisations show, once more, that the Russian biotechnology is still on a low level of activities.

Diversification patterns in the Russian biotechnology sector are, in fact, increasing for the diversification values and the *KSI*. However, the diversification in both terms, namely absolute and relative diversification, is still lagging behind the USA. This results from the lack of governmental support to this knowledge-intensive sector. It is of Russia's interest to change these missing efforts, if it wants to catch-up with the early-movers.

The examination of the innovation networks in the Russian biotechnology sector reveals that it is the most backwarding one within the group of late-comers. The number of external linkages increased between 1986 and 2000. The high level of foreign linkages did not decrease until the last period. However, Russia has just very few linkages at all. The top players of the Russian biotechnology sector are private persons who have very different *degree centralities* and *betweenness centralities* compared to the biotechnology sector of the USA. The inventor network also reveals an unstable development. The different development of the external linkages, compared to the other late-comers, can result from the breakdown of the Soviet Union and the efforts to link to foreign innovators after the opening of the former Eastern Bloc. In general, these findings illustrates that the biotechnology sector in Russia is stagnating sector and needs tremendous efforts to catch up with the US one. The lack of main players plays a crucial role for inefficient innovation network.

10.5.3. National innovation activities with needs for a turn-around

The analysis of Russia in the global technology competition does not deliver promising results for the current status of the *Russian Innovation System*. The only positive finding is the occupation of technological niches. Russian innovation activities concentrate in niches of the early-movers. Findings of the other examinations, however, illustrates that Russia do not spend much efforts to push their innovation system. They rely on the technological legacy of the Soviet Union. In particular, they do not use external knowledge to higher extend, diversification is not developing in the last years and innovation network has an unstable development. As a result Russian technology is not cited frequently. All these facts show that Russia has not reached the stage of an established innovation system yet. Moreover, it even needs to give their efforts to foster innovation a new start. In this case, the transfer of more external knowledge can be initiated and a construction of knowledge-base and innovation environment, including the training of qualified human resources, absorptive capacities and the construction of efficient research institutes can be enforced.

In general it can be concluded for Russia that many positive effects, which are identified for the Asian late-comers, are still missing. For a further development of the national economy, Russian decision-makers need to understand the necessity of a solid innovation environment. In the last years the Russian resource sector has delivered strong economic growth rates. The global economic growth and higher demand on raw materials have been responsible for the flourishing economic development in Russia. However, Russian decision-makers are well advised to invest more financial, as well as political efforts into the innovation system.

10.6. Building a framework for ascension

This section delivers a compact comparison of the technological late-comer countries and draws implications from the patterns of their development. As the Asian late-comers experience a more successful technological development during the last years this section sheds light on the differences of the catch-up processes. Furthermore, these differences are evaluated according to their influences on the catch-up processes. Finally, a discussion of the catch-up processes, as well as an introduction of implications to catch-up processes in general close this section.

10.6.1. Comparing the patterns of technological catch-up

Table 10-1 is a compact summary of the findings for the late-comer countries. It delivers insight into the technological catch-up process of these countries at a glance. In addition, the table also delivers general evaluation of the catch-up process of each country.

The coloured table elements indicate positive or negative findings of each country. Elements in white do not indicate any clear positive or negative aspects. The findings show, for instance, no clear trends or different results for the national or sectoral analysis. This occurs, if general findings indicate a different development than results from the biotechnology sector.

Elements in light green represent positive characteristics. These facts influenced the catch-up of the respective countries in a positive way. In particular, the higher rates of external knowledge at the beginning and, especially, the higher rates of scientific knowledge had a positive effect on the catch-up process of China and India. Moreover, the decreasing number of the use of external knowledge also implies a positive effect on the development of the innovation activities of these countries. Indicators which also show positive developments in the Asian late-comer countries are the high visibility of their technologies and the niche strategy in India. Brazil just shows a positive result for its diversification efforts. The positive result of Russia can be found in its niche occupation. Hence, there are more positive aspects for the two Asian late-comers compared to the other two countries.

In contrary, light red elements are findings of this thesis which indicates negative aspects of technological catch-up of the late-comers. In Brazil, for instance, the low rate of citations of their patents shows that they still need to improve in this stage or even have not reached this stage of innovation activities. Moreover, Brazil should also work on their specialisation focus. China has its disadvantages in the niche strategies. A stronger concentration on some specialisation sectors at the beginning of their innovation activities would have improved the innovation activities in a positive way. Once again, India is the country with the best impressions, as it has no negative result. Lastly, it needs to be stated that Russia left an impression which indicates that it still needs to improve their innovation efforts in many respects. In particular, they do not show any diversification trends, the innovation network of the biotechnology is driven by private persons and has an unstable development and Russian patents are not the source of other international patent citations.

	External knowledge (Chapter 5)	Niche strategies (Chapter 6)	Diversification (Chapter 7)	Networking (Chapter 8)	Knowledge flows (Chapter 9)
Brazil	Higher rates for citations of other patents, but not for non-patent literature. Biotechnology sector does not use more external knowledge.	RSTA close to the German technology profile, but not to the US one. Specialisation sectors also similar to the strengths of the Brazilian industry. In general, no clear niche strategy.	Trends of diversification efforts are clearly observable. Diversification levels of the early-movers are yet not reached. The biotechnology sector is just less diversified.	Innovation network is still in the early-stages. Just few connections. Main drivers of the innovation network are firms and public institutes.	Brazilian patents play a minor role in the global technology competition. Most of their patents are cited by European patents.
China	Higher rates of external knowledge at the beginning, in particular for non-patent literature. Decreasing use of external knowledge. Same holds for the Chinese biotechnology sector.	No clear niche strategy, but at least consistent specialisation focuses after 1995. The biotechnology sector also shows no clear specialisation focuses on US niches.	In the last years China show decreasing diversification. The biotechnology sector converges towards the US biotechnology sector and has diversification trends.	Network activities still very different to the early-movers. Top players are research institutes and universities. External linkages are decreasing.	Chinese technology is already frequently cited by foreign inventors and innovators. They are cited the most by European patents.
India	Higher rates of external knowledge and the exploitation of external knowledge hold on. In the last years the biotechnology sector of India is already one step further. The use of external knowledge is not higher than in the early-mover countries.	Strong niche occupation on the general level and also in the biotechnology sector. Specialisation profiles can be clearly distinguished from the early-mover countries.	Due to the strong specialisation no trend of diversification can be traced on national level. The biotechnology sector, however, is developing towards the US diversification level.	Main players in India are a mixture of firms and public institutes. Foreign linkages are still very important. The innovation network is on the right way, but still needs time to develop.	Indian technology is highly cited. They receive the most citations from North American and European innovators. English seems to play a decisive role in this knowledge transfers.
Russia	External knowledge does not play an important role for Russian technology during the whole period of time. The Russian biotechnology uses external knowledge to higher extend.	Russian innovation activities tend to occupy niches. This can also be stated for the general assumption and the biotechnology sector.	Diversification is still very different to the early-movers. Diversification in the biotechnology sector needs to develop towards the early-movers.	Top players of the Russian innovation network are private persons. The inventor network has an unstable development.	Low rate of patent citations. Russian patents just play a minor role in the global technology competition. Most linkages are with 'Europe'.

Table 10-1: Comparison matrix of late-comer countries

10.6.2. Lessons to learn

The ascension of the Asian late-comer countries refers to the positive results of their technological catch-up process (see Table 10-1). Compared to the other two late-comers their catch-up process delivers more positive aspects. Although the findings indicate that it is not absolutely necessary to run through all steps of the technological catch-up described in this work successfully (see Section 4.4), it is important to fulfil some of these steps to have a steady ascension in the global technology competition. China, for instance, does not focus on certain niches to accelerate their catch-up process, but their technological output show that their innovation activities are raising quickly.

Asian late-comers: Establishing their up-coming innovation systems

According to the findings of the previous chapters, Asian late-comers are still in the stage of establishment of their *NIS*. In this respect, the *Indian Innovation System* is even one step further than Chinese one and, especially, the Indian biotechnology sector, is already on a top level in the international technology competition. Nevertheless, both countries now have to push the works on the establishment. This means that they have to, firstly, broaden their technological portfolio. It is advisable to invest financial and political efforts in new rising sectors, such as the sector of environmental technologies. Moreover, in order to profit from the diversification, these they also have to create inter-sectoral linkages. Secondly, further efforts have to done in the construction of a stronger national innovation network. The interaction of researchers of public institutes and private firms has to be strengthened. In particular, the role of private firms in the innovation network needs to improve.

The findings of Chapter 9 show that China and India already are a source for new innovations. If these two manage to fulfil the latter two aspects to establish their innovation systems they will also play very important roles in the global technology competition in close future.

Tasks for Brazil and, in particular, Russia

In contrary to the Asian late-comer countries, Brazil and Russia are still lagging behind the early-movers. Brazil, however, do not perform too badly in the technological catch-up. Interestingly the diversification process in the Latin American country is already developing, although the initial exploitation of external knowledge and technological niches has not taking part yet. For Brazil it is advisable to go one step backwards and push, once more, the activities of the stage of entry into the technological catch-up. With the help of external knowledge and the focus on some few up-coming and technologies, Brazilian innovation can play an important role in the future.

Russia needs to change the most disadvantages within the group of analysis. Similar to Brazil, they also have to invest more efforts into the stage of entry. The Russian focus on technological niches is an initial point to begin the technological catch-up. However, Russian decision-makers have to deal with an important drawback of their innovation system. The network analysis shows that the most important players of the biotechnology sector are private persons. As a profound scientific base and leading firms are essential for on vital innovation system, Russia basically needs to work on their lack of major players.

General remarks

As aforementioned, a successful technological catch-up has to go through certain steps. It is not necessary that all aspects have to be fulfilled, but it is advisable to follow these aspects. Hence, the hypotheses of this chapter can partly be confirmed. It is shown that successful late-comers, in the case of this analysis the Asian late-comers, have tendencies to develop towards early-movers. Nevertheless, it is important to carry out more analysis of the late-comers in the future, as this analysis shows that even the Asian late-comers are still on the way to establish their innovation systems. More profound results are possible in the future, when the Asian late-comers are even one step further in their technological development.

11. Final conclusion

This dissertation thesis illustrates an empirical analysis of emerging economies, namely of the *BRIC*[64] countries. These countries remarkably affect the global economy in recent years. With the beginning of the new millennium, they have begun to challenge the global economic balance and have made initial shifts towards economic power (see G20). An important question which arises in this context deals with the sustainability of their growth and their future role in the international economy. As sustainable economic growth is based on technological capabilities and a rich knowledge-base, economic catch-up processes include technological catch-up processes. Technology is one of the last domains where developed countries have advantages compared to these emerging economies. This dissertation addresses this topic. For this reason, it deals with the role of these countries within the international technological competition in recent years. It sheds light on their technological capabilities. Moreover, it draws implications for policy makers and indicates the future way of these countries concerning their technological capabilities, and thus, their economic possibilities.

The empirical analysis of this thesis provides an in-depth comparison of technological late-comer countries and the development of their technological capabilities. They are compared vis-à-vis with two technological early-movers, namely the USA and Germany. The whole examination is conducted on national level to deliver a general illustration of the late-comer countries and on sectoral level to gain more insight into the biotechnology sector. This sector is feasible for the analysis as it represents a technology which is knowledge-intensive. Activities in the biotechnology sector need a broad base of intellectual capital, such as qualified workers, access to scientific research etc. Thus, the examination tackles typical functions of an innovation process, for instance, relations of institutions and firms (see Haug, 1995, and Zucker and Darby, 1996), interaction of scientists and other actors etc. (see Malmberg and Maskell, 2002, and Fornahl and Tran, 2009). Moreover, decision-makers of the late-comer countries, as well as in developed countries identify the biotechnology sector as one of the key drivers of future technology and economic development (see Ministry of Science & Technology India, 2007, MOST, 2008 and Fornahl and Tran, 2009).

The complete empirical analysis bases on different well-known innovation indicators and methods. It refers to patent citation analysis to examine different levels of dependencies on external knowledge (forward citation - see Chapter 5), as well as the analysis of the visibility of late-comer knowledge (backward citation - see Chapter

[64] The abbreviation *BRIC* stands for the four countries Brazil, Russia, India and China.

9). The later analysis also consists of an analysis of the influences on knowledge transfer from the late-comer countries. Additionally, the analysis refers to specialisation indicators, such as the *Cosine Index*. This indicator illustrates the technological portfolios of the late-comer countries. The findings demonstrate that niche strategies of late-comer countries are important and enhance their economies to develop a more successful technological base in these niches at the beginning of their technological activities (see Chapter 6). In regard of diversification discussions, this thesis also uses the *Herfindahl-Hirschman-Index* (HHI), also known as the *Herfindahl-Index*, and the *Krugman-Specialisation-Index* (KSI). It shows that technological diversification is one of the weaknesses of these countries. Their technological portfolios are still focused on certain technologies. Hence, they still need to broaden their technological capabilities (see Chapter 7). For the examination of the players within the late-comer countries and the structure of their interaction, the analysis refers to indicators of the *Social Network Analysis* (SNA) (see Chapter 8). Combining these methods and analyses, a framework is developed to clarify the level of technological capabilities of the *BRIC*s, evaluating their technological catch-up process. Moreover, all findings of the analyses are summarised for each country and are discussed in detail (see Chapter 10).

The examination of the late-comer countries bases on an analytical framework which is developed in this thesis. It describes the rise of technological late-comers in three stages and aims at showing the current technological status of a late-comer country. These steps are divided into the early-stages of technological catch-up First, the entry into the technological competition. This is analysed by the use of external knowledge and the occupation of technological niches (see Chapter 5 and Chapter 6). The second stage of the framework deals with a process of establishment within the technological competition. It therefore examines the diversification efforts and the efforts to construct a national innovation network of the late-comer countries (see Chapter 7 and Chapter 8). Finally, the success of these catch-up processes is evaluated for the technological late-comers by analysing the international visibility of their technologies and by exploring the patterns of their development (see Chapter 9 and Chapter 10). This framework is described and illustrated in detail in Chapter 4.

To deliver a brief overview of the analysing steps, the results of each chapter can be summarised as follows[65]:

The use of external knowledge shows that on national level the *BRIC* countries use more external knowledge than the USA and Germany. This difference refers to the use of non-patent literature, for instance, scientific papers and indicates that the four late-

[65] A detailed discussion of each late-comer country is given in Chapter 10.

comers have a higher scientific linkage compared to the early-movers. Within the group of late-comers, the results illustrate that, in particular, the Asian late-comer countries use more scientific knowledge than the early-movers, but also more than Brazil and Russia. This is affected by the higher governmental involvement in these countries. China and India still elaborate *Five-Year-Plans* for their national efforts in science and technology (see Ministry of Science & Technology India, 2007 and MOST, 2008). However, in the course of time, the use of external knowledge of the late-comer countries and the early-movers get more similar to each other. The use of external knowledge in the late-comer countries decreases and they develop towards the early-movers which indicate a positive development for the technological capabilities of these countries. This positive development is strongly indicated by the Asian late-comers. Similar results can be presented for the biotechnology sector. In this knowledge intensive sector, higher numbers in non-patent citations are detectable for all late-comer countries. Interestingly, the Indian biotechnology sector does not show significant differences in the last years of the examined time period. India profits from its concentration on life science since the beginning of their innovation activities.

The examination of the late-comer countries regarding their niche strategies shows that niche strategies are used in all of these countries, but especially in India and Russia. The indications delivered by the *Cosine Index* illustrate that, once again, India experienced a very positive development and focused on technologies which are niches in the global technology competition. Combined with a persistent development of these technologies, India has built up an efficient technology pool in the sectors of 'agriculture and food chemistry', 'chemical industry and petrol industry, basic materials chemistry', 'pharmaceuticals and cosmetics', 'organic fine chemistry' and 'biotechnology'[66]. Meanwhile, the Russian strengths are in the sectors of 'nuclear engineering', 'materials and metallurgy', 'chemical engineering', 'space technology and weapons' and 'environmental technology'. Most of these sectors are classical focuses of the science and technology policy of the former Soviet Union. Once again, this indicates that state-driven forces within the innovation activities in the late-comer countries still play a major role.

The examination of the technological diversification discloses that, in general, the late-comer countries have not reached the diversification of the early-mover countries yet. On national level, the four late-comers are still under-diversified and need to strengthen their efforts to construct a broader technology portfolio. However, China and, in particular, India needs to push its diversification as they already have strong increasing innovation activities. The latter analysis shows that India had positive niche occupation strategies at the beginning of the examined period (see Chapter 6), but

[66] These sectors are derived from the OST/INPI/ISI classification (see Section 3.2).

these efforts still need to extend. In case of the biotechnology sector, India performs well as the technological diversification within this sector already reaches the same level of the US biotechnology sector. China also shows right indications of diversification activities, but lost its diversification activities at the end of the examined time period. This needs to be fixed and turn around to generate a broader Chinese technology portfolio. Brazil also shows positive signs of technological diversification. However, as Brazil's technological output has not reached the ones of India and China, this diversification seems to be a bit too early. It has to develop innovation activities in general and needs to push its technological output. Finally, Russia has to learn to profit from its national strengths and put its efforts in the technologies where they have industrial strengths, but also in new emerging technologies, such as the biotechnology one.

The *Social Network Analysis* (SNA) of the innovation networks illustrates that the networks of the late-comer countries strongly differ from each other. Regarding the linkages to foreign players, the Chinese network shows the most positive indications. It develops to a more autonomous network, as the linkages to foreign players decreases and they have shares of foreign linkages which are comparable with the early-movers. Thus, national innovation efforts without foreign dependencies grow stronger. This analysis also shows that the top players in the late-comer countries still have different statuses compared to the top players of the early-movers. These differences concern their *degree centrality* and *betweeness centrality*. Top players in China, however, also developed most efficiently within the group of late-comers, as they move towards the level of top players of the early-mover countries. Concerning the inventor networks, the SNA of the late-comer countries implies that India and China begin to establish an efficient innovation network. In this respect, Brazil needs to catch up. The analysis of the Russian biotechnology innovation network reveals that Russia's biotechnology stagnates. In general, the SNA shows that the Asian late-comer countries are establishing an efficient innovation network within their countries which also has connections to international players.

The analysis also shows that technology from the late-comers is also used by international competitors to develop new technologies. This is visible in the examination of the backward citation analysis of their patents. Although all countries had astonishing economic growth rates, they played different roles in the global technology competition. In general, it can be stated that all regions of the world (see Chapter 9) use technology of the late-comers. Even more, these citation numbers are still increasing. Citations are mainly driven by 'Europe', 'North America' and 'Asia'. It is interesting that the late-comer countries do not cite each other very often, hence, they do not refer to the each others' knowledge. Once again, the Asian late-comers experienced a much better development between 1986 and 2005. In particular, Indian technology is often cited by other inventors of other countries. That implies that language seems to play a major role in the citation of late-comer patents. This fact is also backed by a regression model that test influences on knowledge diffusion from late-comer countries towards other regions of the world. In general, the regression model shows that language similarities, but in particular technological proximity, influence the knowledge diffusion. In the course of time, the importance of technological proximity even rises. In this respect, language influences only play an important role within the last years of the examined time period. The latter effect is caused by the citations of Indian patents which also increases in the course of time and is the major part of all citations from late-comer countries. The regression model also tests the importance of geographical distance and cultural distance as influences on knowledge diffusion. However, these two influences do not play an important role to the diffusion of knowledge. Thus, the importance of language and, in particular, technology emphasises that absorptive capacity is crucial. In recent years, culture and geographical distance effects just play a minor role in the global technology competition.

To sum up, the Asian late-comer countries have experienced a much better technological progress than Brazil and Russia between 1986 and 2005. Although they are still not at the same technological level compared to the early-movers, their technological progress describes a meaningful development. In particular, the biotechnology sector of India is already recognized on international level (see Chapter 10). Moreover, India has positive indications for the initial stages of a technological catch-up process. They have explored much external knowledge to profit from existing technologies and use niche strategies, on national level as well as on sectoral level, to introduce their technologies. However, India has to diversify the technological portfolio in the future and also needs to strengthen their structured innovation network to experience more efficient national knowledge diffusion (for detailed discussions of India see 10.4). The second Asian late-comer, namely China, also developed well in regard to their technological progress between 1986 and 2005. China has also exploited external knowledge to learn from existing technology. However, China has not focused on certain niches to strengthen their technological catch-up. In this respect, India has experienced a better development between 1986 and 2005. This is also reflected in the visibility of Indian knowledge which means that Indian technology is more often cited by other patent applications than Chinese technology (for a detailed discussion of China see 10.3). The findings of this thesis indicate that the technological progress of Brazil still needs time to develop. It misses some of the positive developments which have been made by the Asian late-comers. However, Brazil needs to focus on its strengths and needs to exploit the international technology pool. Referring to these entry strategies of technological catch-up process, Brazil can also push their own technological capabilities. In this respect, Brazil should stick to its strengths. The industrial structure indicates that the major players of Brazil are companies of the resource sector, such as Petrobas. These players, for instance, can strengthen their efforts to develop new technologies for a more efficient use of resources (for a detailed discussion of Brazil see 10.2). Finally, the findings indicate that Russia still needs the most efforts to construct an innovation-driven economy. Russia lags behind in most of the stages of the technological catch-up process. One positive sign is the niche occupation of Russia's technology portfolio. Russia occupies technological fields which are not at the focus of the early-mover countries. The Russian economy is still dominated by the resource sector. The gas and oil sector occupies the major part of the GDP. However, Russia's chances to speed up technological catch-up rest in these sectors. Similar to Brazil, Russia should enforce the development of new technologies related to these sectors (for a detailed discussion of Russia see 10.5).

The thesis shows that the technological capabilities of the emerging economies are also developing. They do not all show the similar developments, but they are increasing their technological possibilities to challenge the global technological leaders in some years. Leading countries should be aware of these new competitors, in particular of India and China. These two countries are developing well and show also the political efforts to become future innovation driven economies. As the results of this thesis show that the late-comer countries have not reached the same technological level yet, future works on this topic are meaningful. Moreover, future research studies should also enrich this first framework to describe the rise of technological late-comers with more indicators and methods.

References

Abramowitz, M. (1986) 'Catching-up, Forging Ahead, and Falling Behind', *The Journal of Economic History*, Vol. 46, No. 2, The Tasks of Economic History, Jun. 1986, pp. 385-406.

Agnolucci, P. and McDowall, W. (2007) 'Technological change in niches: Auxiliary Power Units and the hydrogen economy', *Technological Forecasting & Social Change*, 74, pp.1394-1410.

Alberts, D.S. and Papp, D.S. (1997) *The Information Age: An Anthology on Its Impact and Consequences*, CCRP Publication Series, 1997.

Altenburg, T., Schmitz, H. and Stamm, A. (2008) 'Breakthrough? China's and India's Transition from Production to Innovation', *World Development*, Vol. 36, No. 2, pp. 325–344.

Ansoff, H.I. (1957) 'Strategies for diversification', *Harvard Business Review*, 35, 5, pp. 113-124.

Argyres, N. (1996) 'Capabilities, Technological Diversification and Divisionalization', *Strategic Management Journal*, Vol, 17, 1996, pp. 395-410.

Arrow, K.J. (1962a) 'The Economic Implications of Learning by Doing', *Review of Economic Studies*, Vol. 29, p155-173.

Arrow, K.J. (1962b) 'Economic Welfare and the Allocation of Resources for Invention', *Science bought and sold*, The University of Chicago Press, Chicago, 2002, pp. 165-180

Arora, A., Fosfuri, A. and Gambardella, A. (2001) *Markets for technology*, MIT Press, Cambridge.

Audretsch, D.B. and Feldman, M.P. (1996) 'R&D Spillovers and the Geography of Innovation and Production', *The American Economic Review*, Vol. 86, No. 3, June 1996, pp. 630-640, American Economic Association.

Balassa, B. (1965) 'Trade liberalisation and revealed comparative advantage', *The Manchester School of Economic and Social Studies*, 33.

Bascavusoglu, E. (2007) 'Innovation and Knowledge Spillover in Developing Countries: A Patent Citation Analysis', Open Discussion Papers in Economics 62, The Open University, Faculty of Social Sciences, Department of Economics.

Baum, J.A.C., Calabrese, T. and Silverman, B.S. (2000) 'Don't go it alone: Alliances network composition and startups' performance in Canadian biotechnology', *Strategic Management Journal*, 21, pp. 267-294.

Berry, M.M.J and Taggart, J.H. (1994) 'Managing technology and innovation: a review', *R&D Management*, 24 (4), pp.341-353.

BMBF (1996) *Biotechnology in Germany*, Bonn.

Breschi, S. and Malerba, F. (1997) 'Sectoral innovation systems: technological regimes, Schumpeterian dynamics, and spatial boundries', *Systems of Innovation – Technologies, Institutions and Organizations, Science*, Technology and the International Political Economy Series, Pinter, London and Washington.

Breschi, S. and Lissoni, F. (2003) ‘Mobility and Social Networks: Localised Knowledge Spillover Revisited’, CESPRI, Working Paper No. 142, March 2003, http://www.nber.org/CRIW/papers/breschi.pdf, 30-08-2010.

Breschi, S., Lissoni, F. and Malerba, F. (2003) ‘Knowledge-relatedness in firm technological diversification’, *Research Policy*, 32, 2003, pp. 69-87.

Bosch, K. (1998) *Statistik-Taschenbuch*, R. Oldenbourg Verlag, 3rd Edition, Oldenbourg, 1998.

Boschma, R. (2005) ‘Proximities and Innovation: A Critical Assessment’, *Regional Studies*, Vol. 39.1, Feb. 2005, pp. 61-74.

Boschma, R. and Iammarino, S. (2009) ‘Related Variety and Regional Growth in Italy’, *Economic Geography*, Vol. 85, Issue 3, pages 289–311, July 2009.

Bullinger, H.-J. (1994) *Einführung in das Technologiemanagement: Modelle, Methoden, Praxisbeispiele*, Teubner, Stuttgart, 1994.

Bush, V. (1945) *Science, The Endless Frontier*, National Science Foundation, Washington, D.C.

Cantner, U. and Graf, H. (2006) ‘The network of innovators in Jena: An application of social network analysis’, *Research Policy*, 35, 2006, pp. 463-480.

Cantwell, J. and Vertova, G. (2004) ‘Historical evolution of technological diversification’, *Research Policy*, 33, 2004, pp. 511-529.

Carpenter, M.P. and Narin, F. (1983), Validation study: Patent Citations as indicator of science and foreign dependence, *World Patent Information*, 5, pp. 180-185.

CEPII (2006), CEPII Distance Database, http://www.cepii.fr/anglaisgraph/bdd/distances.htm, 31-08-2010.

CIA World Fact Book (2009) *The 2008th World Fact Book*, https://www.cia.gov/library/publications/the-world-factbook/, 19-02-2009.

Chang, P. and Tsai, D. (2002) ‘Finding the niche position — competition strategy of Taiwan’s IC design industry’, *Technovation*, Vol. 22, pp. 101-111.

Cho, D., Kim, D. and Rhee, D. (1998) ‘Latecomer Strategies: Evidence from the Semiconductor Industry in Japan and Korea’, *Organization Science*, Vol. 9, No. 4, July, pp. 489-505.

Choung, J.-Y., Hwang, H.-R., Choi, J.-H. and Rim, M.-H. (2000) ‘Transition of Latecomer Firms from Technology User to Technology Generators: Korean Semiconductor Firms’, *World Development*, Vol. 28, No. 5, pp.969-982, 2000

Cohen, W.M. and Levinthal, D.A. (1990) ‘Absorptive Capacities: A New Perspective on Learning and Innovation’, *Administrative Science Quarterly*, Vol. 35, No. 1, Special Issue: Technology, Organizations, and Innovation, Mar. 1990, pp.128-152.

Cook, P., Gomez Uranga, M. and Etxebarria, G. (1997) ‘Regional innovation systems: Institutional and organizational dimensions’, *Research Policy*, 26, 1997, pp. 475-491.

Cooke, P. (2001) ‘Regional Innovation Systems, Clusters, and the Knowledge Economy’, *Industrial and Corporate Change*, Vol. 10, No. 4, 2001, pp.945-974.

Cooke, P. (2001a) ‘New economy innovation systems - Biotechnology in Europe and the USA’, *Industry and Innovation*, Vol. 8, pp. 267-289.

Coulon, F. (2005) 'The use of social network analysis in innovation research: A literature review', DRUID Academy Winter 2005, January 18, 2005.

Cowan, R., David, A.P. and Foray, D. (2000) 'The Explicit Economics of Knowledge Codification and Tacitness', *Industrial and Corporate Change*, Vol. 9, No. 2, 2000.

Dasgupta, P. and David, P.A. (1994) 'Towards a new economics of science', *Research Policy*, 23, p. 487-521.

Edquist, C. (1997) *Systems of Innovation – Technologies, Institutions and Organizations, Science*, Technology and the International Political Economy Series, Pinter, London and Washington

Edquist, C. and Johnson, B. (1997) 'Institutions and organizations in systems of innovation', *Systems of Innovation – Technologies, Institutions and Organizations, Science*, Technology and the International Political Economy Series, Pinter, London and Washington

Edquist, C. (2001) 'The System of Innovation Approach and Innovation Policy: An account of the state of the art', DRUID Conference, Aalborg, June 12-15, 2001

European Council (2004) 'Facing the Challenge - The Lisbon strategy for growth and employment', Report from the High Level Group, November 2004.

Fagerberg, J. (1987) 'A technology gap approach to why growth rates differ', *Research Policy*, No. 16, pp. 87-99.

Fagerberg, J. and Verspagen, B. (2002) 'Technology-gaps, innovation-diffusion and transformation: an evolutionary interpretation', *Research Policy*, 31, pp.1291-1304.

Fagerberg, J. and Srholec, M. (2005) 'Catching Up: What are the critical factors for success?', Globelics Working Paper Series, No. 07-07, The Global Network for Economics of Learning, Innovation, and Competence Building System, www.globelics.org.

Fornahl, D., Haller, I., Tran, C.A. (2008) *'Knowledge Variety and Networks Over Time - How Technologies and Networks Co-evolve in Four German Biotechnology Clusters'*, DIME Workshop Local and sectoral systems of innovations - interdependencies and their development patterns over time, May 22nd-23rd 2008 in Karlsruhe.

Fornahl, D. and Tran, C. A. (2009) '*The development of localglobal linkages in the biotech districts in Germany - Local embeddedness or distance learning?'*, *Business Networks in Clusters and Industrial Districts*, Edited by Belussi, F. and Sammarra, A., Routledge - Regions and Cities, Taylor & Francis Group, London and New York, 2009, pp. 332 – 355.

Forbes, N. and Wield, D. (2000) 'Managing R&D in technology-followers', *Research Policy*, Vol. 29, pp. 1095–1109.

Forbes (2010) 'The Global 2000', http://www.forbes.com/lists/2010/18/global-2000-10_The-Global-2000_Counrty.html, 26-05-2010.

Freeman, C. (1987) *Technology policy and economic performance: Lessons from Japan*, Pinter Publishers, London.

Freeman, C. (2002) 'Continental, national and sub-national innovation systems – complementarity and economic growth', *Research Policy*, 31, 2002, pp. 191-211.

Freeman, C. and Soete, L. (2009) *Developing science, technology and innovation indicators: What we can learn from the past*, Research Policy, 38, pp. 583-589.

Frietsch, R., Köhler, F. and Blind, K. (2008) 'Weltmarktpatente – Strukturen und deren Veränderungen', *Studie zum deutschen Innovationssystem Nr. 7-2008*, Expertenkommission für Forschung und Innovation, www.e-fi.de.

Furman, J. and Hayes, R. (2004) 'Catching up or standing still? National innovative productivity among 'follower' countries, 1978–1999', *Research Policy*, Vol. 33, pp. 1329–1354.

G20 (2008) 'Declaration Summit on Financial Markets and the World Economy', http://www.g20.org/, 02-16-2009.

Gambardella, A. and Torrisi, S. (1998) 'Does technological convergence imply convergence in markets? Evidence from the electronics industry', *Research Policy*, 27, 1998, pp. 445-463.

Garcia-Vega, M. (2006) 'Does technological diversification promote innovation? An empirical analysis for European firms', *Research Policy*, 35, 2006, pp. 230-246.

Giuri, P. and Mariani, M. (2005) 'Everything you always wanted to know about inventors (but never asked): evidence from Patval-EU survey', LEM working paper series, 2005-2020.

Giuri, P. and Mariani, M. (2008) 'Inventors and the Geographical Breadth of Knowledge Spillover', DRUID Working Paper Series, No. 08-01, Danish Research Unit of Industrial Dynamics.

Glass, A. and Saggi, K. (1998) 'International technology transfer and the technology gap', *Journal of Development Economics*, Vol. 55, pp.369–398.

Goldstein, A. (2002) 'EMBRAER: From national champion to global players', *CEPAL Review*, 77, August 2002.

Gomulka, S. (1971) 'Inventive Activity, Diffusion and the Stages of Economic Growth', Skrifter fra Aarhus Universitets Okonomiske Institut, Aarhus.

Graf, H. (2010) 'Gatekeepers in regional networks of innovators', *Cambridge Journal of Economics*, 2010, beq001v1-beq001.

Graf, H. and Henning, T. (2009) 'Public Research in Regional Networks of Innovators: A Comparative Study of Four East-German Regions', *Regional Studies*, 1360-0591, Vol. 43, Issue 10, First published 2009, pp. 1349-1368.

Griliches, Z. (1984), R&D, Patents and Productivity, National Bureau of Economic Research Project Report, The University of Chicago Press.

Griliches, Z. (1990) 'Patent Statistics as Economic Indicators: A Survey', *Journal of Economic Literature*, Vol. 28, No. 4, December, pp. 1661-1707.

Grossekettler, H. (1985) ‚Wettbewerbstheorie. Funktionale Marktprozesse als ordnungspolitische Gestaltungsaufgabe‘, *Preis- und Wettbewerbstheorie. Marktprozesse als analytisches Problem und ordnungspolitische Gestaltungsaufgabe*, Stuttgart (Kohlhammer), p.113–335.

Grossman, G.M. and Helpman, E. (1990) 'Trade, Innovation and Growth', *The American Economic Review*, Vol. 80, No. 2, Papers and Proceedings of the Hundred and Second Annual Meeting of the American Economic Association, 1990, pp.86-91.

Grupp, H. (1994) 'The measurement of technological performance of innovations by technometrics and its impact on established technology indicators', *Research Policy*, 23, pp. 175-193.

Grupp, H. (1996) 'Spillover effects and the science base of innovations reconsidered: an empirical approach', *Journal of Evolutionary Economics*, 6, 1996, pp. 175-197.

Grupp, H. (1998) *Foundations of the Economics of Innovation. Theory, Measurement and Practice*, Chetenham, UK: Edward Elgar.

Grupp, H. and Schmoch, U. (1999) 'Patent statistics in the age of globalisation: new legal procedures, new analytical methods, new economic interpretation', *Research Policy*, Vol. 28, pp. 377–396.

Gu, S. and Lundvall, B.A. (2006) 'China's Innovation System and the Move Toward Harmonious Growth and Endogenous Innovation', DRUID Working Paper, No. 07.

Guellec, D. and van Pottelsberghe de la Potterie, B. (2001) 'The internationalisation of technology analysed with patent data', *Research Policy*, Vol. 30, Issue 8, October 2001, pp. 1253-1266.

Guerrieri, P. and Iammarino, S. (2003) 'The Dynamics of Export Specialization in the Regions of the Italian Mezzogiorno: Persistence and Change', SPRU Electronic Working Paper Series, Paper No. 105, August 2003.

Guriev, S. and Rachinsky, A. (2005) 'The Role of Oligarchs in Russian Capitalism', *The Journal of Economic Perspective*, Vol. 19, No. 1, Winter 2005, pp. 131-150.

Hagedoorn, J. (1993) 'Understanding the Rationale of Strategic Technology Partnering: Interorganizational Modes of Cooperation and Sectoral Differences', *Strategic Management Journal*, Vol. 14, No. 5, July, 1993, pp. 371-385.

Hall, B.M. (2002) 'A note on the bias in the Herfindahl based on count data', *Patents, Citations, and Innovation*, Edited by Jaffe, A. and Trajtenberg, M., MIT Press.

Hall, B.M., Jaffe, A., and Trajtenberg, M. (2005) 'Market Value and Patent Citations', *The RAND Journal of Economics*, Vol. 36, No. 1, Spring 2005, pp. 16-38.

Haller, I. (2009), *Dynamics in Science-Based Markets: Two Phases of Development*, Karlsruhe, University, Dissertation, 2009, http://digbib.ubka.uni-karlsruhe.de/volltexte/1000016599, 31-08-2010.

Harhoff, D., Narin, F., Scherer, F.M., and Vopel, K. (1999) ‚Citation Frequency and the Value of Patented Inventions, *The Review of Economics and Statistics*, Vol. 81, No. 3, Aug. 1999, pp. 511-515.

Harhoff, D., Scherer, F.M., and Vopel, K. (2002) 'Citations, family size, opposition and the value of patent rights', *Research Policy*, Vol. 32, pp. 1343–1363.

Haug, P. (1995) ‚Formation of biotechnology firms in the greater Seattle region: An empirical investigation of entrepreneurial, financial and educational perspectives', *Environment and Planning*, A 27, pp. 249-267.

Hausschildt, J. (1997) *Innovationsmanagement*, Verlag Franz Vahlen GmbH, München, 1997.

Hayek, F. A. von (1978) 'Competition as a Discovery Procedure', *New Studies in Philosophy, Politics, Economics and the History of Ideas*, Chicago, p.179-190.

Hinze, S., Reiss, T. and Schmoch, U. (1997) 'Statistical Analysis on the Distance Between Fields of Technology', Report for European Commission TSER Project, September.

Hobday, M. (1995) 'East Asian Latecomer Firms: Learning the Technology of Electronics', *World Development*, Vol. 23, No. 7, pp. 1171-1 193.

Hobday, M., Rush, H. and Bessant, J. (2004) 'Approaching the innovation frontier in Korea: the transition phase to leadership', *Research Policy*, 33, pp. 1433-1457.

Hullmann, A. (2001) *Internationaler Wissenstransfer und technischer Wandel – Bedeutung, Einflussfaktoren und Ausblick auf technologiepolitische Implikationen am Beispiel der Nanotechnologie in Deutschland*, Physica-Verlag, Heidelberg.

Huntington, S.P. (1996*) The Clash of Civilizations and the Remaking of World Order*, New York, Simon & Schuster, 1996.

Jacobs, J. (1969) *The economy of cities*, New York, Random House.

Jaffe, A.B. (1986) 'Technological Opportunity and Spillovers of R & D: Evidence from Firms' Patents, Profits, and Market Value, *The American Economic Review*, Vol. 76, No. 5, December, 1986, pp. 984-1001.

Jaffe, A.B., Trajtenberg, M. and Henderson, R. (1993), Geographic Localization of Knowledge Spillover as Evidence by Patent Citations, *The Quarterly Journal of Economics*, August 1993, pp. 577-598.

Jaffe, A.B. and Trajtenberg, M. (1999) 'International Knowledge Flows: Evidence from Patents Citations', *Economics of Innovation and New Technology*, Vol. 8, 1999, pp. 105-136.

Jaffe, A.B., Trajtenberg, M. and Fogarty, M.S. (2000), Knowledge Spillovers and Patent Citations: Evidence from a Survey of Inventors, *The American Economic Review*, Vol. 90, No. 2.

Kaufer, E. (1989) *Economics of the Patent System*, Chur, Harwood Academic Publisher, 1989.

Kline, S.J. (1985) 'Research, Invention, Innovation and Production: Models and Reality', Rept. INN-1D Stanford University 1989, pp.1–32.

Kline, S.J. and Rosenberg, N. (1986) 'An Overview of Innovation', *The Positive Sum Strategy – Harnessing Technology for Economic Growth*, National Academy Press, Washington D.C., 1986.

Kuboniwa, M., Tabata, S. and Ustinova, N. (2005) 'How Large is the Oil and Gas Sector of Russia? A Research Report', *Eurasian Geography and Economics*, 46, 1, pp. 68-76.

Koren, M. and Tenreyro, S. (2005) 'Technological Diversification', European Central Bank, Working Paper Series No. 551, November 2005.

Kowalski, P., Dihel, N. and Garcia, M. (2008) 'India', *Globalisation and Emerging Economies*, OECD 2008, Paris.

Krawczyk, O., H. Legler, C. Schadt, R. Frietsch, T. Schubert and D. Schumacher (2007) 'Die Bedeutung von Aufhol-Ländern im globalen Technologiewettbewerb', *Studie zum deutschen Innovationssystem*, Nr. 21-2007.

Krugman, P.A. (1991) 'Myths and Realities' of U.S. Competitiveness, *Science 8*, November 1991, Vol. 254, No. 5033, pp. 811-815.

Krugman, P.A. (1991a) *Geography and Trade*, MIT Press, Cambridge.

Laforgia, F. and Lissoni, F. (2009) 'What do you mean by "mobile"? Multi-applicant inventors in the European biotechnology industry', *Innovation Networks in Industries*,

Edited by Malerba, F. and Vonortas, N.S., Edward Elgar Publishing Ltd., 2009, Cheltenham, UK, pp. 157-176.

Lattimore, R. and Kowalski, P. (2008) 'Brazil', *Globalisation and Emerging Economies*, OECD 2008, Paris.

Laursen, K. (1998) 'Revealed Comparative Advantage and the Alternatives as Measures of International Specialisation', DRUID Working Paper No 98-30, DRUID, 1998.

Leten, B., Belderbos, R. and Van Looy, B. (2007) 'Technological diversification, coherence and performance of firms', Faculty of Economics and Applied Economics, Katholieke Universiteit Leuven, 2007, http://www.whu.edu/csc/paper/Leten,%20Belderbos,%20Van%20Looy.pdf, 17-04-2010.

Lin, B.-W., Chen, C.-J. and Wu, H.-L. (2006) ‚Patent Portfolio Diversity, Technology Strategy, and Firm Value', *IEEE Transactions on Engineering Management*, Vol. 53, No. 1, Feb. 2006.

List, F. (1841) *The National System of Political Economy*, Longman, English Edition, London, 1904.

Lucas, R.E. (1972) 'Expectations and the Neutrality of Money', *Journal of Economic Theory 4*, pp.103-124.

Lucas, R.E. (1988) 'On the Mechanics of Economic Development', *Journal of Monetary Economics*, Vo. 22, 2988, p. 3-42.

Lundvall, B.-A. (1992) *National systems of innovation: towards a theory of innovation and interactive learning*, Pinter, London, 1992

Malerba, F. (2002) 'Sectoral systems of innovation and production', *Research Policy*, 31, 2002, pp. 247-264.

Ministry of Science & Technology India (2007) 'Eleventh Five Year Plan 2008-12', Ministry of Science & Technology India, Department of Science & Technology, http://www.dst.gov.in/about_us/11th-plan/eleventh-plan-index.htm, 16-02-2009.

Machlup, F. (1980) *Knowledge: Its Creation, Distribution, and Economic Significance,* Volume I: Knowledge and Knowledge Production, Princeton.

Malmberg, A. and Maskell, P. (2002) 'The elusive concept of localization economies: towards a knowledge-based theory of spatial clustering', *Environment and Planning A 34*, pp. 429-449.

Marshall, A. (1890) *Principles of Economics*, London, Maxmillan.

Marx, K. (1862) *Zur Kritik der politischen Ökonomie*, MEGA-Ausgabe II.3.6., Berlin, 1982.

Maurseth, P.B. and Verspagen, B. (2002), Knowledge Spillovers in Europe: A Patent Citation Analysis, *Scandinavian Journal of Economics*, 104(4), pp. 531-545.

Meyborg, M. (2010) 'The Impact of FDI on Innovation and Networking Activity in Central and Eastern Europe', European Regional Science Association (ERSA) 2010, Jonkoping, Sweden, 20th August – 22nd August 2010.

Miguélez, E. and Moreno, R. (2010) 'Research Networks and Inventors' Mobility as Drivers of Innovation: Evidence from Europe', IREA, Research Institute of Applied Economics, Working Paper 2010/01.

Mitusch, K., Tran, C.A., Montobbio, F., Cusmano, L. and Malerba, F. (2010) 'National Specialisation Report – Output Paper to the workshop: Innovative industries – Regional and national specialisation patterns and the role of framework conditions', Sectoral Innovation Watch, Europe Innova, 2010, http://www.europe-innova.eu/c/document_library/get_file?folderId=242121&name=DLFE-8910.pdf, 27-09-2010).

Montobbio, F. and Sterzi, V. (2008) 'Inventing Together: Exploring the Nature of International Knowledge Spillovers in Latin America', CESPRI, Working Paper No. 225, November 2008, http://globelics2009dakar.merit.unu.edu/papers/1238428330_FM.pdf, 31-08-2010.

MOST (2008) 'Torch High Technology Industry Development Center', Ministry of Science and Technology, China, http://www.ctp.gov.cn/ctp-eng/index.htm, 20-02-2009.

Mowery, D. and Nelson, R.R. (1999) *Sources of Industrial Leadership: Studies of Seven Industries*, Cambridge University Press, Cambridge.

Murrmann, J.P. and Homburg, E. (2001) 'Comparing evolutionary dynamics across different national settings: The case of the synthetic dye industry, 1857-1914', *Journal of Evolutionary Economics*, 11, Springer-Verlag, 2001, pp. 177-205.

Narula, R. and Jormanainen, I. (2008) 'When a good science base is not enough to create competitve industries: Lock-in and intertia in Russian systems of innovation', United Nations University – Maastricht Economic and Social Research and Training Centre on Innovation and Technology, 2008.

Nelson, R.R. (1993) *National innovation systems: a comparative analysis*, Oxford University Press, New York, 1993.

Nill, J. and Kemp, R. (2009) 'Evolutionary approaches for sustainable innovation policies: From niche to paradigm?', *Research Policy*, 38, pp.668-680.

Niosi, J. (2002) 'National systems of innovation are "x-efficient" (and x-effective) - Why some are slow learners', *Research Policy*, 31, 2002, pp.291-302.

OECD (1996) 'The Measurement of Scientific and Technological Activities Oslo Manual: Guidelines for Collecting and Interpreting Innovation Data', Organisation for Economic Co-operation and Development, European Commission, Eurostat, 1996, http://www.oecd.org/dataoecd/35/61/2367580.pdf, 11-11-2009.

OECD (2005) 'The Measurement of Scientific and Technological Activities Oslo Manual: Guidelines for Collecting and Interpreting Innovation Data, 3rd Edition', Organisation for Economic Co-operation and Development, 2005, http://lysander.sourceoecd.org/vl=1032781/cl=17/nw=1/rpsv/~6683/v2005n5/s1/p1l, 11-02-2010

OECD (2007) 'Compendium of Patent Statistics 2007', Organisation for Economic Co-operation and Development, Issue No. 34, Paris

OECD (2009), 'OECD Patent Statistics Manual', Organisation for Economic Co-operation and Development, 2009, http://oberon.sourceoecd.org/vl=230533/cl=43/nw=1/rpsv/~6683/v2009n1/s1/p1l, 11-02-2010.

Ott, A.E. (1959) *Technischer Fortschritt*, Handwörterbuch der Sozialwissenschaften, Band 10, Stuttgart, Tübingen und Göttingen, Gustav Fischer, J.C.B. Mohr and Vandenhoeck and Rupprecht, pp. 302-316.

Papp, D.S., Alberts, D.S., and Tuyahov, A. (1997) 'Historical Impacts of Information Technologies: An Overview', *The Information Age: An Anthology on Its Impact and Consequences*, CCRP Publication Series, 1997, pp. 13-35.

Pavitt, K. (1985) 'Patent Statistics as Indicators of Innovative Activities: Possibilities and Problems', *Scientometrics*, 7 (1-2), pp. 77-99.

Pavitt, K. (1988) *The Uses and Abuses of Patent Statistics*, Handbook of Quantitative Studies of Science and Technology.

Perillieux, R. (1987) *Der Zeitfaktor im strategischen Technologiemanagement – Früher oder später Einstieg bei technischen Produktinnovationen?*, Berlin, 1987.

Phene, A., Fladmoe-Lindquist, K. and Marsh, L. (2006), 'Breakthrough innovations in the US biotechnology industry: The effects of technological space and geographic origin', *Strategic Management Journal*, 27, pp. 369-388.

Polanyi, M. (1958) *Personal Knowledge: Towards a Post-critical Philosophy*, Routledge and Kegan Paul, London.

Porter, M.E. (1984) *Wettbewerbsstrategie, Methoden zur Analyse von Branchen und Konkurrenten*, 2. Auflage, Campus Verlag, Frankfurt am Main.

Porter, M.E. (1998) 'Clusters and the New Economics of Competition', *Harvard Business Review,* pp. 77-90.

Porter, M.E. (1999) *Wettbewerb und Strategie*, Econ Verlag, Munich.

Posner, M.V. (1961) 'International Trade and Technical Change', *Oxford Economic Papers*, 13, pp. 323-341.

Powell, W.W., White, D.R., Koput, K.W. and Owen-Smith, J. (2005) 'Network Dynamics and Field Evolution: The Growth of Interorganizational Collaboration in the Life Sciences', *American Journal of Sociology*, Vol. 110, No. 4, January 2005, pp. 1132–1205.

Rhoades, S.A. (1995) 'Market share inequality, the HHI, and other measures of the firm-composition of a market', *Review of Industrial Organization*, Springer Netherlands, Volume 10, No. 6, Dec. 1995, pp. 657-674.

Ricardo, D. (1817) *On the Principles of Political Economy and Taxation*, Empiricus Books, 2006.

Roberts, E.B. (1987) *Generating Technological Innovation*, Oxford University Press, New York.

Romer, P. (1986) 'Increasing Returns and Long-run Growth', *Journal of Political Economy*, Vol. 94, 1986, p. 1002-1037.

Romer, P.M. (1990) 'Endogenous technological change', *The Journal of Political Economy*, Vo. 98, No. 5, Part 2: The Problem of Development: A Conference of the Institute for the Study of Free Enterprise Systems, Oct. 1990, pp. S71-S102.

Rutten, V.W. (1959) 'Usher and Schumpeter on Invention, Innovation, and Technological Change', *The Quarterly Journal of Economics*, Vol. 73, No. 4, Nov. 1959, pp. 596-606, The MIT Press.

Saltykov, B.G. (2007) 'Breaking up is hard to do', Russian Science Commentary, pp. 536-537.

Sampath, P. (2006) 'Breaking the Fence: Patent Rights and Biomedical Innovation in 'Technology Followers'', Working Paper Series, No. 08, Maastricht: United Nations University - Maastricht Economic and Social Research and Training Centre on Innovation and Technology.

Schaaper, M. (2004) 'An Emerging Knowledge-Based Economy in China? Indicators from OECD Database', *STI Working Paper*, No. 04, OECD, Paris, 2004.

Schmidt-Tiedemann, K.J. (1982) 'A New Model of Innovation Process', *Research Management*, 25, pp.18-21.

Schmoch, U., Grupp, H. Mannsbart, W., and Schwitalla, B. (1988) *Technikprognosen mit Patentindikatoren*, Verlag TÜV Rheinland GmbH, Köln, 1988.

Schmoch, U. (1990) *Wettbewerbsvorsprung durch Patentinformation – Handbuch für die Recherchenpraxis*, Verlag TÜV Rheinland GmbH, Köln, 1990.

Schmoch, U. (1993), Tracing the knowledge transfer from science to technology as reflected in patent indicators, *Scientometrics*, Vol. 26, No. 1, pp. 193-211.

Schmoch, U., Laville, F., Patel, P., Frietsch, R. (2003) 'Linking Technology Areas to Industrial Sectors', Final Report to the European Commission, DG Research.

Schmoch, U. (2008) 'Concept of a Technology Classification for Country Comparisons', Final Report to the World Intellectual Property Organisation (WIPO).

Schmookler, J. (1951), 'Invention and Economic Development', *Dissertations available from ProQuest.* Paper AAI0007813, January 1, 1951 http://repository.upenn.edu/dissertations/AAI0007813.

Schmookler, J. (1962) 'Economic Sources of Inventive Activity', *The Journal of Economic History*, Vol. 22, No. 1, March 1962, pp. 1-20.

Schumpeter, J.A. (1911) *Theorie der wirtschaftlichen Entwicklung*, München und Leipzig, Verlag von Duncker & Humboldt, 1931.

Schumpeter, J.A. (1934) *The Theory of Economic Development*, Harvard University Press, Cambridge, Massachusetts.

Schumpeter, J.A. (1942) *Capitalism, Socialism and Democracy*, George Allen & Unwin (Publishers) Ltd., London, 1976.

Schwartz, M.A. (1978) *The imitation and diffusion of industrial innovations*, Ann Arbor, 1978.

Schwitalle, B. (1992) *Messung und Erklärung industrieller Innovationstätigkeiten mit empirischen Analysen für die westdeutsche Industrie*, Physica-Verlag, Heidelberg, 1993.

Scott, J. (2000) *Social Network Analysis*, Sage Publications, London.

Shapiro, C. (2000), 'Navigating the Patent Thicket: Cross Licenses, Patent Pools, and Standard-Setting', *Innovation Policy and the Economy*, Vol. 1, 2000, The University of Chicago Press, pp. 119-150, http://www.jstor.org/stable/25056143.

Smith, A. (2003) 'Transforming technological regimes for sustainable development: a role for alternative technology niches?', *Science and Public Policy*, Volume 30, April 2003, Beech Tree Publishing, Guildford, England, pp. 127-135.

Solow, R.M. (1956) 'A Contribution to the Theory of Economic Growth', *The Quarterly Journal of Economics*, Vol. 70, No. 1 (Feb. 1956), pp. 65-94, Published by: The MIT Press.

Stankiewicz, R. (1992) 'Technology as an autonomous, socio-cognitive system', in Grupp (ed.), pp.161-223.

Stavins, J. (2001) 'Price Discrimination in the Airline Market: The Effect of Market Concentration', *The Review of Economics and Statistics*, February 2001, Vol. 83, No. 1, Pages 200-202.

Tarr, D.G. (2008) 'Russia', *Globalisation and Emerging Economies*, OECD 2008, Paris.

Ter Wal, A.L.J. (2009) 'The Spatial Dynamics of the Inventor Network in German Biotechnology: Geographical Proximity Versus Triadic Closure', Economic Geography Research Group, Working Paper Series No. 02.09, http://www.egrg.org.uk/pdfs/egrg_wp0209.pdf, 31-08-2010.

Ter Wal, A.L.J. and Boschma, R.A. (2009) 'Applying social network analysis in economic geography: framing some key analytic issues', *The Annals of Regional Science*, Vol. 43, No. 3, pp. 739-756.

Traistaru, I. and Iara, A. (2002) 'European Integration, Regional Specialization and Location of Industrial Activity in Accession Countries: Data and Measurement', Phare ACE Project P98-1117-R.

Trajtenberg, M. (1990), A Penny for your Quotes, *RAND Journal of Economics*, Vol. 21, 1990, pp. 172-187.

Tran, C.A. (2009), *'BRIC-Countries as a Source of International Knowledge Flows - A Patent Citation Analysis'*, EMAEE 2009: Evolution, Behavior and Organizations, May 21st-23rd 2009, Jena.

Tran, C.A., Beyer, F., Leible, M. and Teubner, T. (2010) *'PATSTAT in a Nutshell'*, Manuscript, Institute of Economic Policy Research (IWW), Karlsruhe Institute of Technology (KIT), Karlsruhe, 2010.

Van de Poel, I. (2003) 'The transformation of technological regimes', *Research Policy*, 32, pp. 49-68.

Vollrath, T.L. (1991) 'A Theoretical Evaluation of Alternative Trade Intensity Measures of Revealed Comparative Advantage', *Review of World Economics*, Volume 127, Number 2, Springer Berlin/Heidelberg, June 1991, pp. 265-280.

Wasserman, S. and Faust, K. (1994) *Social Network Analysis: Methods and Applications*, Cambridge University Press, Cambridge.

Wilson, D. and Purushothaman, R. (2003) 'Dreaming with the BRICs: The Path to 2050', Global Economics Paper No. 99, Goldman Sachs.

Wong, P.-K. (1999) 'National Innovation Systems for Rapid Technological Catch-up: An analytical framework and a comparative analysis of Korea, Taiwan and Singapore', DRUID Summer Conference on National Innovation Systems, Industrial Dynamics and Innovation Policy, Rebild, Denmark, June 9-12, 1999.

World Bank (2009), Gross Domestic Product 2008, World Development Indicators database, World Bank, 7 Oct. 2009, http://siteresources.worldbank.org/DATASTATISTICS/Resources/GDP.pdf.

Zander, I. (1997) 'Technological diversification in the multinational corporation – historical evolution and future prospects', *Research Policy*, 26, 1997, pp. 209-227.

Zhang, Y. (2009) 'Alliance-based Network View on Chinese Firms' Catching-up: Case Study of Huawei Technologies Co. Ltd.', Working Paper Series, No. 2009-039, United Nations University – Maastricht Economic and Social Research and Training Centre on Innovation and Technology, 2009.

Zucker, L. G. and Darby, M. R. (1996) 'Star scientists and institutional transformation: patterns of invention and innovation in the formation of the biotechnology industry', *Proceedings of the National Academy of Sciences*, 93, pp. 12709-12716.

Appendix

Appendix 1: Technological sectors of the OST[67]/INPI[68]/ISI[69] Concordance

Tech. Sector	Sector name
1	Electrical machinery and apparatus, electrical energy
2	Audiovisual technology
3	Telecommunications
4	Information technology
5	Semiconductors
6	Optics
7	Analysis, measurement, control technology
8	Medical technology
9	Nuclear engineering
10	Organic fine chemistry
11	Pharmaceuticals, cosmetics
12	**Biotechnology**
13	Agriculture, food chemistry
14	Materials, metallurgy
15	Surface technology, coating
16	Macromolecular chemistry, polymers
17	Chemical industry and petrol industry, basic materials chemistry
18	Chemical Engineering
19	Materials processing, textiles, paper
20	Handling, printing
21	Agricultural and food machinery and apparatus
22	Environmental technology
23	Machine tools
24	Engines, pumps, turbines
25	Thermal processes and apparatus
26	Mechanical elements
27	Transport
28	Space technology, weapons
29	Consumer goods and equipment
30	Civil engineering, building, mining

[67] Observatoire des Science et Techniques
[68] Institute de la Propriété Industrielle
[69] Fraunhofer Institut für System- und Innovationsforschung

Appendix 2: PATSTAT-IWW

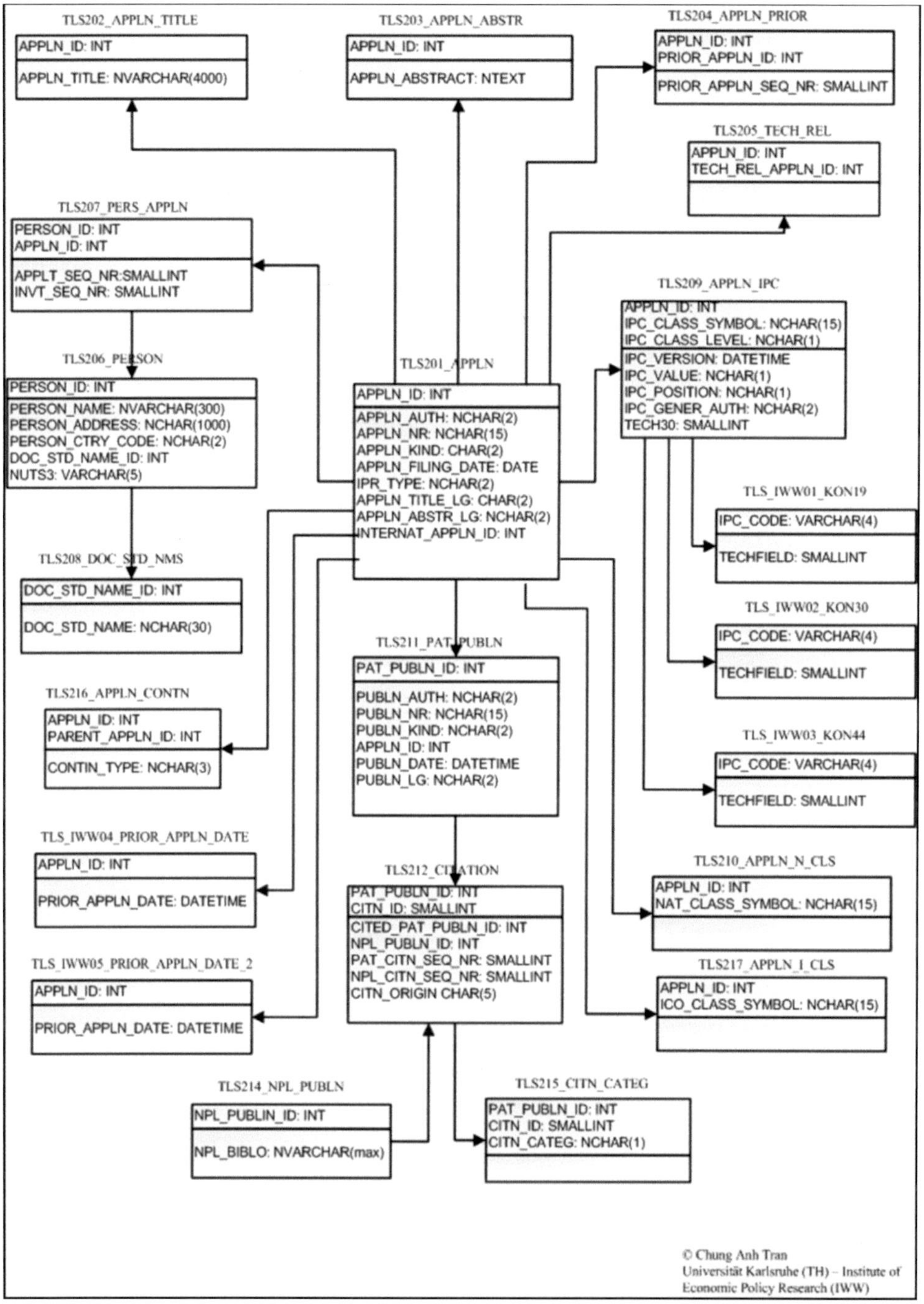

Appendix 3: Mean value of all citations

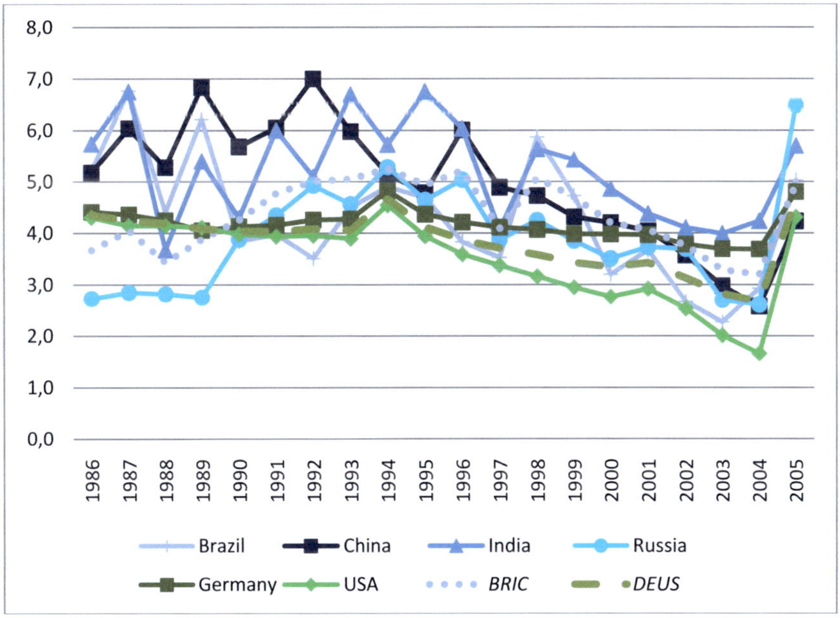

Appendix 4: Mean value of patent publication citations

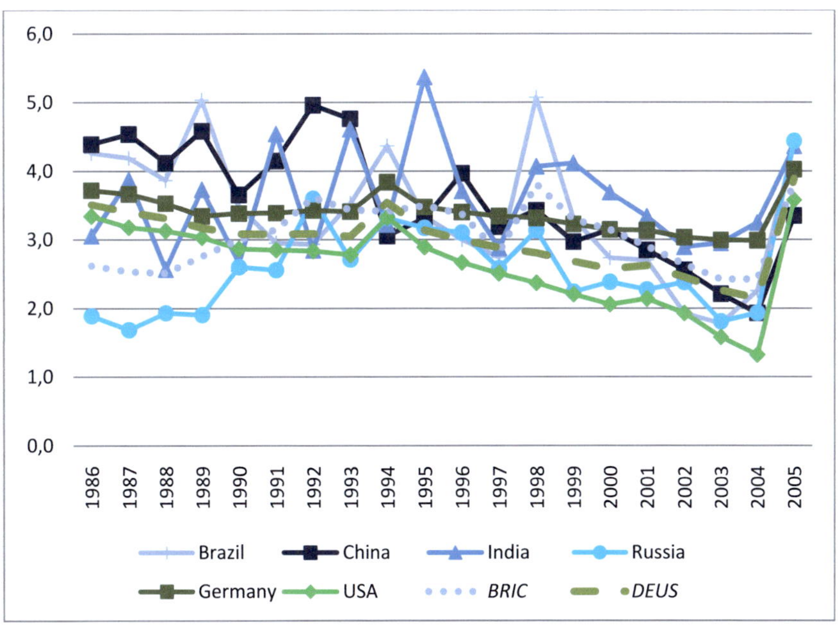

Appendix 5: Mean value of non-patent literature citations

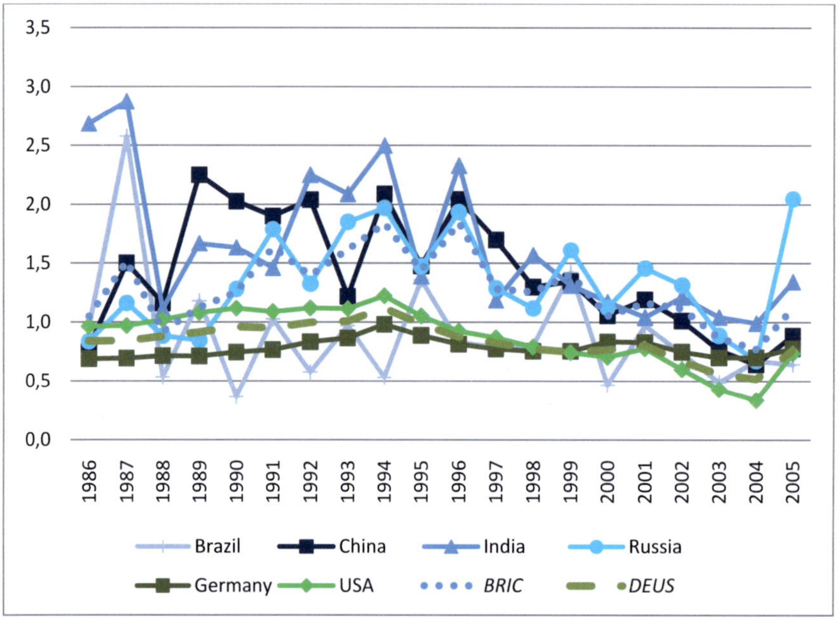

Appendix 6: Development of RSTA correlation

1986-1990	BRIC	Brazil	China	India	Russia
DEUS	-0.9691***	-0.3029	-0.2384	-0.3679**	-0.8829***
Germany	0.2334	0.1571	0.0636	-0.4032**	0.2941
USA	-0.2442	-0.101	-0.0579	0.4478**	-0.31*
1991-1996	**BRIC**	**Brazil**	**China**	**India**	**Russia**
DEUS	-0.9197***	-0.088	-0.7262***	-0.1659	-0.8661***
Germany	0.303	0.6886***	0.1235	-0.1795	0.2596
USA	-0.2363	-0.6823***	-0.0806	0.2543	-0.2007
1996-2000	**BRIC**	**Brazil**	**China**	**India**	**Russia**
DEUS	-0.9354***	-0.3665**	-0.1858	-0.6957***	-0.4442**
Germany	-0.2942	0.2513	-0.3132*	-0.3699**	-0.1524
USA	0.3269*	-0.2824	0.3242	0.3665**	0.2011
2001-2005	**BRIC**	**Brazil**	**China**	**India**	**Russia**
DEUS	-0.8838***	-0.2557	-0.4987***	-0.8123***	-0.3094*
Germany	-0.5441**	0.4053**	-0.4968***	-0.4468**	-0.2396
USA	0.4637***	-0.4401**	0.4291**	0.3583*	0.2974

Standard errors: *p<0.1, **p<0.05 and ***p<0.01

Appendix 7: RSTA values 1986-2005

Technological field	Brazil	China	India	Russia	Germany	USA	*BRIC*	*DEUS*
Electrical machinery and apparatus, electrical energy	-11.848	24.138	-92.729	19.578	15.441	-14.885	*-24.412*	*0.466*
Audiovisual technology	-58.648	62.872	-87.468	-36.080	-28.541	19.873	*1.154*	*-0.025*
Telecommunications	-76.701	82.043	-39.188	-41.370	-34.233	21.496	*38.135*	*-1.052*
Information technology	-84.482	17.275	-1.056	-49.512	-59.000	34.733	*-11.103*	*0.223*
Semiconductors	-94.890	-4.201	-92.788	-39.252	-31.255	22.742	*-52.647*	*0.933*
Optics	-81.691	-17.005	-99.004	29.336	-40.110	26.955	*-41.088*	*0.746*
Analysis, measurement, control technology	-54.920	-50.191	-76.418	16.935	2.025	-0.359	*-42.134*	*0.763*
Medical technology	7.134	-60.229	-86.672	14.104	-46.760	30.104	*-43.447*	*0.784*
Nuclear engineering	-96.932	-78.570	-96.864	93.939	-13.816	9.244	*34.084*	*-0.906*
Organic fine chemistry	10.735	-13.443	84.730	6.168	-8.843	4.194	*52.730*	*-1.702*
Pharmaceuticals, cosmetics	8.276	12.429	87.271	0.798	-39.396	22.712	*59.651*	*-2.115*
Biotechnology	-2.178	1.322	34.227	37.715	-36.083	23.201	*22.030*	*-0.533*
Agriculture, food chemistry	73.648	23.993	96.604	33.612	-32.057	13.716	*85.116*	*-5.490*
Materials, metallurgy	46.706	-35.383	-39.504	78.128	11.483	-12.472	*22.803*	*-0.554*
Surface technology, coating	-52.859	-62.332	-82.897	50.620	-2.882	3.578	*-32.766*	*0.608*
Macromolecular chemistry, polymers	-12.188	-51.403	-53.381	-51.434	-1.920	3.228	*-47.699*	*0.853*
Chemical industry and petrol industry, basic materials chemistry	70.531	-43.260	87.450	-1.139	1.892	-5.648	*58.702*	*-2.053*
Chemical Engineering	13.458	-26.003	-41.923	56.381	12.330	-12.326	*1.408*	*-0.030*
Materials processing, textiles, paper	54.873	-62.725	-50.083	-47.602	19.327	-19.280	*-36.527*	*0.671*
Handling, printing	21.078	-68.984	-63.844	-76.011	16.671	-15.169	*-58.150*	*1.022*
Agricultural and food machinery and apparatus	9.690	-66.604	-91.707	-22.796	27.232	-29.721	*-58.155*	*1.022*
Environmental technology	-10.709	-47.916	-49.047	53.674	23.901	-26.577	*-11.100*	*0.223*
Machine tools	-6.397	-25.917	-94.914	37.396	34.658	-43.514	*-28.724*	*0.540*
Engines, pumps, turbines	49.573	-72.681	-91.592	42.658	29.987	-35.264	*-29.632*	*0.556*
Thermal processes and apparatus	37.218	8.843	-97.977	23.861	34.896	-44.490	*-16.365*	*0.322*
Mechanical elements	19.095	-84.175	-97.923	-57.795	36.430	-44.972	*-75.095*	*1.310*
Transport	-16.803	-81.188	-95.176	-68.057	42.410	-57.078	*-78.372*	*1.370*
Space technology, weapons	-28.303	-92.355	-97.454	55.925	18.089	-17.323	*-46.896*	*0.840*
Consumer goods and equipment	43.245	72.135	-53.318	-20.290	20.354	-23.963	*31.459*	*-0.818*
Civil engineering, building, mining	-2.005	-54.063	-99.329	-2.817	40.068	-53.015	*-56.691*	*0.999*

Appendix 8: Inner country correlation of RSTA

BRIC	1986-1990	1991-1995	1996-2000	2001-2005	All
1986-1990	1				
1991-1995	0.641***	1			
1996-2000	0.325*	0.598***	1		
2001-2005	0.123	0.162	0.792***	1	
All	0.281	0.378**	0.885***	0.959***	1

Brazil	1986-1990	1991-1995	1996-2000	2001-2005	All
1986-1990	1				
1991-1995	0.526***	1			
1996-2000	0.502***	0.707***	1		
2001-2005	0.326*	0.700***	0.640***	1	
All	0.534***	0.844***	0.894***	0.895***	1

DEUS	1986-1990	1991-1995	1996-2000	2001-2005	All
1986-1990	1				
1991-1995	0.473***	1			
1996-2000	0.204	0.544***	1		
2001-2005	0.145	0.109	0.804***	1	
All	0.229	0.276	0.875***	0.980***	1

China	1986-1990	1991-1995	1996-2000	2001-2005	All
1986-1990	1				
1991-1995	0.292	1			
1996-2000	0.202	0.069	1		
2001-2005	0.107	-0.087	0.845***	1	
All	0.172	-0.039	0.875***	0.988***	1

Germany	1986-1990	1991-1995	1996-2000	2001-2005	All
1986-1990	1				
1991-1995	0.957***	1			
1996-2000	0.920***	0.963***	1		
2001-2005	0.881***	0.925***	0.976***	1	
All	0.949***	0.97***	0.992***	0.978***	1

India	1986-1990	1991-1995	1996-2000	2001-2005	All
1986-1990	1				
1991-1995	0.804***	1			
1996-2000	0.712***	0.762***	1		
2001-2005	0.783***	0.848***	0.928***	1	
All	0.774***	0.829***	0.959***	0.98***	1

USA	1986-1990	1991-1995	1996-2000	2001-2005	All
1986-1990	1				
1991-1995	0.959***	1			
1996-2000	0.938***	0.974***	1		
2001-2005	0.920***	0.957***	0.985***	1	
All	0.965***	0.986***	0.991***	0.985***	1

Russia	1986-1990	1991-1995	1996-2000	2001-2005	All
1986-1990	1				
1991-1995	0.527***	1			
1996-2000	0.377**	0.757***	1		
2001-2005	0.327*	0.682***	0.894***	1	
All	0.625***	0.856***	0.921***	0.896***	1

Standard errors: *p<0.1, **p<0.05 and ***p<0.01

Appendix 9: IPC classes of the biotechnology sector analysis

A01C	B01F	B44C	C08H	D03D	F21S	G06N
A01F	B01J	B44F	C08J	D04B	F21V	G06Q
A01G	B01L	B60N	C08K	D04H	F22B	G06T
A01H	B02B	B60R	C08L	D06B	F23G	G07C
A01K	B02C	B61D	C09B	D06F	F23N	G07D
A01M	B03B	B61K	C09C	D06L	F23R	G07F
A01N	B03C	B62D	C09D	D06M	F24F	G08B
A01P	B03D	B64C	C09G	D06N	F24J	G08C
A21B	B04B	B64D	C09H	D06P	F25B	G08G
A21C	B04C	B65B	C09J	D06Q	F25C	G09B
A21D	B05B	B65C	C09K	D21B	F25D	G09C
A22B	B05C	B65D	C10C	D21C	F26B	G09F
A22C	B05D	B65F	C10G	D21D	F27B	G09G
A23B	B06B	B65G	C10H	D21F	F27D	G10H
A23C	B07B	B66B	C10L	D21H	F28D	G10K
A23D	B07C	B67B	C10M	E01C	F28F	G10L
A23F	B08B	B67C	C11B	E01F	F28G	G11B
A23G	B09B	B67D	C11C	E01H	F41B	G11C
A23J	B09C	B81B	C11D	E02B	F41C	G12B
A23K	B21D	B81C	C12C	E02D	G01B	G21C
A23L	B21F	B82B	C12F	E04B	G01C	G21F
A23N	B21J	C01B	C12G	E04D	G01D	G21H
A23P	B22C	C01C	C12H	E04G	G01F	G21K
A24B	B22F	C01D	C12J	E05F	G01G	H01B
A24D	B23B	C01F	C12L	E05G	G01J	H01C
A41D	B23K	C01G	C12M	E21B	G01K	H01F
A45C	B23P	C02F	C12N	F01D	G01L	H01G
A45D	B24B	C03B	C12P	F01L	G01M	H01J
A47C	B24C	C03C	C12Q	F01M	G01N	H01L
A47J	B25B	C04B	C12S	F02B	G01P	H01M
A47K	B25H	C05B	C13D	F02C	G01R	H01Q
A47L	B25J	C05C	C13F	F02M	G01S	H01R
A61B	B26B	C05D	C13K	F02P	G01T	H01S
A61C	B26D	C05F	C14C	F04B	G02B	H02K
A61D	B27K	C05G	C21C	F04C	G02C	H02M
A61F	B27L	C06B	C22B	F04D	G02F	H02N
A61G	B27N	C07B	C23C	F04F	G03B	H02P
A61H	B28B	C07C	C23F	F15B	G03C	H03B
A61J	B28C	C07D	C23G	F15C	G03F	H03F
A61K	B29B	C07F	C25B	F16D	G03G	H03K
A61L	B29C	C07G	C25D	F16F	G03H	H04B
A61M	B29D	C07H	C30B	F16J	G05B	H04J
A61N	B30B	C07J	C40B	F16K	G05D	H04L
A61P	B32B	C07K	D01C	F16L	G05F	H04N
A61Q	B41J	C08B	D01D	F16M	G06F	H04Q
A62B	B41M	C08C	D01F	F17B	G06G	H04R
A62D	B41N	C08F	D01H	F17C	G06K	H05B
B01D	B42D	C08G	D02G	F21K	G06M	H05H
						H05K

Appendix 10: Inner biotechnology technology ranking

Brazil	Total	Share	China	Total	Share	India	Total	Share	Russia	Total	Share
12	57.48	60.50	12	194.12	54.68	12	261.44	67.04	12	183.20	62.53
11	11.07	11.65	11	58.88	16.59	10	44.71	11.46	11	31.95	10.90
10	10.43	10.98	10	37.75	10.63	11	34.63	8.88	10	29.55	10.09
13	5.09	5.36	7	30.26	8.52	7	16.44	4.22	7	15.41	5.26
7	3.41	3.59	13	11.56	3.26	13	13.80	3.54	18	6.80	2.32
17	2.88	3.03	18	5.86	1.65	17	8.22	2.11	13	5.58	1.90
16	1.92	2.02	17	3.75	1.06	19	2.73	0.70	17	4.26	1.45
18	1.24	1.31	21	3.09	0.87	16	1.43	0.37	16	3.75	1.28
19	0.70	0.74	8	2.02	0.57	22	0.98	0.25	4	3.14	1.07
22	0.11	0.12	15	1.04	0.29	21	0.82	0.21	8	1.80	0.61
1	0.00	0.00	19	1.00	0.28	15	0.67	0.17	19	0.98	0.33
2	0.00	0.00	22	0.83	0.23	4	0.64	0.17	21	0.96	0.33
3	0.00	0.00	16	0.58	0.16	8	0.62	0.16	1	0.80	0.27
4	0.00	0.00	20	0.50	0.14	18	0.24	0.06	22	0.67	0.23
5	0.00	0.00	5	0.41	0.12	29	0.20	0.05	30	0.43	0.15
6	0.00	0.00	4	0.25	0.07	1	0.00	0.00	15	0.14	0.05
8	0.00	0.00	23	0.25	0.07	2	0.00	0.00	2	0.00	0.00
9	0.00	0.00	29	0.25	0.07	3	0.00	0.00	3	0.00	0.00
14	0.00	0.00	14	0.14	0.04	5	0.00	0.00	5	0.00	0.00
15	0.00	0.00	6	0.07	0.02	6	0.00	0.00	6	0.00	0.00
20	0.00	0.00	1	0.00	0.00	9	0.00	0.00	9	0.00	0.00
21	0.00	0.00	2	0.00	0.00	14	0.00	0.00	14	0.00	0.00
23	0.00	0.00	3	0.00	0.00	20	0.00	0.00	20	0.00	0.00
24	0.00	0.00	9	0.00	0.00	23	0.00	0.00	23	0.00	0.00
25	0.00	0.00	24	0.00	0.00	24	0.00	0.00	24	0.00	0.00
26	0.00	0.00	25	0.00	0.00	25	0.00	0.00	25	0.00	0.00
27	0.00	0.00	26	0.00	0.00	26	0.00	0.00	26	0.00	0.00
28	0.00	0.00	27	0.00	0.00	27	0.00	0.00	27	0.00	0.00
29	0.00	0.00	28	0.00	0.00	28	0.00	0.00	28	0.00	0.00
30	0.00	0.00	30	0.00	0.00	30	0.00	0.00	29	0.00	0.00
Germany	**Total**	**Share**	**USA**	**Total**	**Share**	***BRIC***	**Total**	**Share**	***DEUS***	**Total**	**Share**
12	8430.23	58.64	12	17726.45	50.83	12	763.56	65.37	12	26156.68	53.11
11	1920.05	13.36	11	6793.45	19.48	10	129.40	11.08	11	8713.50	17.69
10	1551.49	10.79	10	4606.72	13.21	11	112.28	9.61	10	6158.21	12.50
7	1204.77	8.38	7	3285.73	9.42	7	51.72	4.43	7	4490.50	9.12
13	278.34	1.94	17	452.64	1.30	13	38.27	3.28	13	730.60	1.48
18	274.55	1.91	13	452.26	1.30	17	23.59	2.02	18	656.93	1.33
17	172.53	1.20	18	382.38	1.10	18	8.53	0.73	17	625.17	1.27
16	94.67	0.66	8	287.45	0.82	16	8.52	0.73	8	372.50	0.76
8	85.05	0.59	21	214.84	0.62	19	7.14	0.61	21	283.92	0.58
21	69.08	0.48	16	133.01	0.38	4	4.43	0.38	16	227.68	0.46
22	68.41	0.48	4	118.59	0.34	8	3.04	0.26	4	144.52	0.29
19	51.17	0.36	19	80.87	0.23	22	2.73	0.23	19	132.04	0.27
4	25.93	0.18	22	48.38	0.14	21	2.59	0.22	22	116.80	0.24
14	14.79	0.10	14	24.94	0.07	15	1.48	0.13	14	39.73	0.08
1	13.27	0.09	6	17.77	0.05	1	0.80	0.07	6	30.88	0.06
6	13.11	0.09	20	17.44	0.05	30	0.43	0.04	1	30.67	0.06
20	7.65	0.05	1	17.40	0.05	29	0.40	0.03	20	25.09	0.05
15	6.73	0.05	5	16.37	0.05	2	0.00	0.00	5	23.07	0.05
5	6.70	0.05	15	13.86	0.04	3	0.00	0.00	15	20.59	0.04
25	3.29	0.02	2	6.96	0.02	5	0.00	0.00	25	9.30	0.02
29	2.91	0.02	29	6.10	0.02	6	0.00	0.00	29	9.01	0.02
26	1.90	0.01	25	6.01	0.02	9	0.00	0.00	2	8.09	0.02
24	1.62	0.01	23	5.28	0.02	14	0.00	0.00	9	6.33	0.01
30	1.61	0.01	9	4.89	0.01	20	0.00	0.00	23	6.24	0.01
9	1.44	0.01	26	4.16	0.01	23	0.00	0.00	26	6.06	0.01
2	1.13	0.01	24	3.71	0.01	24	0.00	0.00	24	5.33	0.01
23	0.96	0.01	3	3.39	0.01	25	0.00	0.00	3	3.93	0.01
3	0.54	0.00	27	3.09	0.01	26	0.00	0.00	27	3.49	0.01
27	0.40	0.00	30	1.78	0.01	27	0.00	0.00	30	3.39	0.01
28	0.11	0.00	28	0.33	0.00	28	0.00	0.00	28	0.44	0.00

Appendix 11: Inner country correlation of RSTA for the biotechnology sector

BRIC	1986-1990	1991-1995	1996-2000	2001-2005	All
1986-1990	1				
1991-1995	0.759***	1			
1996-2000	0.314*	0.378**	1		
2001-2005	0.397**	0.235	0.564***	1	
All	0.589***	0.504***	0.691***	0.769***	1

Brazil	1986-1990	1991-1995	1996-2000	2001-2005	All
1986-1990	1				
1991-1995	0.907***	1			
1996-2000	0.539***	0.453**	1		
2001-2005	0.386**	0.368**	0.805***	1	
All	0.513***	0.456**	0.864***	0.977***	1

DEUS	1986-1990	1991-1995	1996-2000	2001-2005	All
1986-1990	1				
1991-1995	-0.024	1			
1996-2000	-0.114	-0.130	1		
2001-2005	-0.106	-0.145	0.479***	1	
All	-0.045	0.093	0.441**	0.545***	1

China	1986-1990	1991-1995	1996-2000	2001-2005	All
1986-1990	1				
1991-1995	0.765***	1			
1996-2000	0.374**	0.274	1		
2001-2005	0.302	0.253	0.359*	1	
All	0.326*	0.247	0.556***	0.898***	1

Germany	1986-1990	1991-1995	1996-2000	2001-2005	All
1986-1990	1				
1991-1995	0.333*	1			
1996-2000	0.231	0.464***	1		
2001-2005	0.198	0.214	-0.051	1	
All	0.439**	0.724***	0.528***	0.633***	1

India	1986-1990	1991-1995	1996-2000	2001-2005	All
1986-1990	1				
1991-1995	0.411**	1			
1996-2000	0.378**	0.406**	1		
2001-2005	0.584***	0.259	0.573***	1	
All	0.439**	0.313*	0.817***	0.847***	1

USA	1986-1990	1991-1995	1996-2000	2001-2005	All
1986-1990	1				
1991-1995	0.004	1			
1996-2000	0.036	-0.020	1		
2001-2005	0.126	0.369**	0.119	1	
All	0.309*	0.517**	0.577***	0.616***	1

Russia	1986-1990	1991-1995	1996-2000	2001-2005	All
1986-1990	1				
1991-1995	0.748***	1			
1996-2000	0.347*	0.464***	1		
2001-2005	0.291	0.159	0.161	1	
All	0.644***	0.629***	0.428**	0.695***	1

Standard errors: *p<0.1, **p<0.05 and ***p<0.01

Appendix 12: *DIV* values 1986-2005

	86	87	88	89	90	91	92	93	94	95	96	97	98	99	00	01	02	03	04	05
BRIC	0.94	0.94	0.94	0.94	0.94	0.95	0.95	0.95	0.94	0.95	0.95	0.95	0.94	0.94	0.94	0.93	0.93	0.92	0.91	0.91
Brazil	0.90	0.91	0.92	0.92	0.92	0.92	0.93	0.92	0.92	0.93	0.93	0.92	0.92	0.93	0.94	0.95	0.95	0.95	0.94	0.93
China	0.92	0.92	0.92	0.92	0.92	0.92	0.92	0.91	0.92	0.93	0.93	0.94	0.93	0.93	0.93	0.92	0.91	0.89	0.85	0.82
India	0.78	0.79	0.84	0.85	0.84	0.86	0.88	0.89	0.88	0.86	0.86	0.87	0.88	0.87	0.86	0.86	0.87	0.87	0.88	0.87
Russia	0.93	0.93	0.93	0.94	0.94	0.94	0.94	0.94	0.94	0.94	0.95	0.95	0.94	0.95	0.95	0.95	0.95	0.95	0.95	0.94
DEUS	0.95	0.95	0.95	0.95	0.95	0.95	0.95	0.95	0.95	0.95	0.95	0.95	0.95	0.95	0.95	0.95	0.95	0.95	0.95	0.95
DE	0.95	0.95	0.95	0.95	0.95	0.95	0.95	0.95	0.95	0.95	0.95	0.95	0.95	0.95	0.95	0.95	0.95	0.95	0.95	0.95
USA	0.95	0.95	0.95	0.95	0.95	0.95	0.95	0.95	0.95	0.95	0.95	0.95	0.94	0.94	0.94	0.94	0.94	0.94	0.94	0.93

Appendix 13: *DIV* values for the biotechnology sector 1986-2005

	86	87	88	89	90	91	92	93	94	95	96	97	98	99	00	01	02	03	04	05
Brazil	0.84	0.58	0.45	0.43	0.64	0.81	0.67	0.51	0.54	0.66	0.65	0.48	0.44	0.54	0.57	0.57	0.60	0.60	0.67	0.88
China	0.67	0.58	0.61	0.70	0.67	0.58	0.57	0.60	0.62	0.63	0.57	0.52	0.56	0.65	0.69	0.68	0.66	0.63	0.60	0.59
India	0.67	0.67	0.68	0.65	0.60	0.58	0.63	0.67	0.61	0.49	0.43	0.45	0.52	0.58	0.59	0.56	0.48	0.43	0.40	0.29
Russia	0.68	0.67	0.64	0.61	0.64	0.67	0.70	0.72	0.71	0.61	0.55	0.56	0.55	0.51	0.49	0.53	0.54	0.43	0.32	0.34
DE	0.66	0.66	0.65	0.65	0.65	0.66	0.66	0.67	0.67	0.66	0.65	0.64	0.64	0.63	0.62	0.59	0.58	0.56	0.52	0.48
USA	0.68	0.69	0.70	0.69	0.69	0.69	0.69	0.69	0.68	0.68	0.67	0.67	0.68	0.69	0.68	0.68	0.64	0.58	0.52	0.50

Appendix 14: *KSI* values 1986-2005

	86	87	88	89	90	91	92	93	94	95	96	97	98	99	00	01	02	03	04	05
BRIC	0.54	0.52	0.49	0.48	0.47	0.45	0.43	0.43	0.41	0.40	0.39	0.40	0.46	0.50	0.48	0.49	0.51	0.52	0.57	0.67
Brazil	0.92	0.78	0.71	0.72	0.71	0.76	0.74	0.73	0.75	0.64	0.59	0.64	0.65	0.60	0.57	0.56	0.53	0.52	0.59	0.73
China	0.78	0.74	0.68	0.75	0.76	0.70	0.74	0.78	0.69	0.62	0.60	0.52	0.49	0.47	0.46	0.49	0.53	0.57	0.66	0.77
India	1.35	1.25	1.12	1.06	1.06	1.03	0.95	0.86	0.88	0.97	0.96	0.93	0.96	1.01	1.04	1.03	0.97	0.92	0.95	1.07
Russia	0.76	0.73	0.67	0.65	0.65	0.63	0.62	0.59	0.53	0.49	0.51	0.51	0.50	0.48	0.42	0.37	0.37	0.39	0.44	0.54
DEUS	0.00	0.00	0.00	0.00	0.00	0.00	0.00	0.00	0.00	0.00	0.00	0.00	0.00	0.01	0.01	0.01	0.01	0.02	0.02	0.03
DE	0.22	0.23	0.25	0.26	0.27	0.28	0.29	0.30	0.30	0.30	0.28	0.27	0.27	0.27	0.26	0.25	0.26	0.28	0.25	0.19
USA	0.19	0.20	0.21	0.21	0.20	0.21	0.21	0.22	0.22	0.22	0.22	0.22	0.23	0.23	0.22	0.22	0.22	0.23	0.26	0.32

Appendix 15: *KSI* values for the biotechnology sector 1986-2005

	86	87	88	89	90	91	92	93	94	95	96	97	98	99	00	01	02	03	04	05
Brazil	0.28	0.76	0.90	0.78	0.52	0.30	0.47	0.72	0.69	0.52	0.51	0.59	0.63	0.64	0.55	0.45	0.42	0.41	0.32	0.11
China	0.73	0.78	0.65	0.61	0.58	0.48	0.50	0.51	0.45	0.43	0.42	0.41	0.35	0.30	0.26	0.20	0.19	0.21	0.26	0.33
India	0.59	0.48	0.39	0.33	0.33	0.37	0.33	0.32	0.40	0.54	0.60	0.52	0.49	0.48	0.43	0.40	0.42	0.38	0.32	0.35
Russia	0.64	0.75	0.60	0.42	0.38	0.42	0.44	0.46	0.53	0.62	0.57	0.40	0.38	0.47	0.55	0.50	0.41	0.40	0.40	0.37
De	0.20	0.21	0.21	0.20	0.22	0.23	0.24	0.20	0.15	0.18	0.20	0.18	0.19	0.21	0.23	0.23	0.18	0.14	0.13	0.14

Appendix 16: Top ten late-comer biotechnology applicants

	degree centrality				betweenness centrality			
Brazil	I	II	III	IV	I	II	III	IV
Fundacao Oswaldo Cruz (Fiocruz)	-	-	-	0.167	-	-	-	0.015
FAPESP	-	-	-	0.333	-	-	-	0.076
Universidade Federal de Minas Gerais-Ufmg	-	-	-	-	-	-	-	-
PHB Industrial S.A.	-	-	-	0.167	-	-	-	0.000
Petroleo Brasileiro S.A. Petrobras	-	-	-	-	-	-	-	-
Universidade Federal do Rio de Janeiro	-	-	0.333	0.083	-	-	0.067	0.000
EMBRAPA	1.000	-	-	-	0.000	-	-	-
Alellyx S.A.	-	-	-	-	-	-	-	-
Biobras S.A.	-	-	0.167	-	-	-	0.000	-
Biolab Sanus Farmaceutica Ltd.	-	-	-	0.167	-	-	-	0.000
China								
Tsinghua University	-	-	0.182	0.026	-	-	0.182	0.000
CapitalBio Corporation	-	-	0.091	0.026	-	-	0.000	0.000
The Chinese University of Hong Kong	-	-	-	0.026	-	-	-	0.000
Shanghai Institute of Biochemistry Chinese Aca.	-	-	-	-	-	-	-	-
Guangdong Center for Disease Control and Prev.	-	-	-	0.158	-	-	-	0.000
Hong Kong DNA Chips Limited	-	-	-	-	-	-	-	-
Peking University	-	-	0.182	-	-	-	0.182	-
Yu, Long	-	-	-	-	-	-	-	-
Oakville Hong Kong Co., Limited	-	-	-	-	-	-	-	-
Yang Sheng Tang Company, Ltd.	-	-	-	-	-	-	-	-
India								
Council of Scientific & Industrial Research	-	-	0.231	0.120	-	-	0.026	0.017
Hindustan Lever Limited	-	-	0.154	0.080	-	-	0.000	0.000
Avestha Gengraine Technologies Pvt. Ltd	-	-	-	0.040	-	-	-	0.000
Biocon Limited	-	-	-	-	-	-	-	-
Reliance Life Sciences Pvt. Ltd.	-	-	-	-	-	-	-	-
Ranbaxy Laboratories Limited	-	-	-	-	-	-	-	-
National Institute of Immunology	-	-	0.077	-	-	-	0.000	-
All India Institute of Medical Sciences	-	-	0.077	0.040	-	-	0.000	0.000
Nicholas Piramal India Limited	-	-	-	0.040	-	-	-	0.000
Ramakrishna, Nirogi, Venkata, Satya	-	-	-	-	-	-	-	-
Russia								
Frank, Ludmila	-	-	-	-	-	-	-	-
Markova, Svetlana	-	-	-	-	-	-	-	-
Vysotski, Eugene	-	-	-	-	-	-	-	-
Institute of Protein Research	-	-	0.200	0.091	-	-	0.000	0.000
Dorokhov, Yurii	-	-	-	0.182	-	-	-	0.000
Ivanov, Peter	-	-	-	0.182	-	-	-	0.000
Atabekov, Joseph	-	-	-	0.182	-	-	-	0.000
Bonch-Osmolovskaya, Elizaveta	-	-	-	-	-	-	-	-
Institut Molekulyarnoi Biologii	-	-	-	-	-	-	-	-
Skulachev, Maxim	-	-	-	0.182	-	-	-	0.000

Appendix 17: Top ten early-mover-comer biotechnology applicants

	degree centrality				betweenness centrality			
Germany	I	II	III	IV	I	II	III	IV
Bayer AG	0.018	0.014	0.021	0.010	0.000	0.004	0.018	0.006
BASF AG	-	0.010	0.028	0.014	-	0.001	0.018	0.006
Max Planck Gesellschaft	0.089	0.062	0.053	0.024	0.014	0.018	0.028	0.017
Degussa AG	0.054	0.005	0.018	0.004	0.029	0.000	0.009	0.001
Genencor International GmbH	0.018	0.005	0.002	-	0.000	0.000	0.000	-
Aventis Behring GmbH	-	-	0.003	0.014	-	-	0.000	0.000
Schering AG	-	0.010	0.005	0.003	-	0.001	0.000	0.000
Hoechst AG	0.054	0.010	-	-	0.005	0.000	-	-
Chiron Behring GmbH & Co.	-	-	-	0.004	-	-	-	0.000
Epigenomics AG	-	-	-	0.004	-	-	-	0.008
USA								
Merck & Co. Inc.	0.007	0.012	0.013	0.003	0.013	0.013	0.012	0.001
Regents of the University of California	0.042	0.089	0.075	0.045	0.091	0.164	0.175	0.103
Genentech Inc.	0.031	0.026	0.028	0.004	0.028	0.021	0.034	0.002
Human Genome Sciences	-	0.006	0.027	-	-	0.003	0.030	-
Inctye Genomics, Inc.	0.035	-	-	0.010	0.000	-	-	0.000
Department of Health and Human Services	0.035	0.069	0.041	0.039	0.067	0.113	0.084	0.087
Pfizer Inc.	0.003	0.006	0.012	0.006	0.000	0.000	0.017	0.005
Du Pont Pharmaceuticals Company	0.017	0.002	0.008	0.009	0.022	0.000	0.007	0.005
Abbott Biotech, Inc.	0.007	0.004	0.003	-	0.004	0.003	0.005	-
Becton Dickinson and Company	0.017	0.012	0.001	0.039	0.000	0.022	0.000	0.000

Appendix 18: Inventor networks characteristics 2000-2005

		2000	2001	2002	2003	2004	2005	Mean
Brazil	*density*	0.1042	0.1051	0.1005	0.1150	0.1527	-	0.0963
	degree cent.	0.1702	0.0783	0.0912	0.1354	0.1429	-	0.1030
	between. dentraliz.	0.0357	0.0000	0.0000	0.0293	0.0771	-	0.0237
	average degr.	3.54	4.10	2.71	4.71	4.28	-	3.2245
China	*density*	0.0575	0.0233	0.0270	0.0302	0.0338	0.1349	0.0511
	degree cent.	0.0941	0.0555	0.0604	0.1631	0.0683	0.0387	0.0800
	between. dentraliz.	0.0041	0.0033	0.0049	0.0203	0.0132	0.0000	0.0076
	average degr.	5.00	5.06	4.68	4.90	5.35	4.72	4.9510
India	*density*	0.0436	0.1020	0.0216	0.0307	0.0322	0.0513	0.0469
	degree cent.	0.0406	0.2104	0.0491	0.0432	0.0405	0.0665	0.0750
	between. dentraliz.	0.0020	0.0008	0.0028	0.0024	0.0019	0.0025	0.0020
	average degr.	4.19	14.17	3.39	3.77	5.79	3.54	5.8094
Russia	*density*	0.0548	0.0641	0.0781	0.0576	0.1207	0.1880	0.0939
	degree cent.	0.0778	0.0928	0.1549	0.1097	0.2580	0.0877	0.1301
	between. dentraliz.	0.0212	0.0147	0.0198	0.0121	0.1366	0.0007	0.0341
	average degr.	4.00	5.39	5.46	5.24	8.45	4.89	5.5720
Germany	*density*	0.0019	0.0019	0.0020	0.0024	0.0024	0.0032	0.0023
	degree cent.	0.0177	0.0077	0.0147	0.0095	0.0108	0.0179	0.0131
	between. dentraliz.	0.0006	0.0005	0.0007	0.0008	0.0008	0.0009	0.0007
	average degr.	4.79	4.97	4.71	4.86	4.59	4.23	4.6906
USA	*density*	0.0008	0.0010	0.0008	0.0009	0.0010	0.0110	0.0026
	degree cent.	0.0187	0.0205	0.0141	0.0056	0.0075	0.0275	0.0156
	between. dentraliz.	0.0007	0.0009	0.0001	0.0001	0.0000	0.0018	0.0006
	average degr.	5.99	5.27	4.69	4.69	4.59	4.58	4.9686

Appendix 19: Citation numbers of the top citing countries

Brazil	1986-1989	1990-1993	1994-1997	1998-2001	China	1986-1989	1990-1993	1994-1997	1998-2001
AT	1.00	0.00	0.00	1.67	AT	0.00	0.00	2.50	5.00
AU	1.00	2.50	0.00	0.00	AU	1.00	1.00	1.00	5.00
BE	1.85	3.50	0.20	1.00	BE	0.00	0.00	0.17	6.33
BR	2.83	10.10	2.00	13.29	BR	0.00	0.00	0.00	0.67
CA	2.00	1.00	2.25	1.00	CA	1.00	2.00	2.00	6.40
CH	0.25	2.00	2.60	2.50	CH	0.67	1.00	1.85	12.58
CN	0.00	0.00	0.00	0.00	CN	8.50	5.50	10.22	98.46
DE	12.90	6.00	22.00	15.79	DE	6.00	11.25	27.00	105.45
DK	1.00	0.00	1.00	1.00	DK	0.00	0.20	0.00	7.00
ES	0.00	2.00	2.00	3.00	ES	0.00	0.00	5.00	7.67
FI	0.00	0.00	7.00	0.00	FI	0.00	0.00	1.00	16.75
FR	4.00	1.00	6.67	1.00	FR	2.33	7.00	7.00	26.33
GB	3.50	3.33	9.40	2.00	GB	8.00	1.00	10.56	56.18
HK	0.00	0.00	0.00	0.00	HK	1.00	2.00	1.00	16.14
IL	0.00	0.00	0.00	0.00	IL	0.00	0.00	1.00	2.00
IN	0.00	0.00	0.00	0.00	IN	0.00	0.00	0.00	3.25
IT	2.00	0.00	9.80	7.00	IT	2.00	6.75	3.00	9.00
JP	6.00	7.00	20.00	3.00	JP	18.00	4.12	18.33	34.77
KR	0.00	0.00	0.00	3.00	KR	1.00	0.00	1.67	36.58
NL	0.00	3.00	2.00	3.00	NL	1.00	1.00	2.25	18.20
RU	0.00	0.00	0.00	0.00	RU	0.00	0.00	0.00	1.00
SE	0.00	1.00	5.00	0.75	SE	0.00	5.40	1.00	16.63
TW	0.00	0.00	0.00	0.00	TW	0.00	5.17	1.00	20.33
US	18.42	27.23	47.42	17.33	US	37.50	38.96	49.95	152.85
Russia	**1986-1989**	**1990-1993**	**1994-1997**	**1998-2001**	**India**	**1986-1989**	**1990-1993**	**1994-1997**	**1998-2001**
AT	3.00	1.00	2.83	0.67	AT	0.75	0.00	1.00	11.40
AU	1.00	2.00	12.67	1.00	AU	2.00	0.00	0.00	2.00
BE	6.00	0.50	9.25	3.33	BE	1.50	2.00	0.00	14.58
BR	0.00	0.17	0.67	0.00	BR	0.00	0.00	0.00	4.17
CA	2.00	0.14	5.83	0.50	CA	0.00	3.00	5.50	4.08
CH	3.25	3.40	15.33	2.70	CH	0.00	2.00	5.83	16.24
CN	0.00	1.00	1.00	0.00	CN	0.00	0.00	0.00	18.61
DE	37.75	47.32	57.37	74.52	DE	9.25	19.00	16.80	124.24
DK	1.00	0.00	0.00	6.50	DK	0.00	0.00	0.00	6.11
ES	1.00	1.00	3.00	1.00	ES	0.00	4.75	1.20	24.45
FI	1.00	1.00	2.00	0.00	FI	1.00	0.00	0.00	8.33
FR	8.50	6.75	17.33	5.00	FR	2.00	4.00	7.99	44.58
GB	4.67	4.00	18.50	7.13	GB	8.80	1.50	13.00	176.26
HK	0.00	0.00	0.00	0.00	HK	0.00	0.00	0.00	0.00
IL	1.67	7.22	9.78	0.00	IL	1.00	0.00	3.00	32.83
IN	0.00	0.00	0.00	1.00	IN	13.47	1.00	26.01	366.28
IT	2.00	5.00	16.30	8.40	IT	1.00	8.00	8.67	25.70
JP	12.00	15.25	22.89	14.39	JP	2.92	26.00	14.00	50.34
KR	0.00	1.75	0.25	1.00	KR	0.00	1.00	0.80	12.20
NL	4.33	3.50	6.00	23.27	NL	2.00	0.00	0.80	72.58
RU	1.00	36.05	71.18	40.00	RU	0.00	0.00	1.00	0.69
SE	2.00	1.00	6.66	2.00	SE	0.00	0.00	3.00	6.00
TW	0.00	0.00	0.00	1.00	TW	0.00	0.00	1.00	2.00
US	33.75	56.97	121.43	24.67	US	29.32	40.50	47.20	287.20